Evaluation Research

An Introduction to Principles, Methods and Practice

Alan Clarke *with* Ruth Dawson

SAGE Publications
London • Thousand Oaks • New Delhi

SAGE Publications Ltd
6 Bonhill Street
London EC2A 4PU

SAGE Publications Inc.
2455 Teller Road
Thousand Oaks, California 91320

SAGE Publications India Pvt Ltd
32, M-Block Market
Greater Kailash – I
New Delhi 110 048

British Library Cataloguing in Publication data

A catalogue record for this book is available
from the British Library

ISBN 0 7619 5094 X
ISBN 0 7619 5095 8 (pbk)

Library of Congress catalog record available

Typeset by Mayhew Typesetting, Rhayader, Powys
Printed in Great Britain by The Cromwell Press Ltd,
Trowbridge, Wiltshire

Contents

Preface

The primary aim of this book is to introduce the reader to some of the fundamental principles of evaluation. Basically, we see the enterprise of evaluation as drawing heavily upon research methods and methodologies found in the social sciences. For us, what distinguishes evaluation research from other types of social research activity has nothing to do with research design, techniques of data collection or methods of data analysis. Indeed, by and large, evaluation involves the application of the methods of social research. What serves to distinguish an evaluative study from other forms of social research is simply a question of purpose. An evaluation is action oriented. It is conducted to determine the value or impact of a policy, programme, practice, intervention or service, with a view to making recommendations for change.

It is essential that evaluators have a good understanding of the strengths and weaknesses of various research methods and methodologies if they are to be able to apply them in imaginative and creative ways to address evaluation issues. The first three chapters of the book provide an introduction to the major methodological perspectives and describe some of the more commonly used methods of data collection.

Chapter 1 presents an introduction to the general field of evaluation and evaluation research. There is a description of summative and formative approaches, followed by a discussion of the general social context in which evaluations are conducted. In many evaluation settings there are multiple stakeholder groups. The chapter looks at the characteristics of stakeholder-based evaluation and the implications this has for the role of the evaluator. The issue of the importance of theory in the evaluation process is also addressed.

As a discipline, evaluation research does not have a methodology of its own. In Chapter 2 we provide an overview of what evaluation theorists have labelled the 'paradigm problem' or 'paradigm wars'. This involves outlining the characteristic features of the quantitative and qualitative perspectives on the logic and method of social inquiry, as well as describing their impact on research design in programme evaluation. As far as the quantitative approach is concerned we outline the strengths and weaknesses of experimental and quasi-experimental methods when used to evaluate social interventions. In discussing qualitatively-oriented methodologies we describe the salient features of the interpretivist and constructivist approaches to evaluation. We warn against taking a doctrinaire stance in the paradigm debate and welcome what we see as a move towards methodological pluralism in evaluation research.

Evaluation involves the application of the methods of social research. In Chapter 3 we describe features of the main methods of both quantitative and qualitative data collection. This covers the basic principles behind questionnaire design, observation, interviewing and documentary methods. As many evaluations have multi-method research designs, we discuss aspects of triangulation and the benefits to be gained from combining quantitative and qualitative methods. In the final section of the chapter we note the importance of linking theory and methods in evaluation research designs.

The following three chapters focus on evaluation activity in three substantive areas: criminal justice, health care and education. The emphasis is not on the findings of evaluation studies in these different fields, but on the methodological issues, practical difficulties and related problems encountered when conducting evaluations. Chapter 4 focuses on evaluation research on two main topics: the impact of non-custodial sentences and the evaluation of community-based crime prevention initiatives. In the case of the former, there is some discussion about the selection of outcome measures and whether the reconviction rate is a reliable and accurate measure of effectiveness. Evaluations of crime prevention programmes are described in order to illustrate the different types of research validity, the importance of theory-focused evaluations and the contribution the scientific realist perspective can make to evaluation research design.

A number of conceptual and methodological issues are raised in Chapter 5. It is noted that health and well-being are not easy concepts to define or measure. Mention is also made of the limitations associated with using randomized control trials for determining the effectiveness of treatment. Some conceptual issues in economic approaches to evaluating health are also discussed. Given the increasing use of patient evaluation surveys to measure the quality of care, we comment on the nature, scope and content of patient satisfaction questionnaires and describe their role in evaluating health care.

Inspection is a neglected aspect of evaluation. Chapter 6 describes the part played by the Office for Standards in Education (OFSTED) in providing a national inspection system for schools in England and Wales. The chapter considers the extent to which these inspections can be considered to meet the four major attributes of effective evaluation namely, utility, propriety, feasibility and accuracy.

Evaluation, as a form of applied research, is intended to be used. The final chapter discusses the utilization problem in evaluation research. The major factors affecting utilization are described and ways of maximizing utlization are discussed.

Our experience as both teachers and researchers has been invaluable in writing this book. Through our individual contributions we hope to provide the reader with an introduction to some of the fundamental principles and practices of evaluation research. Chapters 2, 4 and 5 were written by Alan Clarke, who also wrote Chapters 1, 3 and 7 with contributions from Ruth Dawson. Chapter 6 was written by Ruth Dawson with a contribution from Alan Clarke.

Finally, we would like to express our gratitude to the various people who have helped us during the course of writing this book. Particular thanks are due to Nigel Fielding for his comments on Chapters 2 and 4, and also Roger Tarling for his comments on Chapter 4. Individually we are especially grateful for the constant support and encouragement we have received from our respective partners, Christine Clarke and Dave Dawson. Our thanks also to the staff of Sage, in particular Simon Ross, Stephen Barr and Miranda Nunhoffer. Finally, we acknowledge that we are solely responsible for any deficiencies in the book.

Alan Clarke	**Ruth Dawson**
School of Human Sciences	Education Services
Department of Sociology	Southampton City Council
University of Surrey	

1   Understanding Evaluation

What is evaluation?

The term 'evaluation' is used in a myriad of contexts, settings and circumstances. For example, we might apply the term evaluation to any of a number of diverse activities, such as: assessing the literary merits of a new novel; determining the rehabilitative impact of prison sentences; judging the aesthetic value of a work of art; monitoring the standards and quality of service provided by a private company or public sector organization, or comparing the advantages of one holiday destination over another. Furthermore, in our more introspective moments we may practise self-evaluation by subjecting our own behaviour to some form of personal appraisal. Indeed, 'evaluation' can be described as 'an elastic word that stretches to cover judgements of many kinds' (Weiss, 1972: 1). Whether we are referring to the formal systematic examination of a planned social intervention, as undertaken by a professional evaluator, or the kind of informal subjective assessments people make in the course of their everyday lives, the activity involves judging the value, merit or worth of something. However, the former type of evaluation is clearly distinguishable from the latter by the very nature of the manner in which it is conducted. Formal evaluation is defined as a form of 'disciplined inquiry' (Lincoln and Guba, 1986: 550) that applies scientific procedures to the collection and analysis of information about the content, structure and outcomes of programmes, projects and planned interventions.

Many of the most influential texts on the fundamental principles and techniques of evaluation originate from the United States of America, where evaluation has been recognized as a specialist activity for a number of years. The literature is replete with definitions of evaluation, of which the following are examples.

Program evaluation is the systematic collection of information about the activities, characteristics, and outcomes of programs for use by specific people to reduce uncertainties, improve effectiveness, and make decisions with regard to what those programs are doing and affecting. (Patton, 1986: 14)

Evaluation is a type of policy research, designed to help people make wise choices about future programming. Evaluation does not aim to replace decision makers' experience and judgement, but rather offers systematic evidence that informs experience and judgement. Evaluation strives for impartiality and fairness. At its best, it strives to represent the range of perspectives of those who have a stake in the program. (Weiss, as quoted in Alkin, 1990: 83)

Evaluation is usually defined as the determination of the worth or value of something – in this case, of educational and social programs, policies, and personnel – judged according to appropriate criteria, with those criteria explicated and justified. (House, 1993: 1, paraphrasing Scriven, 1991a)

Evaluation research is the systematic application of social research procedures for assessing the conceptualization, design, implementation, and utility of social intervention programs. (Rossi and Freeman, 1993: 5)

Each of the definitions emphasizes different aspects of evaluation through the use of the terms evaluation, evaluation research and pro- gramme evaluation. The major characteristic features of the evaluation enterprise can be gleaned from these few definitions. Evaluation is presented as a form of applied social research, the primary purpose of which is not to discover new knowledge, as is the case with basic research, but to study the effectiveness with which existing knowledge is used to inform and guide practical action. As stated by Stufflebeam and Shinkfield, 'The most important purpose of evaluation is not to prove but to improve' (1985: 151). Similarly, according to Weiss, 'evalu- ation, unlike the basic sciences, does not aim for "truth" or certainty. Its aim is to help improve programming and policy making' (1997: 516). It is this practical orientation that constitutes one of the major distin- guishing features of evaluation. As a form of inquiry it is very much action oriented. The view that evaluation research differs from other types of research, more in terms of its intended objective than in the nature of its design or the method of its execution, is shared by many evaluation theorists (Suchman, 1967; Rossi and Freeman, 1993; Berk, 1995).

Evaluators rely heavily upon existing social science research methods and methodologies for obtaining information. This is a prac- tice that has led some commentators to assert that there is no single research strategy unique to evaluation research (Robson, 1993). As described above, what distinguishes evaluation research from other forms of social research is not the methods evaluators employ but the purpose to which the methods are put (Babbie, 1995). As Rossi and Freeman assert, a 'commitment to the "rules" of social research is at the core of our perspective on evaluation' (1993: 6). Indeed, social science makes an important contribution to the evaluation enterprise. It pro- vides knowledge of research methods, methodological know-how and theoretical insight. Bulmer describes programme evaluation as 'the most scientific conception of applied social research, the "hard" end of applied social science' (1982: 159).

The idea that the roots of evaluation research are firmly embedded within the social sciences gains wide support throughout the evaluation community. There can be little doubt that applied social science is the dominant paradigm in evaluation studies. In the words of two distinguished exponents:

> All social science fields have contributed to the development of evaluation research methods. It is not surprising, therefore, that the best evaluation research and the best evaluators draw on a number of disciplines, using an eclectic repertoire of concepts and methods. (Berk and Rossi, 1990: 12)

However, not all theorists accept that evaluation should be treated as a specialist area of applied social research. For example, Scriven (1991a) considers evaluation to be a key analytical process with its own identity: a 'transdiscipline' on the verge of becoming a discipline in its own right. House also defines evaluation as 'a loose or "almost" discipline' (1993: 77) and agrees with Scriven that the social sciences do not currently provide an appropriate basis for evaluation. However, for House, the solution is not to be found by separating evaluation from the social sciences, but through a radical reform of the social sciences.

Although evaluators make use of an impressive repertoire of concepts and methods drawn from the social sciences, evaluation research and academic research differ in a number of respects. Evaluation is primarily concerned with determining the merit, worth or value of an established policy or planned intervention. This makes it a unique form of social inquiry. Emphasis is placed on providing practical knowledge to aid the decision-making process; a feature that has led to evaluation being seen as a type of policy research. By virtue of its practical orientation and policy focus, evaluation not only has political effects, but is also influenced by political forces. This has implications for the nature of the relationship between the researcher and the researched. In an evaluation study there will be numerous individuals and groups who have vested interests in the programme under review. It is not uncommon to encounter a range of diverse viewpoints reflecting conflicting interests. Thus, 'unlike most other social scientists, who assume an audience of peers/scholars, evaluators must negotiate whose questions will be addressed and whose interests will be served by their work' (Greene, 1994: 531). Few would dispute Rossi and Freeman's (1993) view that evaluation research is not just about the application of methods, but is also a political activity.

Both the terms 'evaluation' and 'evaluation research' are used in the definitions provided above. While there is a tendency for these terms to be used interchangeably, there are some evaluation theorists who make a point of distinguishing between the two. For Suchman (1967), evaluation refers to the goal of establishing the value or worth of an action, intervention or programme, whereas evaluative research is said to take place when scientific methods are employed in the process of carrying out an evaluation. Similarly, Cordray and Lipsey (1986) see evaluation and research as performing different functions as far as evaluation studies are concerned. They distinguish between programme evaluation and programme research. The former is 'essentially a service-oriented, practical mode of inquiry that primarily has evaluative intent' (1986: 19). As an approach, it is directly responsive to the needs of programme administrators and managers. Its main aim is to establish the merit or value of a programme or intervention. In comparison, programme research is described as 'an applied social science study of social programs with no pretensions to be evaluative, responsive, or useful (at least in the short term)' (1986: 20). Emphasis is placed on ascertaining cause-and-effect relationships between programme activities and outcomes. The idea is not just to discover whether a programme works, but to explain how it works. However, while distinguishing between an evaluation perspective and a research perspective in this way allows us to appreciate differences in method and purpose, Cordray and Lipsey acknowledge that when it comes to the practice of evaluation there is considerable overlap between the two approaches.

Patton (1986) also draws on the distinction between evaluation and research when defining programme evaluation. Although programme evaluators use research methods to gather data on specific programmes, their primary intention is to provide information for those responsible for making decisions about the future development of those programmes. Thus, the emphasis is on 'utility, relevance, practicality, and meeting the information needs of specific decision makers' (1986: 15). This is in contrast to evaluation research where, according to Patton, 'there is relatively greater emphasis on generalizability, causality, and credibility within the research community' (1986: 15).

It should be apparent by now that it is not possible to provide a simple definitive answer to the question, what is evaluation? As Patton commented sometime ago, 'no single-sentence definition will suffice to fully capture the practice of evaluation' (1982: 35). More recently, Pawson and Tilley have suggested that 'the term carries so much baggage that one is in danger of dealing not so much with a methodology as with an incantation' (1997: 2). One way of dealing with this definitional problem and developing a greater understanding of the nature and scope of evaluation is to consider it in relation to monitoring, auditing and inspection.

Auditing, monitoring and inspection as methods of evaluation

In comparing and contrasting auditing and evaluation, Chelimsky (1985) notes that programme effectiveness evaluation addresses three broad categories of questions: these are labelled descriptive, normative and cause-and-effect. At the descriptive level the evaluator wants to know how many people are engaged in particular programme activities and what form their participation takes. Normative questions involve inquiring as to the extent to which a programme is operating as originally intended. For example, are patients receiving the prescribed number of home visits within the time frame recommended by the programme? Cause-and-effect questions are designed to ascertain whether or not a programme has worked. The evaluator seeks to discover which of the observed changes can be seen as resulting from specific programme interventions. According to Chelimsky (1985), although all three types of questions feature in evaluation, auditing rarely involves descriptive questions, never addresses cause-and-effect questions but concentrates on normative questions.

Evaluation then is not the same as audit. Both may follow systematic procedures, look at a programme's outcomes and share the same ultimate aim of improving the quality of a programme, but they approach the task in different ways. An evaluation examines a programme from a number of different perspectives and looks for causal linkages between programme activities and outcomes. Programme evaluation is a theory-focused activity that also considers the relevance of the various components of a programme and makes predictions about future developments. By comparison, an audit is much less ambitious; it concentrates on checking what actually happens against prescribed normative standards. The information provided by an audit can be considered to be evaluative insofar as equalling or surpassing a predicted target figure is deemed preferable to falling beneath it. As a method of evaluation, audits are widely used in the monitoring of quality assurance in health care, as discussed in Chapter 5.

Monitoring and evaluation are closely linked. According to Phillips et al., monitoring involves 'the systematic and continuous surveillance of a series of events' (1994: 1). It concentrates on examining the procedures and processes involved in the delivery of a programme. Information is collected on a regular basis to provide feedback about the level of performance. Monitoring can be carried out throughout the implementation stage of a programme with a view to making changes should there be any significant deviation from the planned goals or programme objectives. Thus, monitoring plays an integral part in process evaluation. Rossi and Freeman (1993) not only comment on how it has become increasingly difficult to distinguish between process evaluations and programme monitoring for management purposes, but they use the terms interchangeably.

Although monitoring is part of the evaluation process, it is possible to distinguish between monitoring and evaluation. In comparing the two, Connor (1993) states that monitoring is essentially a value free activity. The emphasis is on collecting information about what a programme is doing without questioning the logic or structure of the programme design. Monitoring might generate data for use in an evaluation study but it is evaluation that is concerned with judging the merit or worth of an intervention or programme activity. An evaluation takes the form of an in-depth study of a programme at a certain point in its life cycle, whereas monitoring is an on-going activity.

Performance monitoring requires the identification of measurable indicators; these are sometimes referred to as key performance indicators. They provide information about inputs, outputs and outcomes relating to a programme's activities or the performance of an organization. This kind of performance measurement usually takes place on an annual basis to provide data to assist in budget decision-making. In public sector organizations outcome-related performance indicators are used in the interests of public accountability. There are three broad types of accountability: fiscal, process and programme accountability (Day, 1993). The first is concerned with inputs and is about making sure that public funds are used in accordance with the appropriate rules. Process accountability is about efficiency and as such focuses on service or programme outputs. The issue here is one of the efficient management of public resources. Programme accountability concerns outcomes, it is about establishing whether or not a funded activity succeeds in reaching its intended goals.

All the main public sector service providers publish annual performance figures: the health authorities provide information on waiting lists and aspects of patient care, police services publish data on crime trends, detection rates and response times and education authorities publish the examination results of schools. Clearly, data of this kind are useful to the evaluator who is assessing an institution or a programme. However, there are important questions of validity and reliability surrounding performance measurement. 'Performance' itself is an elusive concept. Wholey considers it to be a socially constructed concept when he asserts that performance 'is not an objective reality out there somewhere waiting to be measured and evaluated . . . [it] exists in people's minds if it exists anywhere at all' (1996: 146). Thus, performance needs to be defined before it can be measured.

Outcome performance measurement relies primarily on quantitative indicators but this does not mean that it is entirely objective and value free. The critical evaluator needs to look at who defined the performance indicators in the first place and for what purpose. In drawing attention to the limited usefulness of official statistics, Dingwall notes how performance indicators are 'indicators of the performance of the organisation in constructing its activities in their terms' (1992: 163), thus effectively casting doubt on the claims that quantitative performance measures reflect an indisputable objective reality. To illustrate his point, he comments that if the performance of a hospital were to be judged on the basis of its mortality rate, then it is likely that the staff would attempt to find ways of making sure that patients were recorded as dying elsewhere. Monitoring schemes are therefore not neutral reporting devices. Smith (1995), in a study of the impact of performance review on the maternity services in the UK, describes how the use of a system of performance indicators can actually have dysfunctional effects on an organization's performance. Such schemes may encourage managers to strategically manipulate performance measures, indulge in forms of 'creative' reporting, concentrate on short-term issues as opposed to longer-term goals and avoid pursing innovative but potentially risky initiatives. Wholey (1996) sees a role for evaluators in advising programme managers and policy decision-makers on how to set up appropriate performance measurement systems.

Inspection as a method of evaluation is not particularly well documented (Wilcox, 1992). Like monitoring it can be described as a top-down approach that checks that codes of practice are adhered to and minimum standards are achieved. In general, inspection represents a form of external evaluation in that those responsible for carrying out the inspection are usually from outside the institution. For example, there are inspection units located in social service departments that are responsible for inspecting residential homes both in the public and private sectors. Schools are also subjected to regular inspections as described in Chapter 6.

Auditing, monitoring and inspection are all capable of generating data that can be used in evaluation, but in themselves they do not constitute an evaluation. As described above, evaluation goes well beyond these activities, by seeking not just to describe how a programme is operating but also aiming to explain the underlying logic behind a programme. In the following sections we describe the basic types of evaluation, outline the various roles performed by the evaluator and emphasize the importance of a theory-guided approach to evaluation.

Basic types of evaluation

Scriven (1967) is often credited with introducing one of the most popular, fundamental and enduring distinctions between types of evaluation when he used the terms formative and summative to describe two approaches to the evaluation of educational curricula. This dichotomy was eventually applied to programme evaluation in general.

According to Scriven, formative evaluation is evaluation 'done to provide feedback to people who are trying to improve something' (1980: 6). It refers to a particular type of evaluation activity, in which the primary objective is 'to support the process of improvement' (1991b: 20). Consequently, in a formative study, the emphasis is on identifying the strengths and weaknesses of a programme or intervention. Essentially this involves the evaluator gathering information on programme design

TABLE 1.1 *Formative and summative evaluation: a comparison*

	Formative	Summative
Target audience	programme managers/ practitioners	policy-makers, funders, the public
Focus of data collection	clarification of goals, nature of implementation, identifying outcomes	implementation issues, outcome measures
Role of evaluator	interactive	independent
Methodology	quantitative and qualitative (emphasis on latter)	emphasis on quantitative
Frequency of data collection	continuous monitoring	limited
Reporting procedures	informal via discussion groups and meetings	formal reports
Frequency of reporting	throughout period of observation/study	on completion of evaluation

Source: Adapted from Herman et al. (1987: 26)

and implementation. In particular, the emphasis is on the perceptions and experiences of programme planners, practitioners and participants. Ultimately the aim is to ascertain if any changes are needed in order to improve the programme. This differs from summative evaluation, where basically the principal aim of the exercise is to determine the overall effectiveness or impact of a programme or project, with a view to recommending whether or not it should continue to run. As Patton observes, 'summative evaluations tend to be conclusion-oriented whereas formative evaluations tend to be action-oriented' (1986: 66).

To capture the essential elements of these two formal approaches to evaluation, Herman et al. (1987) present them as two ideal or pure types situated at opposite ends of a continuum. The salient features of the formative/summative dichotomy are summarized in Table 1.1. By contrasting the two ideal types in this way, it is possible to highlight some of the major differences between formative and summative evaluation strategies. As the table illustrates, at the two extremes there are clearly recognizable differences. These are particularly pronounced in areas such as overall methodological orientation, the choice of research methods, the frequency with which data is collected, the opportunities for reporting research findings, and the nature of the relationship between the evaluator and those engaged in programme activities.

In the case of a formative evaluation the target audience consists of those who have a responsibility for planning, managing and delivering a programme. The formative evaluator works closely with programme staff, not only to develop an understanding of how a particular programme is interpreted and implemented, but also in order to be in a position to provide feedback on problems and progress, as and when the need arises. This information-providing function is a fundamental feature of formative evaluation. Using both qualitative and quantitative methods, the formative evaluator focuses on programme processes. For some, it is this emphasis on process that serves to distinguish formative from summative approaches. As Patton notes, 'formative evaluations often include a process evaluation strategy' (1987: 28). The idea behind such a strategy is to describe how a programme actually operates, particularly during its early stages. The task facing the evaluator working in this mode is to ascertain 'why certain things are happening, how the parts of the program fit together, and how people perceive the program' (Patton, 1986: 139).

The primary purpose of a formative evaluation is to identify ways in which a social programme or intervention might be improved. Thus, at the outset it is essential that the evaluator clarifies the aims, content and structure of the programme. This entails not only identifying the different components of the programme but also developing an understanding of how the various elements are expected to produce the desired effects. Once the programme mechanisms have been identified, the evaluator can explore the extent to which the programme's objectives are met by the planned activities. If some activities are found to be more successful than others in achieving programme goals, this can be reported to programme staff and the programme can be adjusted accordingly. By its very nature the formative evaluation process, which makes heavy use of qualitative data gathering techniques, is fairly time-consuming. It involves the evaluator maintaining close contact with the programme, collecting data over a continuous period of time and regularly feeding information back to those responsible for running the programme.

In many respects this differs from a summative approach to evaluation. As previously noted, a summative evaluation is primarily concerned with determining the effectiveness of a treatment or planned intervention. Such evaluations are usually commissioned by policy-makers and funders to help them to reach a decision on the future of a particular project. Given this focus on ascertaining the extent to which a programme achieves its stated objectives, data collection is dominated by an emphasis on quantitative outcome measures. The need to determine whether or not a programme works means that summative evaluators have a tendency to favour experimental and quasi-experimental research designs. Constructing objective indicators of success and conducting field experiments can give rise to a number of practical and technical difficulties, as highlighted in later chapters.

The choice of research design and the selection of data collection methods are not the only areas where it is possible to detect differences between formative and summative evaluation strategies. The researcher engaged in a summative study adopts a more independent, detached role, in comparison to the formative evaluator who often interacts with programme staff on a regular basis throughout the evaluation. In the case of a formative study it is normal practice for the researcher to offer information and advice to programme staff at regular intervals during the monitoring period, whereas in a purely summative evaluation, feedback generally takes the form of a single, formal written report presented to the commissioning body on completion of the evaluation exercise. As Scriven observes, while a summative evaluator reports *on* a programme, a formative evaluator reports *to* a programme (1991a: 340).

There are clearly discernible differences between the formative and summative approaches; however, it is important not to treat the formative/summative dichotomy as being synonymous with the distinction between process evaluation and outcome evaluation. Patton (1982) comments on how, due to a lack of precision in the use of terminology, formative evaluation came to be seen as exclusively process-oriented and summative evaluation was defined as singularly outcome-focused. Scriven states quite categorically that, 'formative evaluations are not a species of process evaluation' and summative evaluations are not exclusively concerned with outcomes: indeed, either may focus on process or outcome (1996: 152). For example, Rossi and Freeman (1993) note how small impact evaluations, designed to provide an estimate of the likely outcome of a proposed intervention, may be conducted as part of an overall formative evaluation strategy. Similarly, Scriven refers to one of the most effective kinds of formative evaluation as 'early-warning summative' in nature (1991a: 169).

While the identification of two contrasting types of programme evaluation enables us to appreciate how evaluators might focus an evaluation, it nevertheless raises some fundamental questions about the comparative contribution the two approaches make to the evaluation enterprise and the nature of the relationship between them. For example, are formative and summative evaluations of equal importance? Do they constitute mutually exclusive categories or can they be combined within a single research design?

When it comes to choosing between formative and summative evaluations there are evaluators who readily express a strong preference for one or the other. Ever since he first introduced the formative/summative dichotomy, Scriven has accorded summative evaluation something of a pre-eminent status. In his view, the primary purpose of a formative study is to prepare a programme for summative assessment. As he asserts, 'formative evaluation is worth nothing at all unless it at least includes a preview of good summative evaluation' (1991b: 53). However, in defending himself against the charge that in advocating summative evaluation he actively undermines the value of formative evaluation (Chen, 1996), Scriven makes the point that he has found himself making a case more often for summative evaluation simply because it is this type of evaluation which has come in for the most criticism in the literature. Not only does he claim to enjoy undertaking formative studies, but he also contends that 'summative and formative evaluation are each valuable in the appropriate circumstances' (Scriven, 1996: 154). In other words, both types of evaluation have their uses and it is wrong to assume that one is intrinsically superior to the other; whichever is the more appropriate can only be decided when the circumstances of the evaluation inquiry are known. Thus, for Scriven, the formative/summative distinction can be said to be context-dependent. Furthermore, he acknowledges the possibility that both formative and summative issues can be addressed within a single evaluation.

Some evaluators hold the view that although Scriven's original distinction still has its uses, it is of limited value when it comes to considering the wide range of types of programme evaluations currently in use (Chambers et al., 1992). To quote Patton: 'The field of professional evaluation practice has become too rich and varied to be pigeon-holed into a single dichotomy' (1996: 142). He contends that there are some activities performed by evaluators that cannot be easily categorized as formative or summative in nature. This is also the case when evaluation research is used not to evaluate the effectiveness of a specific programme, but to generate knowledge about the basic principles underlying effective programme development and implementation. According to Patton, this is knowledge-generation for conceptual use. Unlike formative and summative strategies, where research findings can be instrumental in bringing about changes in a programme, knowledge-generating evaluation research can help planners and practitioners to clarify how they think about a particular programme. This may not result in changes being made to the programme, but the fact that they are clearer about the aims and objectives of the programme will have implications for future developments.

Chen (1996) is also of the opinion that the formative/summative distinction has its limitations. He feels that a more comprehensive conceptual framework is required in order to capture the variety of evaluation types. As shown in Figure 1.1, his typology of basic types of evaluation distinguishes between two broad elements: the function(s) performed by an evaluation and the programme stage focused upon. What is immediately apparent from this fourfold typology is that it neither limits process evaluation to issues of programme improvement, nor restricts outcome evaluation to focusing purely on assessing the merit or overall effectiveness of a programme. Consequently, given that it identifies new types of evaluation, it provides a broader conceptual framework than that offered by Scriven's original formative/summative dichotomy.

In briefly outlining the four basic types of evaluation we draw heavily from Chen (1996: 124–5). In describing process-improvement evaluation he recognizes that evaluation information can be used for either instrumental or conceptual purposes. The former applies when

Evaluation functions

		Improvement	Assessment
Programme stages	Process	Process-improvement evaluation	Process-assessment evaluation
	Outcome	Outcome-improvement evaluation	Outcome-assessment evaluation

FIGURE 1.1 *Basic types of evaluation (Chen, 1996: 123)*

the aim of an evaluation is to detect strengths and weaknesses in programme processes, with a view to making recommendations for altering the structure, or adjusting the implementation, of a programme. As Chen asserts, although the evaluation data collected are of instrumental value, it is not usually the purpose of a process-improvement evaluation to provide a full-blown assessment of the success or failure of a programme implementation strategy.

What serves to distinguish process-improvement evaluation from formative evaluation is the way in which the former makes use of evaluation information in a conceptual sense, such as when evaluation findings from a specific study are used to inform decision-making at a more general level. Chen provides a hypothetical example of a process-improvement evaluation of a family planning programme in an under-developed country in order to illustrate the distinction between the instrumental use and conceptual use of evaluation findings. Preliminary investigations may reveal that couples are more likely to adopt certain birth control methods if they receive help and guidance from local counsellors, rather than from health workers from outside their community. As Chen notes, although this finding is not based on a full evaluation of the implementation of the programme, it can be put to both instrumental and conceptual use. In the case of the former, those responsible for running the programme may decide to train local people to provide information and advice on the use of contraceptive methods, thereby ensuring a greater take-up of the service. As regards the conceptual use of the information, this will apply in cases where the findings are used to inform debates about the development of similar programmes in other locations.

Process-assessment evaluation is the second type of process evaluation identified by Chen. Here the emphasis is on ascertaining whether or not a programme has actually been successfully implemented. He cites quality control as a good example, on the basis that quality control techniques are designed not only to control the quality of products (in this case the programme is the product), but also to control the quality of the process leading to the production and implementation of the programme.

Chen also identifies two types of outcome evaluation; one focuses on programme improvement and the other on the overall assessment of a programme. Outcome-improvement evaluation concentrates on how the component parts of a programme affect programme outcomes and involves taking implementation issues into account. As a single programme usually incorporates a number of different treatments or elements, this type of evaluation attempts to identify which elements are more successful at producing the desired outcomes. This does not constitute a summative evaluation, as there is no formal assessment of the effectiveness of the programme as a whole. The evaluation information provided is used to help programme planners identify areas where a programme may benefit from some form of adjustment. In contrast, the other type of outcome evaluation does encompass summative evaluation. According to Chen, the primary purpose of outcome-assessment evaluation 'is to provide an overall judgement of a program in terms of its merit or worth' (1996: 125).

An important feature of Chen's fourfold typology is the fact that it illustrates that programme implementation and programme effectiveness are not the only two dimensions of programme evaluation. For example, as described above, process-improvement evaluations can make a significant contribution to programme planning, design and development. Furthermore, Chen notes that the basic types of evaluation can be purposefully mixed within a single comprehensive evaluation strategy.

Chen is quick not to undermine the importance of Scriven's original formative/summative conceptual formulation; indeed he acknowledges that the distinction is 'both inspiring and useful' (1996: 130). However, he feels that given the growth in the scope and nature of evaluation activity over recent years a broader, more all-embracing, conceptual framework is required.

Chen is not the only one to produce a basic classification of the varying types of evaluation. Patton (1982: 44) refers to an earlier presentation of six broad and enduring categories identified by the former Evaluation Research Society. Formative and summative evaluations were included among the six basic types, with the latter being subsumed under the general heading of impact evaluation. The remaining four types were labelled front-end analysis, evaluability assessment, programme monitoring and evaluation of evaluation.

Front-end analysis refers to evaluations undertaken before an intervention is introduced or a programme adopted. Basically, evaluations in this category provide information that will help those responsible for programme planning and implementation. This type of analysis is sometimes conducted to determine whether or not a programme should be launched in the first place.

Rossi and Freeman describe evaluability assessment as a form of 'pre-evaluation' undertaken prior to conducting a formal, full-blown evaluation (1993: 145). It entails the evaluator carrying out a preliminary investigation to estimate the technical difficulties, practical implications and financial costs associated with various evaluation research designs. In short, it involves the evaluator examining the feasibility of different evaluation approaches in a given context.

Programme monitoring involves the systematic collection of information relating to the performance of a programme. However, the central objective is not to establish whether a programme has an impact, but to provide basic data about how a programme is delivered and ascertain the extent to which it can be considered to be reaching those groups in the population it was specifically designed to benefit. The final category, evaluation of evaluation, covers meta-evaluation. Scriven (1991a) describes how evaluators can evaluate their own work, or the work of other evaluators, using an evaluation-specific checklist designed for this very purpose.

As Patton (1982) observes, the evaluation activities included in each of the six categories are not mutually exclusive. Indeed, while it is possible that they all might feature at one time or another during the course of a single evaluation study, combinations of activities from the different categories are to be found in the majority of evaluations. Take for example summative evaluations or impact assessments. In order to interpret the findings of such studies it is essential to have knowledge about, among other things, the coverage of a programme, the characteristics of its recipients and the general context in which it is introduced. This information can be obtained through programme monitoring and will be helpful when it comes to explaining why a programme did or did not produce the desired effect.

Chambers et al. (1992) provide a classification of evaluation types based on the fact that social programmes have a number of different aspects and research on each aspect constitutes a different type of evaluation. All in all, they identify five broad types of evaluation: studies of programme outcomes; cost-effectiveness studies and cost–benefit analysis; implementation studies; consumer satisfaction studies and needs studies.

These different types of evaluation serve different purposes. First there are studies of programme outcomes. In one sense, an outcomes-based study is designed with the intention of ascertaining the extent to which a planned intervention or programme actually works. Summative evaluations, with their focus on the achievement of programme objectives, are therefore included in this category. However, Chambers et al. also include under this heading evaluation activities undertaken prior to programme implementation, that is during the planning or design stages of a programme, which attempt to estimate the likely impact of a proposed intervention.

Achieving stated objectives is only one aspect, albeit an important one, of a social programme. There is also the important issue of the costs involved. At the planning stage it may be necessary to predict the economic efficiency of a programme prior to its implementation by estimating net outcome in relation to costs. On the completion of a programme, when data on actual costs and benefits are available, it may be possible to calculate the costs incurred in achieving the programme goals and compare these to the costs associated with similar intervention strategies or the costs of not having a programme at all.

A third aspect of evaluation research is evaluating whether a programme has been installed as actually intended. This is the province of formative evaluation and is included by Chambers et al. under the general heading of implementation studies. Also included in this category are evaluability studies and feasibility studies. In the case of the latter, the evaluator investigates the practical aspects of implementation prior to the launch of the programme.

Evaluating the reactions and responses of programme recipients is a fourth aspect of the evaluation process. Largely as a result of the emergence of quality assurance mechanisms, consumer satisfaction surveys have almost become a routine feature of the information gathering systems of many public sector organizations involved in providing a range of health care and social welfare services.

As social programmes are purposefully designed to meet perceived need within a specific client population or locality, evaluators sometimes find themselves called upon to conduct a needs assessment exercise. Chambers et al. include needs assessment studies as a type of evaluation when they assert that 'we can speak of *evaluating* the extent to which some important human need exists in the surrounding community population' (1992: 9). In this sense, needs studies are part of what Rossi and Freeman (1993) refer to as diagnostic evaluation research. They can be used to diagnose the nature and extent of a particular problem prior to policy-makers embarking upon a search for solutions. Furthermore, the diagnostic data produced by such studies can help programme planners to estimate the appropriateness of different programme initiatives or intervention strategies.

Needs assessment is not something that is only carried out prior to the design and implementation of a social programme. It can, in fact, be conducted at any stage during the life of a project. Indeed, as Herman et al. (1987) observe, many requests for evaluators to evaluate programmes that are up and running call for some form of needs assessment to be undertaken. A formative or summative research strategy is not always the most appropriate in meeting the information needs of programme planners and sponsors. For example, it may be the case that 'the sponsor wants to discover weaknesses or problem areas in the current situation which can eventually be remedied or to project future conditions to which the program will need to adjust' (1987: 15). It is essential at the outset that the evaluator obtains a clear understanding as to what the client requires from the evaluation and develops the evaluation research design accordingly.

A needs study can be undertaken on its own or as part of a full-blown evaluation. A variety of methods, both quantitative and qualitative, are employed in this type of exercise. It is, however, a field of study which gives rise to much controversy. There are some complex philosophical and methodological debates surrounding the conceptualization, definition and measurement of need (McKillip, 1987).

The social context of evaluation

Although it is possible to identify a number of basic types of evaluation, it should not be assumed that one only has to follow systematically a set of methodological guidelines to produce the perfect evaluative study. The evaluator not only has to contend with technical issues and methodological problems when designing and implementing a piece of evaluation research, but must also deal with the practical difficulties that can be encountered in the field. Indeed, it has been widely acknowledged for some time that evaluation research is greatly influenced by the very nature of the social context in which it is performed. According to Levine and Levine, this influence is evident at all stages of the evaluation process: 'The social context modifies and influences the process of the research, the inferential process, the final report, the participants, and the varied uses to which evaluation may be put' (1977: 533). In recognition of the important influence of social and political contexts, particularly with regard to the utilization of research findings, Rossi and Freeman exhort evaluators 'to continually assess the social ecology of the arena in which they work' (1993: 406).

A common feature of many evaluation settings is the existence of a number of distinct groups, each having an interest in the outcome of the evaluation. The term 'stakeholders' is normally used to describe these groups. According to Patton, 'stakeholders are people who have a stake – a vested interest – in evaluation findings' (1986: 43). In any programme or policy evaluation there are multiple stakeholders representing a wide variety of interests. In the first place, there are those who commission evaluation studies. This group ranges from policy-makers and senior officials in government departments, charged with the responsibility of formulating and monitoring large-scale policy initiatives across a wide range of social welfare issues, to boards of directors of small charitable trusts or local voluntary organizations, trying to determine how they might make the best use of their limited resources. Programme managers, administrators and steering committees constitute another interest group. There are also the workers who are engaged in actually delivering the programme on a day-to-day basis. It is this group with whom the evaluator usually has the most contact, as they often provide the primary source of evaluation data. Stakeholders also come in the form of service users, programme recipients or pressure groups representing the interests of the target population. Where programmes are funded from public coffers, taxpayers may also be included among the group of multiple stakeholders.

Given the nature of the phenomenon of multiple stakeholders it should come as no surprise that conflicts of interest are a regular occurrence. As Rossi and Freeman (1993) observe, this can cause problems for the evaluator in a number of ways. First, there is the issue as to which of the different stakeholder approaches should be incorporated in the evaluation research design. For example, there may be a lack of consensus regarding the relative importance attached to the various programme objectives, which ultimately has implications for the selection of outcome measures. Second, as every programme has both its supporters and critics, it is impossible for the evaluator to please everyone. Whatever the findings of an evaluation, they will be welcomed by some groups and rejected by others. The situation can be particularly difficult when the findings do not confirm the positive expectations of those who commissioned the research and have a vested interest in the continuation of the programme. Finally, the evaluator may encounter problems communicating with different stakeholder groups and misunderstandings may arise, especially when attempting to explain evaluation practices and procedures to widely differing lay audiences. Clearly, there is potential for conflict throughout the evaluation process, hence Berk and Rossi's advice that 'evaluation research should not be undertaken by persons who prefer to avoid controversy, or who have difficulty facing criticism' (1990: 14).

Smith et al. (1997) offer the would-be evaluator some general guidance by identifying five key points that need to be addressed when conducting a formal evaluation. The first of these concerns the handling of conflict. It is important that any conflict between the different stakeholder perspectives is openly acknowledged and not ignored, because there is a danger of research findings being discounted if there is any misunderstanding among the participating groups. Second, it is deemed advisable to allow the various stakeholders to have some input into the research design process. Third, there is the importance of maintaining contact with the participating groups throughout the course of the evaluation. Fourth, the nature and scope of the project or programme must be clearly defined and understood in order to enable stakeholders to identify what objectives have been achieved. Finally, the evaluator needs to give some consideration to the situational factors in evaluation practice, that is the organizational conditions and political circumstances in which evaluations are conducted, as these will undoubtedly have a bearing on the dissemination and implementation of the findings.

Many evaluators strongly advocate the involvement of multiple stakeholder groups in the various stages of the evaluation process (Guba and Lincoln, 1981; Weiss, 1983a; Patton, 1987). This is a feature of a number of well-established models of evaluation, such as responsive evaluation (Stake, 1975) and utilization-focused evaluation (Patton, 1986). These models are sometimes referred to as examples of stakeholder-based evaluation or participatory evaluation. Mark and Shotland use the term stakeholder-based evaluation to describe those evaluations that 'involve stakeholder groups, other than sponsors, in the formulation of evaluation questions and in any other evaluation activities' (1985: 606). Similarly, Fink (1993) describes participatory evaluation as an approach whereby those groups who are likely to be affected by the outcome of an evaluative study are invited to take an active part in the process. The idea is that primary stakeholders are consulted on matters such as the identification of the evaluation questions, the definition of what constitutes a successful outcome and how programme effectiveness will be measured.

According to Mark and Shotland (1985), there are three major reasons for pursuing a collaborative approach and encouraging stakeholder participation. First there is the question of the utilization of evaluation research findings: an issue uppermost in the minds of all evaluators. Indeed, in promoting his utilization-focused model of evaluation, Patton comments that 'concern for utilization should be the driving force in an evaluation' (1986: 57). In stakeholder-based evaluation the central assumption is that by working closely with those groups who have a vested interest in the programme, the evaluator is able to identify and address what are seen as the salient issues from the perspectives of the different stakeholders. Also, consulting with different groups at critical stages in the evaluation is likely to make them feel that they are active participants in the whole process. Thus, if stakeholders feel that an evaluation addresses the relevant issues and they are committed to the exercise, then it seems reasonable to assume that there will be an increased likelihood that they will act upon the findings.

A second reason for adopting a stakeholder-based approach is that it represents an attempt to come to terms with the realities of the policy-making process. The notion that there is one 'right' or 'objective' interpretation of a particular programme is firmly rejected, in favour of the view that multiple participants will generate a plurality of perspectives. As Mark and Shotland observe, when policy decisions are made they often involve 'not single unitary choices, but rather the accumulation of numerous choices by multiple parties' (1985: 610–11). It is reasonable to assume that the aims and goals of an evaluation will be perceived differently by different stakeholder groups. Although there may be an element of consensus surrounding some issues, the evaluation questions generated by a particular group will, in the main, be a reflection of their primary interests and concerns. In this context, decision-making is all about conflict and negotiation. As Cronbach et al. affirm, 'most action is determined by a pluralistic community, not by a lone decision maker. . . . When there are multiple participants with multiple views, it is meaningless to speak of one action as rational or correct action. The active parties jockey towards a politically acceptable accommodation' (1980: 84).

A third reason advanced in favour of a stakeholder-based approach is that it offers an opportunity for a wide range of groups to bring their concerns to the attention of those who have the power to change existing programmes or authorize the development of new policy initiatives. The need to capture the diversity of interests is recognized by House when he asserts that, 'Evaluations should serve the interests not only of the sponsors but also of the larger society, and of various groups within society, particularly those most affected by the program under review' (1993: 128). Thus, in serving a range of audiences, this approach to evaluation research displays a potential for democratizing the decision-making process. For example, it provides a mechanism through which the least powerful stakeholder groups can make their feelings known. In this sense, stakeholder-based evaluation may be thought of as an enabling, motivating resource; a way of empowering relatively powerless stakeholder groups.

The plurality of perspectives and the existence of competing interest groups help to give evaluation activity a political dimension. As Law asserts, 'every evaluation is a political act, political in the sense that there is a continuing competition for stakes among the clients of an evaluation' (Alkin, 1990: 51). Within any programme context there will be various groups representing different institutional, professional and ideological perspectives. One approach to evaluation research that readily acknowledges this situation as a potential source of conflict, and lays considerable emphasis upon the importance of eliciting the views of programme planners, providers and participants, is 'pluralistic evaluation' (Smith and Cantley, 1985a). Smith and Cantley describe how they adopted this approach in their evaluation of a new psychogeriatric day hospital. As they assert,

> The central point we are making is that if we are to understand and evaluate the part played by the several different groups involved in the care of a client group then we must understand how they use different criteria of success in their own interests and how 'success' thus operates in the social context of its use. (Smith and Cantley, 1985b: 12)

This requires the evaluator to be aware of, and sensitive to, the different sets of interests encountered within a particular policy or programme setting. A comprehensive evaluation is not simply about identifying a set of objective, quantitative indicators that can be used to measure success, but is also about describing the nature of the interaction that takes place between the different stakeholder groups. Thus, both qualitative and quantitative research methods are used when conducting a pluralistic evaluation. Qualitative data collection techniques are particularly useful for exploring the views and perspectives of the different interest groups found within a specific policy context.

Smith and Cantley describe the major characteristic features of the pluralistic approach to evaluation as follows. In terms of its theoretical and intellectual roots, the approach 'draws quite heavily both upon theories of political pluralism and upon the "subjectivist" school within sociology' (1985a: 158). Consequently, one of the first steps in the evaluation research process is to identify the main groups with a stake in the policy or programme under review. The evaluator then compares them with each other in terms of how they define the situation, what their principal objectives are and what tactics they employ to protect or further their interests. A further feature of this approach is its focus upon collecting data to illustrate the different ways in which the constituent groups define what counts as a success. For the pluralist evaluator 'success' is clearly not a unitary concept. Data relating to the plurality of definitions of success are a key element in this evaluation strategy. As Smith and Cantley assert, 'an attempt to disentangle the meanings and pursuit of "success" is an intrinsic part of the evaluation exercise' (1985b: 173).

The existence of a plurality of perspectives clearly has implications when it comes to choosing which data collection methods to employ. Smith and Cantley observe that some data sources are 'interest-bound', insofar as they represent the views and interests of a particular set of stakeholders. Take, for example, quantitative outcome measures and key performance indicators used by organizations to evaluate whether or not they are achieving their stated goals. These measures are portrayed as providing hard, objective, factual information for decision-making purposes. However, it needs to be remembered that organizations are made up of groups representing diverse and conflicting interests who may have different views regarding the definition of organizational objectives (Hickson, 1987). As Goddard and Powell proclaim, 'such objectives are value-laden, and often constructed by a very few individuals. Any results from such studies merely measure the service in terms of what those who set the objectives deem important' (1994: 474). It follows that the final choice of indicators or measures of success is often the result of the ability of a particular group to impose their definition of the situation. Invariably this ability derives from the power held by the group, and is not necessarily an acknowledgement that their chosen measures are the most appropriate in all circumstances. It is recommended that the pluralistic evaluator should use a wide range of data collection methods in order to ensure that the views of all the major stakeholder groups are reflected in the final analysis.

For Smith and Cantley, pluralistic evaluation has a number of advantages over more traditionally oriented approaches to evaluative research. Many of these advantages stem from the fact that one of its key characteristics is its attempt to address the interests and concerns of those groups with a vested interest in the programme or policy under consideration. It is claimed that not only does a pluralistic strategy reveal different ways of determining and measuring success, but it also provides information that helps in accounting for why success or failure occurs in a particular context. As Smith and Cantley claim, 'Pluralistic evaluation says a good deal about why some outcomes but not others take place' (1985b: 13). This makes it much easier to establish how current practices might be altered to improve programme performance, and enables those responsible for planning and providing services to identify the kinds of new initiatives that are needed to improve the situation.

Furthermore, supporters of this approach argue that because it encourages the involvement of significant stakeholder groups in the evaluation process and gives them an opportunity to express their views, it stands a realistic chance of producing what may be interpreted as a politically neutral assessment. In other words, a pluralistic orientation provides a safeguard against an evaluation being accused of only reflecting the interests and opinions of one or two strategically placed groups. Clearly, this has implications when it comes to the implementation of evaluation findings. If an evaluation takes into account the diverse interests of the major groups involved, then it is less likely that the findings will be opposed by groups claiming that their particular interests have not received due consideration.

The stakeholder concept features prominently in mainstream evaluation. Without a doubt, there are positive aspects to stakeholder participation, for example it increases the range and quantity of information available to the evaluator, and it provides an opportunity for diverse interest groups to feed their views into the decision-making process. However, it should not be assumed that the stakeholder approach is capable of resolving the conflicts that can characterize the relationships between various interest groups (Weiss, 1983b). Indeed, a particular social programme may have an impact on a number of disparate groups, some of which have diametrically opposed expectations and competing interests. As the focus of a stakeholder-based evaluation is largely determined by the questions and concerns raised by the participating groups, it is important to understand something about the way in which stakeholders are selected for participation and the relationship between the evaluator and the various stakeholder groups. This raises the wider question of the role the evaluator plays in the evaluation process, to which we now turn our attention.

The role of the evaluator

As Rossi and Freeman proclaim, 'Evaluation research is more than the application of methods. It is also a political and managerial activity'

(1993: 15). Consequently, there is more to the role of the evaluator than simply that of a technical expert. Indeed, there are many aspects to the role the evaluator performs in the process of conducting an evaluation. A fundamental distinction is usually drawn between external and internal evaluation roles. An external evaluator is an independent consultant who is commissioned to undertake an evaluation on behalf of a service-providing agency or funding organization. For example, staff involved in running a community-based drug rehabilitation programme may employ an outside consultant to examine the relative success of different treatment strategies. When funding a social programme or welfare initiative, a charitable trust or government department may stipulate that some form of external evaluation is conducted. As Patton observes, 'The defining characteristic of external evaluators is that they have no long-term, ongoing position within the program or organization being evaluated' (1986: 309). In contrast, internal evaluators are full-time employees who carry out evaluations within their own organizations as directed by senior management.

The advantages and disadvantages associated with the external–internal evaluator dichotomy are captured in Table 1.2.

Although internal and external evaluators use the same research methods and encounter similar methodological problems, their relationship to the organization or agency in which they carry out their evaluations is very different. This can have implications for the nature and content of their respective research roles. For example, Patton (1986) describes how the formal evaluation skills of internal evaluators are often under-utilized, especially when they are asked to produce information as part of a public relations exercise or expected to undertake nothing more than general monitoring activities.

As useful as the internal–external dichotomy is for helping us to appreciate some of the ways in which the organizational context might influence the evaluator's role, it should not be assumed that the two approaches are mutually exclusive. Patton (1986) maintains that there are opportunities for combining the two in a single evaluation, thus effectively benefiting from the advantages that each has to offer. There is also the view that not all evaluator roles are embraced by the internal–external dichotomy. For example, when discussing participatory evaluation, Mathison (1994) describes how it is possible for an external evaluator, who has worked with a particular organization over a long period of time, to enter into a form of partnership. The evaluator comes to identify with the aims of the organization, in this case the provision of better educational programmes, and becomes 'an involved collaborating participant in the evaluation' (1994: 304).

As the theory and practice of evaluation research has developed, different aspects of the evaluator's role have been emphasized. Initially, the evaluator was viewed as a technical expert, a value-neutral scientist who was able to provide decision-makers with information to help them

TABLE 1.2 *The advantages and disadvantages of using internal or external evaluators*

Advantages

Internal evaluators will be:

- familiar with the history, background, policies, issues and culture of the organization;
- likely to be more committed to implementing evaluation recommendations, having been responsible for producing them;
- likely to focus on the central concerns as perceived by management.

External evaluators have:

- an independent stance and offer a fresh perspective;
- an objective, critical approach;
- an overview of numerous organizations to serve as comparisons;
- a knowledge and experience of a wide range of evaluation techniques;
- a resilience to intimidation by management.

Disadvantages

Internal evaluators may:

- have a vested interest in a particular outcome;
- often be over-influenced by the history and knowledge of organizational issues;
- sometimes be over-influenced by the known views of management;
- be unlikely to have had experience of a broad range of evaluation techniques;
- be less committed to the need for evaluation;
- be inclined to favour programmes developed within their own unit or section;
- find it difficult to encourage stakeholders in their own organization to actively participate in the evaluation process.

External evaluators may be:

- ignorant of internal matters so that judgements may not reflect the complex reality of the situation;
- unaware as to who are the key players in a particular setting and thus more easily misled by interested parties;
- more interested in a report than its implementation;
- influenced by the need to secure future contracts;
- insensitive to organizational norms and internal relationships;
- primarily responsible to an external organization.

Sources: Adapted from Feek (1988) and Love (1991)

modify existing programmes and policies. Campbell (1988) sees the role in a passive sense, as one of servant-evaluator or 'servant-methodologist' (Shadish et al., 1991: 141), in which the evaluator's expertise is used to inform decision-makers about the failure or success of existing programmes. The evaluator is depicted as a neutral, objective analyst, an 'expert witness' (Rossi and Freeman, 1993: 417) who provides information but does not make policy decisions. In the words of Rossi and Freeman, 'the proper role of evaluation is to contribute the best possible knowledge on evaluation issues to the political process . . . and evaluators should not attempt to supplant that process' (1993: 420).

Acting as an information broker is a major feature of the evaluator's role. However, Scriven (1993) warns against the dangers of identifying too closely with the interests of decision-makers and thus effectively overlooking the concerns of other stakeholder groups. The evaluator needs to be 'multi-partisan' and act as both an informant and educator to all parties in an evaluation (Cronbach et al., 1980). This involves making information available to all those groups with a vested interest in a particular programme and not just providing information for those with the power to make decisions. The educative function of the evaluator's role is also stressed by Stake and Trumbull (1982) when they assert that the programme evaluator is there to support practitioners and help them to arrive at new understandings of situations and contexts. In what Stake (1975) calls responsive evaluation the emphasis is clearly on evaluation as a service and the evaluator as a facilitator. The evaluator is encouraged to identify and concentrate on the practical concerns of programme practitioners and participants, rather than focus on the concerns of distant policy-makers who are far removed from actual programme activities, as this is more likely to produce information relevant for programme improvement.

How the evaluator perceives his or her role may not only influence the choice of research methods, but will probably also have implications for the nature of the relationship the evaluator has with the various stakeholder groups. For example, Stake (1981) is a strong advocate of case study methodology employing qualitative methods, which he sees as the most appropriate way of obtaining rich experiential understandings of specific programme contexts; these understandings provide a basis for naturalistic generalizations which influence action choices. Working in the responsive mode requires the evaluator to have direct contact with programme practitioners and participants in order to identify the value positions and primary practical problems within a particular evaluation context. The evaluator is there to provide a service and meet the needs of his or her clients; a concerted effort is made to ensure that the information needs of the clients are clearly identified. As a facilitator the evaluator's task is to help those engaged in a programme to articulate their concerns, describe what they see as the core issues and develop their own solutions. The responsive evaluator does not approach an evaluation with any preconceived ideas as to what the evaluation questions should be or how the success of a programme can be measured. Through detailed and systematic observational fieldwork, and in-depth interviews with programme participants, key evaluation issues are allowed to emerge. In this way, the views of various stakeholder groups are represented in the evaluation process.

The evaluator can also be seen as a stakeholder insofar as she or he is concerned with producing a methodologically sound piece of work that addresses the salient evaluation issues and makes a worthwhile contribution to the decision-making process. As the existence of multiple stakeholder groups with divergent interests produces the potential for conflict, when it comes to deciding on the priorities in a particular evaluation context, the evaluator may have to take on the role of mediator or 'consensus generator' (Chen, 1990: 78). This requires that the evaluator use his or her expertise to encourage the various stakeholders to appreciate each other's viewpoint and come to a consensus concerning the focus of a proposed evaluation. As Chen notes, 'Evaluators cannot passively accept the values and views of the other stakeholders; as evaluation experts, they should present their professional views, having in mind the planning of a useful evaluation' (1990: 78).

The idea of a collaborative role for the evaluator is developed in the work of Guba and Lincoln (1981, 1989) and is an integral feature of what they term fourth-generation evaluation. They describe this type of evaluation as 'a socio-political process that is simultaneously diagnostic, change-oriented and educative for all the parties involved' (Lincoln and Guba, 1985: 141). Essentially it constitutes a participatory form of evaluation in which the evaluator collaborates with programme stakeholders through all stages in the evaluation process. Stakeholders are not viewed as merely sources of data but are seen as having an important part to play in deciding the nature, form and content of the evaluation itself. For example, as Guba and Lincoln maintain, 'Evaluators are subjective partners with stakeholders in the literal creation of evaluation data' (1989: 110). Part of the fourth-generation evaluator's role involves facilitating communication among the multiple stakeholder groups and creating opportunities for them to formulate their own ideas and participate in the collection, analysis and interpretation of data. Given the fact that different stakeholder groups have different value systems, the evaluator is cast in the role of a mediator engaged in a process of negotiation to establish a value consensus, or some common ground, around which an evaluation can be constructed. As Greene declares, for Guba and Lincoln the 'evaluator's role is not so much one of describer and consultant as one of negotiator and social change catalyst' (1994: 540).

Collaboration is also a fundamental feature of empowerment evaluation, which is 'creating a new niche in the intellectual landscape of evaluation' (Fetterman, 1994a: 11). Basically, it is a democratic approach designed to promote self-determination. The idea is that evaluation concepts and research techniques can be applied in such a way as to give programme participants a voice in evaluation. According to one advocate,

> Empowerment evaluation is the use of evaluation to help others help themselves. It is designed to foster self-determination, rather than dependency. Empowerment evaluation focuses on improvement, is collaborative, and requires both qualitative and quantitative methodologies. (Fetterman, 1994b: 305)

Although empowerment evaluation can be distinguished from other approaches to evaluation, it can take a number of different forms. Its advantages become apparent once we examine the type of roles performed by the evaluator working within this particular perspective.

In one sense, evaluators can help to empower groups by acting as their advocates or spokespersons when reporting evaluation findings. This is particularly relevant when the groups concerned are socially marginalized, economically disadvantaged and powerless. According to Fetterman, evaluators have a moral responsibility to act as advocates for powerless stakeholder groups. This advocate role does not only influence the dissemination of research findings but also has implications for how the evaluation is conducted. As Fetterman describes, 'Advocate evaluators allow participants to shape the direction of the evaluation, suggest ideal solutions to their problems, and then take an active role in making social change happen' (1994a: 6).

Four basic procedural steps to empowerment evaluation are outlined by Fetterman (1994b) as follows. First, there is the initial task of establishing how things stand with a programme at the outset; this involves identifying the major strengths and weaknesses of a programme. Second, there is the question of determining what the programme hopes to achieve, this entails determining programme goals and setting objectives. The third step involves the evaluator working closely with programme staff and participants to help them to develop programme practices and strategies to achieve the principal aims and objectives. Finally, the evaluator helps programme staff to identify the kind of information they need to gather in order to evaluate the extent to which a particular programme is achieving its stated goals. As Fetterman states, the idea is to encourage those staff engaged in programme activities to embrace evaluation so as it becomes a natural and integral part of the whole process of programme design, planning and management.

Given their expert knowledge and technical skills, evaluators have been referred to as 'power merchants' (Fein et al., 1993). However, in empowerment evaluation, the emphasis is on empowering stakeholders. Rather than relying on professional evaluators to identify the evaluation issues and construct and implement evaluation study designs, this approach stresses self-determination and self-evaluation. The evaluator takes on the role of trainer-facilitator, whose primary objective is to ensure that the interests served by the evaluation are those of the programme participants. Stakeholders are encouraged to identify their own evaluation needs and develop the skills and techniques necessary to become active participants in the evaluation process. Ultimately, this can lead to programme staff acquiring the ability to carry out their own evaluation studies in the future. In this way, evaluation becomes an integral part of programme design and planning.

As Fetterman suggests, empowerment evaluation can be a liberating experience for individuals, groups, organizations and communities. By working in close partnership with stakeholders, evaluators are able to set up mechanisms to support self-evaluation activities presided over by the stakeholders themselves. This can apply across a range of evaluation settings. Cracknell (1996) describes procedures for evaluating the innumerable small overseas projects funded by the United Nations. The UN relies on self-evaluation at the local level, complemented by advice and support from professionally qualified evaluators based at headquarters. Arrangements such as these ensure that local programme staff not only develop a sense of commitment to evaluation but also come to feel a sense of ownership of the evaluation process itself.

Participation and empowerment also feature in some action research designs. In general terms action research can be described as 'a cyclical inquiry process that involves diagnosing a problem situation, planning action steps, and implementing and evaluating outcomes' (Elden and Chisholm, 1993: 124). As a research strategy it incorporates elements of research, action and evaluation. This suggests that there is some commonality between evaluation research and action research, making it possible for an action research strategy to be employed as part of a formative evaluation research design. Patton (1988b) describes his utilization-focused evaluation as a combination of an action research and stakeholder-oriented approach. On the whole, action research is a collaborative enterprise aimed at finding solutions to practical problems. In this context evaluation data are used for diagnostic purposes, they help in ascertaining the impact of planned interventions and also inform decision-making regarding future changes. Collaboration between the professional researcher and those individuals and groups working in the area under investigation can occur at all stages of the research process, from the identification of the problem right through to the analysis and interpretation of the findings.

One form of action research in which full collaboration is encouraged between practitioners and researchers is known as participatory action research. This has been described as follows:

> In participatory action research (PAR), some of the people in the organization or community under study participate actively with the professional researcher throughout the research process from the initial design to the final presentation of results and discussion of their action implications. PAR thus contrasts sharply with the conventional model of pure research, in which members of organizations and communities are treated as passive subjects, with some of them participating only to the extent of authorizing the project, being its subjects, and receiving the results. PAR is *applied* research, but it also contrasts sharply with the most common type of applied research, in which the researchers serve as professional experts, designing the project, gathering the data, interpreting the findings, and recommending action to the client organization. Like the conventional model of pure research, this is an elitist model of research relationships. In PAR, some of the members of the

organization we study are actively engaged in the quest for information and ideas to guide their future actions. (Whyte, 1991: 20)

In essence, participatory action research implies that the relevant stakeholders or their representatives play an active part in the research process. However, as Greenwood, Whyte and Harkavy (1993) assert, a researcher working within this methodological framework is not in a position to dictate that a participatory action research design will be employed. A participatory approach must be allowed to emerge, it cannot be imposed from the outset. They see participatory action research as existing at one end of a continuum from 'expert research'. In the extreme case of the latter, the researcher exercises full control over the design and execution of the research. At the opposite end of the continuum, design and execution are part of a highly collaborative process involving researchers and project or programme practitioners and participants.

All this has implications for the nature and content of the interaction between professional evaluators or researchers and practitioners and participants. In order to understand how the collaborative process works, it is necessary to know something about the respective roles performed by researchers and participants in specific programme contexts. Elden and Levin (1991) suggest distinguishing between insider and outsider frameworks. A framework is described as a way of understanding. Insiders are the project workers or programme staff who have first-hand experience of a particular situation. They have their views about programme goals and problem solutions. The outsiders are the external researchers, the social scientists, who bring a battery of research skills and a wealth of theoretical ideas: 'The richness and quality of the research depends on the ability of the insiders and outsiders to play their different frameworks and expertise against each other to create a new, third explanatory framework' (1991: 132). According to Elden and Levin, this new way of understanding is a product of the collaborative process and could not have evolved singly from within the existing frameworks. The new, shared framework is generated from a merging of existing frameworks.

Elden and Levin (1991) note how participatory forms of action research provide empowerment through learning in three main ways. First, active involvement in research enables participants to acquire new insights and reach new levels of understanding. Carr and Kemmis (1986) describe action research as a form of 'self-reflective enquiry'. Second, by participating in the research experience stakeholders learn how to learn. Finally, the whole experience can be a liberating one insofar as participating stakeholders discover how to create new opportunities for action. Thus, participatory action research, like empowerment evaluation, has the potential to be both illuminating and liberating.

Clearly, there is much to commend in the stakeholder-based approach to evaluation with its emphasis on creating a collaborative partnership between the evaluator and the principal stakeholders. However, this approach has its challenges. For example, identifying the different 'worlds of meaning' and encouraging disparate groups to arrive at a common vision of the future (Fetterman, 1994b) is no easy task for the evaluator. Not only might some stakeholder groups be suspicious of the whole idea of evaluation and distrustful of the involvement of external evaluators, but there might also be conflicts of interest among the major stakeholder groups themselves. Often the evaluator needs to work at establishing and maintaining a climate of trust and co-operation. It may be particularly difficult to achieve this especially when dealing with groups who feel that their views have been ignored in the past (O'Neill, 1995).

More fundamentally, there is the general question as to whether this approach actually gives programme participants a real and influential voice in the evaluation process. As Mark and Shotland (1985) assert, stakeholder participation can lead to pseudo-empowerment. This can come about in two ways. First, in any given evaluation situation stakeholder groups are not guaranteed equal representation. Stakeholder selection involves basic value judgements on the part of the evaluator. According to Mark and Shotland (1985), the evaluator's perceptions of the level of power held by a group and the legitimacy accorded to a particular group's interests will influence their chances of selection. It follows therefore that the evaluator plays a large part in determining the nature and the extent of the involvement of stakeholder groups. If the evaluator favours particular groups, such as those that appear to be more accessible or co-operative, this will influence the subsequent focus of the evaluation and lead to the exclusion of some groups. Secondly, participation may be limited in the sense that although stakeholders are granted a say in the actual evaluation, some groups may find that they are given little, if any, opportunity to influence the programme itself. Thus, while involving stakeholders in the evaluation may give the impression of empowerment, it could be argued that,

> Viewed cynically, this possible effect of stakeholder-based evaluation could be seen as a means of social control, rather than empowerment, by which the powerful appease the less powerful by giving the appearance of control without relinquishing any actual power. (Mark and Shotland, 1985: 618)

It is possible to see the evaluator in the role of a 'benevolent dictator', with power permeating downwards from the evaluator to the stakeholders, producing what can be described as a form of 'autocratic power sharing' (1985: 618).

Irrespective of the type of evaluation being conducted, the professional evaluator can take on any of a number of roles including 'collaborator, trainer, group facilitator, politician, organizational analyst, internal colleague, external expert, methodologist, information broker, communicator, change agent, diplomat, problem solver and creative consultant' (Patton, 1986: 319). Ultimately the choice of roles will depend on the circumstances surrounding the evaluation, as well as the evaluator's own personal characteristics and previous professional experience. The roles are not necessarily mutually exclusive and the evaluator may occupy a different combination of roles at various stages in the course of a single evaluative study.

The role of theory

To appreciate fully the role of the evaluator it is necessary to have some understanding of the contribution theory makes to evaluation. This is a topic often overlooked by many introductory texts where evaluation is portrayed as an atheoretical, methods-oriented enterprise. However, the importance of theory is stressed by a number of evaluators who represent different perspectives within the discipline (Patton, 1989; Chen, 1990; Pawson and Tilley, 1997; Weiss, 1997). In a general sense, theory performs many functions and is a vital element in the evaluation process. For example, it can provide evaluators with a rationale for choosing particular research methods and methodological approaches in specific evaluation contexts. Theory can also help to focus an evaluation by directing the evaluator to certain issues and problems.

When exploring the relationship between theory and evaluation it is important to distinguish between theory *about* evaluation and theory *in* evaluation. It is the former that is of interest to Shadish et al. (1991) in their exposition of some of the basic theories underlying practical programme evaluation. As they assert:

> Evaluation theory tells us when, where, and why some methods should be applied and others not, suggesting sequences in which methods could be applied, ways different methods can be combined, types of questions answered better or less well by a particular method, and benefits to be expected from some methods as opposed to others. Evaluation theories are like military strategy and tactics; methods are like military weapons and logistics. (Shadish et al., 1991: 34)

In describing the evolution of evaluation theory, through a study of the writings of seven major evaluation theorists, Shadish et al. maintain that a sound and comprehensive theory of evaluation should contain five major components. They describe these as social programming, knowledge construction, knowledge use, valuing and practice.

Essentially the term evaluation theory refers to theory as it is applied to the actual practice of evaluation. In other words, it is theory about the doing of evaluation. This is very different to focusing on programme theory *in* evaluation, where the emphasis is on specifying how a particular intervention or programme is supposed to operate. Weiss (1972) was one of the first evaluation theorists to raise the issue of theory-focused programme evaluation. The theory-guided approach is commonly referred to as theory-driven (Chen and Rossi, 1981) or theory-based evaluation (Weiss, 1995). To understand the implications of a theory-driven perspective for evaluation practice and the role of the evaluator it is necessary to take a closer look at programme theory. We need to know what it is, why it is important, where it comes from and what its major attributes are.

As mentioned at the beginning of this chapter, evaluation research is concerned with discovering whether or not social programmes or planned interventions work. Interventions or programmes constitute an organized response to a perceived problem. For example, a firm may introduce a health and safety initiative to reduce the number of workplace accidents; a school may institute a mentoring scheme for difficult and disruptive pupils; anger management courses and behavioural skills training may be made available to individuals convicted of crimes involving violence to the person. No matter what the programme context, those responsible for designing and implementing a programme will not only have some idea of what they hope to achieve (i.e. the desired outcomes) but will also have some notion as to how they expect a programme to actually produce the desired impact. As Fitz-Gibbon and Morris state, 'The term "theory-based" evaluation . . . means an evaluation based on a model, theory, or philosophy about how the program works; a model, theory, or philosophy which indicates the causal relationships supposedly operating in the program' (1996: 178). Programme theory is generally made up of a combination of hunches, beliefs, intuitive assumptions and knowledge founded on practical experience.

In reality, the theory behind a programme is not always made explicit nor is it fully articulated by policy-makers or programme designers. An early task facing the evaluator is to identify the beliefs and assumptions underlying a planned intervention. As Wholey (1987) maintains, a programme cannot be properly evaluated unless there is some understanding of its underlying theoretical basis. It is this focus on theory that separates evaluation research from other forms of evaluation activity such as periodic inspection, systematic monitoring and auditing. In evaluation research the evaluator engages in the specification and testing of theory. This emphasis on theory clearly has implications for the kind of role performed by the evaluator, as indicated by Chen and Rossi (1981) when they argue that the conventional 'official-goal-fixed approach' to evaluation should be replaced by the 'multi-goal, theory-driven approach'. In the case of the former, the evaluator concentrates on a fairly limited number of outcome measures as prescribed by programme planners and practitioners. The alternative approach creates a more active and integrated role for the evaluator. Under the theory-driven approach, the evaluator seeks to 'actively search for and construct a theoretically justified model of the social problem' (1981: 43) so as to help to specify the mechanisms by which a programme can be expected to produce change. Thus, developing a programme theory is a step towards clarifying the relationship between a programme's activities and its effects. Using theory in this way helps to structure an evaluation.

Chen (1990) advocates the replacing of the method-oriented approach to evaluation with a theory-driven perspective; in so doing he distinguishes between two broad types of programme theory, descriptive and prescriptive. The former is concerned with linking theory, process and outcomes through an exploration of a programme's causal mechanisms and is therefore referred to as causative theory. It is this type of theory that features in evaluations of programme effectiveness and seeks to explain how, and under what conditions, a programme works. The evaluator working with causative theory is concerned with the elaboration of treatment–outcome relationships. In contrast, prescriptive or normative theory looks at what form the structure of a programme should take. As Chen observes, 'The evaluation of normative theory . . . requires only that the consistency between the theoretical program structure and the implemented program structure be assessed' (1990: 44). Here the evaluator is concerned with identifying problems in the design, implementation and operation of a programme.

The movement towards theory-driven evaluations has recently been given an impetus by the introduction of Pawson and Tilley's (1997) brand of scientific realist evaluation. It is their contention that 'the careful enunciation of program theory is the prerequisite to sound evaluation' (1997: 56–7). Realist social explanation provides a model for the specification of the theory underlying a social programme based on a conceptual configuration of mechanisms, contexts and outcomes. As they maintain, simply showing that a specific outcome follows a particular intervention does not necessarily lead to a full causal explanation as to why a programme works. There is more to measuring programme success than merely monitoring the patterning of inputs and outputs. Realist evaluators stress that it is the actions of individuals and groups that make interventions work. The evaluator needs to understand how, and under what conditions, a programme's causal potential is released. This is achieved by thinking in terms of context-mechanism-outcome configurations. Such a configuration is described as 'a proposition stating what it is about a program which works for whom and in what circumstances' (1997: 217). These propositions are an integral feature in the development and testing of programme theory. Ultimately, theory provides guidelines for establishing the key issues in an evaluation and determines what the most appropriate research methods are for addressing those issues.

Evaluation research is very much a theory-testing endeavour, but how does the evaluator arrive at the theory in the first place? Weiss identifies four basic sources of information that help in the generation and specification of programme theories: 'documents, people, prior research and logical reasoning' (1997: 508). First, the evaluator can acquire an insight into the objectives of a programme by studying the available documentary evidence; this includes internal reports, minutes of committee meetings, applications for funding and literature disseminated by the programme. However, this material is of limited usefulness, as programme theories are not always made explicit. Consequently, as Weiss states, many evaluators begin theory-based evaluations by talking to programme administrators, practitioners and planners. Identifying a programme's theory of change becomes a collaborative process in which both evaluators and stakeholders are active participants. Realist evaluators claim that the interview has an important role to play in the testing and refining of theory: 'Its key aspect is the creation of a situation in which the theoretical postulates and conceptual structures under investigation are open for inspection in a way that allows the respondent to make an informed and critical contribution to them' (Pawson and Tilley, 1997: 182). Through interviews with principal stakeholders the evaluator can construct a tentative model of the links between activities, mechanisms, contexts and outcomes. This view of programme theorizing as an interactive process is also a feature of utilization-focused evaluation (Patton, 1986). Although the evaluator's own theories may be used to help to clarify a programme's theory of action, in this case primary importance is given to the theories espoused by the major stakeholders.

Previous research findings are a third source of information available to the evaluator. Chen (1990) is an enthusiastic advocate of the use of social science theory in the construction of programme theory. While he acknowledges the value of stakeholder contributions he maintains that programme theory based exclusively on the stakeholders' viewpoint may fail to identify some potential causal links. Knowledge of social science theory gives the evaluator an important edge when it comes to understanding not only the contexts within which programmes operate, but also how social processes can influence outcomes. A view endorsed by Bulmer when he asserts that good evaluation research design is achieved by successfully blending 'the potential effects as defined by the programme with possible effects derived from social science knowledge and theory' (1986: 179). However, Weiss is less optimistic about the potential contribution of social science theory in general, which she sees as being 'at a high level of abstraction . . . and not very useful at the level of specificity at which programs operate' (1997: 509). Past research studies of programmes similar to the one currently under review are seen as offering the evaluator a better source of information from which to fashion a series of causal assumptions and theoretical propositions.

The fourth source of basic information for programme theory building recognized by Weiss is logical reasoning. There is an element of this in the other three information sources mentioned.

Clearly, programme theory performs a number of important functions in the evaluation process. It helps to identify the key evaluation questions, determine what research methods are most appropriate and clarify the nature and content of the relationship between a programme's activities and its outcomes. Despite its advantages, a theory-based approach is not the automatic choice in every evaluation situation. As Weiss (1997) points out, theory-based evaluation has its costs; collecting, collating, analysing and interpreting the requisite data can be both time-consuming and expensive. In small-scale evaluations, where resources are limited, theory-driven evaluation may not be a practical proposition. However, a theory-based approach is essential if the objective of the exercise is to establish how and why a social programme succeeds or fails. Before a theory of change can be subjected to an evaluation it needs to meet three criteria (Connell and Kubisch, 1997). First, it must be 'plausible', that is the postulated relationship between the proposed programme activities and the intended outcomes must appear coherent and logical. Second, the planned change should be 'doable'. In other words, there must be sufficient resources available and the necessary expertise on hand to see the initiative through. Finally, the theory of change must be 'testable', that is it must be amenable to empirical investigation and verification.

Summary

There are many dimensions to evaluation. According to Berk and Rossi, 'commonsense program evaluation has evolved into "evaluation *research*", a heterogeneous mix of substantive issues and procedures' (1990: 8). The purpose of this chapter has been to explore some of those issues and procedures. During the course of conducting an evaluation an evaluator can be called upon to perform a variety of roles and serve the needs and interests of a diverse collection of stakeholders. It is important to be aware of the social and political context in which evaluation research is undertaken. As regards research methods and methodological perspectives, the social sciences provide a rich source of practical advice, technical information and theoretical insight. The following two chapters deal with some of the methodological issues and methods decisions facing evaluators.

2 Quantity and Quality: Paradigmatic Choices in Evaluation Methodology

Evaluation research is a form of applied research which aims to produce information about the implementation, operation and ultimate effectiveness of policies and programmes designed to bring about change. In contrast to what may be termed basic research, the primary objective is not the discovery of new knowledge but rather the study of the effectiveness with which existing knowledge is used to inform and guide practical action. What distinguishes evaluation from basic research is the purpose for which data are collected. Evaluation research has no methodology of its own: 'it differs from nonevaluative research more in objective or purpose than in design or execution' (Suchman, 1967: 82). As Patton (1986) argues, while basic scientific research is concerned with adding to an existing body of knowledge, 'program evaluation is undertaken to inform decisions, clarify options, reduce uncertainties, and provide information about programs and policies' (1986: 14). He considers the difference in objectives to be abundantly clear when he categorically asserts that, 'Research is aimed at truth. Evaluation is aimed at action' (1986: 14).

Whether they are monitoring performance, conducting a medical or social audit, carrying out a consumer satisfaction survey or undertaking a formal evaluation using scientific methods, evaluators are engaged in collecting and processing information. Consequently, they have been appropriately described as 'active information brokers' involved in 'the business of knowledge construction' (Shadish et al., 1991). Information is obtained by making extensive use of a wide variety of well-established social research methods. If evaluators are to avail themselves of these methods then it is imperative that they are aware of the methodological and philosophical debates surrounding the use of such methods in the social sciences, particularly insofar as these have implications for evaluation practice. For example, it is only by appreciating the strengths and weaknesses of the various methods that the evaluator can be expected to formulate an evaluation design and research strategy capable of producing meaningful findings. It needs to be acknowledged that different methods may produce contradictory results when applied to the same evaluation problem. Inappropriate methods can produce findings that are misleading, which in turn may influence decision-making culminating in a recommendation for the continuation of an ineffective programme or intervention. As Patton (1982) asserts, it is vital that evaluators make informed methods choices, and this can only be achieved if they have an appreciation of the philosophical issues surrounding research methods and methodologies in the social sciences.

Consideration needs to be given to wider philosophical issues not merely in the interests of making better methods choices but also in order to develop evaluation theory. If evaluation is to present itself as a practical scientific undertaking then it needs a theoretical foundation. Chen (1990) maintains that for too long evaluation research has been so excessively preoccupied with methodological questions that it has acquired an atheoretical focus. His proposal for a theory-driven approach is based on the premise that programme evaluation involves more than a collection of diverse methods and data gathering techniques:

> As a discipline, program evaluation must emphasize and develop its own unique, systematic, and theoretically based body of knowledge. Instead of being treated as ends in themselves, methods should be considered to be the means for facilitating the development of knowledge. (Chen, 1990: 30)

As Shadish et al. (1991) note, any emergent theory of evaluation must incorporate a theory of knowledge.

There are four key elements to our understanding of knowledge construction. First, there are issues surrounding methods, such as, which techniques to use for collecting data and which analytical procedures are the most appropriate. Second, there are considerations of general methodology, which relate to the overall logic of inquiry and cover the general principles by which research tools and techniques are applied. For example, whether or not to employ an experimental research design. Third, there are questions of ontology which are concerned with being and the nature of reality. Finally, there are matters of epistemology which are concerned with questions of knowing and the nature and limits of knowledge. While the first two key elements address the practicalities of knowledge construction, the latter two concentrate on the philosophical assumptions underlying research practice.

Although 'terms like *ontology* and *epistemology* bore many evaluators, because they conjure up images of sterile philosophical debates' (Shadish et al., 1991: 42) they cannot be ignored if evaluation is to become more theory-oriented. Indeed, as will be seen, the debates are far from sterile especially given that contemporary evaluation studies are becoming increasingly characterized by epistemological and methodological pluralism (Fetterman, 1988).

The paradigm problem

Within the social sciences there is a long-established debate about the relative merits of quantitative and qualitative methods. Given the extent to which evaluation research has utilized such methods it is understandable that this debate has found its way into the evaluation literature. It constitutes what is known as 'the great paradigm wars' (Gage, 1989) or the 'paradigm problem' (Chambers et al., 1992).

Drawing on the work of Thomas Kuhn (1970), Patton (1986) describes the concept of paradigm:

> A paradigm is a world view, a general perspective; a way of breaking down the complexity of the real world. As such, paradigms are deeply embedded in the socialization of adherents and practitioners: Paradigms tell them what is important, legitimate and reasonable. Paradigms are also normative, telling the practitioner what to do without the necessity of long existential or epistemological consideration. (Patton, 1986: 181)

A paradigm not only advances a set of assumptions about the world but also provides a philosophical framework for the study of that world. As such paradigms serve a positive function by guiding the process of inquiry and forming a 'basis for the practice of science' (Kuhn, 1970: 6). They direct the researcher towards those research methods and methodologies that are considered appropriate, given the nature of the phenomena under investigation.

There is also a negative side. Once a paradigm dominates a discipline it can suppress new lines of inquiry or stifle creativity. However, dominant paradigms do not go unchallenged. 'Scientific revolutions' (Kuhn, 1970) or 'paradigm shifts' occur when new modes of thought successfully challenge an existing paradigm and replace it with an alternative. It has been claimed that the increasing use of qualitative methods by evaluators is of paradigmatic proportions and represents 'a silent scientific revolution in evaluation' (Fetterman, 1988: 4). Thus it can be seen that a paradigm not only embraces a particular philosophical world view but also determines the choice of research methods.

For some the paradigms debate is seen as something of a distraction and evaluators are exhorted to concentrate on actual research while leaving the philosophical arguments to others (Miles and Huberman, 1988). Although a strong commitment to practical work is essential, evaluators need to have a clear understanding of the fundamental features of the competing paradigms in order to make suitably informed methodological decisions. Knowledge of the paradigmatic nature of decision-making will 'help make evaluators more aware of their methodological biases and paradigmatic assumptions so that they *can* make flexible, sophisticated, and adaptive methodological choices' (Patton, 1988a: 119). An insight into the paradigms debate is essential if evaluators are to avoid becoming slavishly attached to one particular paradigm. This will hopefully ensure that the methods chosen will be determined by the nature of the research problem rather than by the methodological prejudices of the researcher. Throughout the 1980s Patton, in numerous articles and books, criticized much evaluation practice in the United States of America because it was based on habit; he emphasized the need for greater creativity in the use of methods and a willingness on the part of practitioners to give more consideration to the specific context in which an evaluation is conducted (Patton, 1980, 1982, 1986, 1988a). Thus it can be seen that the paradigms debate, far from being solely an exercise in metaphysics, has practical relevance.

At the centre of the debate is the issue of the relative merits and demerits of what are sometimes presented as two divergent paradigms, namely, the quantitative and qualitative. Numerous terms have been used to describe the quantitative paradigm, such as, traditional, conventional, scientific, experimental, positivist, empiricist and hypothetico-deductive (Patton, 1986; Guba and Lincoln, 1988; Creswell, 1994). The qualitative paradigm has been variously labelled naturalistic (Guba and Lincoln, 1981), constructivist (Guba and Lincoln, 1989), interpretivist (Smith, 1989), postpositivist (Quantz, 1992), holistic-inductive and alternative (Patton, 1975). Within the social sciences, particularly sociology, there is a substantial literature devoted to exploring the nature of the differences between the quantitative and qualitative traditions in research. The two traditions have been referred to as scientific and humanistic (Martindale, 1974), positivistic and humanistic (Hughes, 1976) and positivistic and interpretive (Giddens, 1976). An understanding of the philosophical assumptions behind these two paradigms is essential if researchers are to be able to identify appropriate methodological guidelines for effective evaluation practice across a variety of policy settings.

It is not possible within the confines of the current chapter to provide a detailed account of the philosophical assumptions characteristic of each paradigm; the subject area is much too complex. However, it is possible to identify what may be considered a dominant set of philosophical tenets which influence and guide social inquiry. The following discussion is merely intended to provide a general overview of the more salient assumptions made by supporters of each of the two approaches. A more detailed treatment of the subject from a general social science perspective can be found in Hughes (1976) and Bryman (1988). The debate as it relates to evaluation research is covered in Cook and Reichardt (1979), Guba and Lincoln (1981), Lincoln and Guba (1985) and Guba (1990).

The quantitative and qualitative paradigms adopt different ontological positions when it comes to the question of the nature of reality. In the case of the former, reality is something which is objective; it exists independently of human perception. It is assumed that there is in fact a single reality, which can be uncovered by applying the same logic of inquiry as found in the natural sciences. A central tenet of this position is that social research should be scientific in the mode of the natural sciences. Although there is one social reality it can be divided and the constituent parts studied independently. By following rational methods of empirical inquiry the social researcher can find regularities and relationships and discover the causes of social phenomena. This is how truth is established, by the application of rigorous and systematic scientific investigation.

Truth is a much more elusive concept for supporters of the qualitative paradigm who reject the notion of a single objective reality existing 'out there'. For them, there are multiple, subjective realities:

> 'Reality' resides neither with an objective external world nor with the subjective mind of the knower, but within dynamic transactions between the two. (Barone, 1992: 31, quoted in Greene, 1994)

As Guba and Lincoln (1988: 93) observe the quantitative or conventional paradigm is based on a 'realist' ontology, whereas the qualitative or alternative paradigm is founded on a 'relativist' ontology. Thus for the qualitative researcher reality is not a single entity which can be subjected to objective measurement. Individuals and groups will construct their own version of reality. The task facing the researcher is not to attempt to identify which version corresponds to the 'truth', but to ensure that the different versions are accurately recorded and reported.

There are also differences between the two paradigms at the epistemological level. The quantitative paradigm assumes that it is possible to separate the researcher from the researched. It is held that the investigator can easily adopt an objective stance and remain detached from the phenomenon under study. This is achieved by using survey methods and experimental research designs which limit the interaction that takes place between the investigator and the investigated and by employing systematic sampling techniques in order to control for bias. Thus the research strategies used are interventionist by nature.

Conversely, qualitative evaluators reject the conventional view that quantitative research methods provide an adequate safeguard against bias and help researchers to maintain an objective stance in the search for the truth. They believe that there are fundamental differences between natural and social phenomena that make the methods associated with the scientific paradigm inappropriate for investigating the social world. The task of the qualitative researcher is to acquire insight and develop understanding. The researcher actually getting close to the data in order to understand the actors' point of view obtains social knowledge. This is very much in contrast to the conventional paradigm, which demands the researcher adopt a stance of scientific detachment. The issue is one of scientific objectivity versus phenomenological subjectivity.

These ontological and epistemological differences have given rise to two distinct methodological postures. One promotes a quantitative methodology by favouring what has been termed the hypothetico-deductive approach, in which causal explanation and prediction follow, in the main, a deductive form of logic. The research process starts with a theory that consists of a set of interconnected general propositions. By a process of logical reasoning the researcher formulates a hypothesis, or tentative explanation, based on the theoretical propositions. The next step is to test the hypothesis. This involves collecting facts to confirm or disprove the hypothesis. These procedural rules dictate that research hypotheses are specified before any data collection takes place. The hypotheses under investigation remain fixed throughout the research exercise. The other methodological stance advocates an inductive, as opposed to deductive, research strategy. Rather than collect data to test previously formulated hypotheses qualitative researchers aim to derive broad generalizations from observed data.

Patton (1986) outlines the implications these two strategies have for evaluation research:

> In evaluation the classic deductive approach is measuring relative attainment of predetermined clear goals in a randomized experiment that permits precise attribution of goal attainment to identifiable program treatments. In contrast, the classic inductive approach is goal-free evaluation, in which the evaluator gathers qualitative data on actual program impacts through direct observations of program activities and in-depth interviews with participants, all without regard to stated, predetermined goals. (Patton, 1986: 194)

The deductive approach requires that the evaluator decides in advance what constitutes a successful programme outcome and determines how such outcomes will be measured. There is no room for such a priori reasoning within the inductive approach. Here the assumption is that a clear understanding of the programme and its outcomes can only be obtained by gaining an insight into the individual experiences of programme participants. Thus the two approaches are associated with different research methods. The quantitative evaluator uses research instruments, such as highly structured questionnaires or interview schedules, which contain predetermined, standardized categories into which individual responses are fitted. The qualitative evaluator wishes to elicit the views of programme participants without imposing pre-existing expectations. This entails choosing methods, such as in-depth interviewing, which allow respondents more freedom of expression. The idea is to explore the impact of programmes by concentrating on the accounts of individuals who have been subjected to the programmes, as opposed to focusing on a number of objective outcome measures.

Care needs to be taken to separate the debate over the two supposedly distinct and opposing methodological paradigms from the debate about the relative advantages and disadvantages of two types of research methods. Evaluators should be aware not only of the assumptions behind the two approaches, but also have an insight into how to choose between the two when conducting an evaluation, as well as knowing when, and under what circumstances, the two approaches can be combined in a single study. An understanding of these issues is essential if the evaluator is to develop the necessary 'practice principles' which will guide them in their work (Chambers et al., 1992: 305).

The quantitative approach

Shadish et al. (1991), in a wide-ranging review of theories of evaluation practice, identify three broad stages in the evolution of evaluation theory in the United States of America. In the first of these stages they observe that the focus of attention was on the need to adopt the logic and rules of scientific method in order to establish the effectiveness of a policy intervention. For some exponents the idea of evaluation as a scientific endeavour is a core defining characteristic, as portrayed by Suchman (1967) when he distinguishes between evaluation and evaluation research:

> *evaluation* [is] the general process of judging the worthwhileness [sic] of some activity regardless of the method employed, and *evaluation research* [is] the specific use of the scientific method for the purpose of making an evaluation. (Suchman, 1967: 31)

Consequently evaluation research came to be dominated by the natural science paradigm which extolled the virtues of objective quantitative measurement, experimental research design and hypothesis testing. These procedures constitute what is known as the hypothetico-deductive approach to research.

Under this paradigm 'the idea of causality lies at the heart of all policy evaluation' (Nachmias, 1979: vii). The ultimate aim of summative evaluation is to establish whether or not there is a cause-and-effect relationship. Policy-makers and professional practitioners frequently raise questions of causality in a variety of settings. For example: Does the introduction of staff–inmate liaison groups improve relations between prison officers and inmates? Do study skills courses improve the academic performance of first year undergraduate students? Which of three health education programmes is more successful in encouraging individuals to adopt a healthier lifestyle? In these examples the policy which is the subject of the evaluation is the independent variable (the cause), while the planned change is the dependent variable (the effect). For some theorists assessing the impact of a policy and ascertaining causality amount to one and the same thing:

> The problem of establishing a program's impact is identical to the problem of establishing that the program is a cause of some specified effect. Hence, establishing impact essentially amounts to establishing causality. (Rossi and Freeman, 1993: 218)

Furthermore, Rossi and Freeman maintain that experimental research designs, utilizing quantitative methods, provide the best way of arriving at causal explanations.

Experimental design

In what has become a classic text on experimental research designs Campbell and Stanley describe the experiment 'as the only available route to cumulative progress' (1963: 3). As a result of its impact on evaluation practice this work has been referred to as the evaluator's 'bible' (Rossi and Wright, 1979). Of the various experimental designs available true experiments are the most strongly recommended. A central feature of true experiments is the random assignment of cases to experimental or control conditions. Randomized experiments have been referred to as 'the flagships of evaluation' (Rossi and Freeman, 1993: 294). With random assignment each individual or case has an equal probability of being placed in a control group or treatment group. In order to appreciate the significance of randomization procedures when it comes to making causal inferences it is necessary to understand the concept of internal validity (Cook and Campbell, 1979). As Berk and Rossi (1990: 82) remark, the 'gold standard' for internal validity requires random methods to be used when allocating units to treatment and control groups. According to Mark and Cook 'internal validity is concerned with the accuracy of inferences about whether the treatment as manipulated caused any change in the outcome as measured' (1984: 75). In programme evaluation, the purpose of an experimental design is to obtain an estimate of the effect of a treatment or intervention by comparing the outcome measures or scores from one or more experimental (i.e. treatment) group(s) with those produced by the control group(s). The measured effect is what is actually observed by the researcher. However, not all the effect may be attributable to the treatment received. In other words there can be a discrepancy between the change produced by the programme and the total change observed by the evaluator. Factors unrelated to a particular intervention may be responsible for observed differences. As Reichardt and Gollob (1989) state, anything that produces a discrepancy between a (true) treatment effect and its estimate constitutes a threat to internal validity.

The problem facing the evaluator is that causal effects cannot be directly observed but must be inferred, this creates the possibility of inferential errors. Take for example the hypothetical case of an evaluation of a training programme designed to help the unemployed find work. An evaluator may attempt to measure the causal effect of the programme by comparing the future employment records of individuals participating in the programme with the records of unemployed adults living either in an area where no such training is available or residing in the same area but not receiving the training. However, before claiming that any observed improvement in employment prospects is a direct result of involvement in the training programme the evaluator needs to take steps to eliminate alternative explanations. For example, if enrolment in the programme is voluntary it could be argued that those who elect to take part are more likely to be the short-term unemployed who are reasonably still optimistic about the prospects of finding work and still have a positive self-image. Their motivation and enthusiasm may give them the edge over the long-term unemployed who may have a more fatalistic outlook. It may be the case that those deciding to join the training course would have found employment even if the course had not been available. If the experimental and control groups were located in different areas consideration would have to be given to factors capable of influencing the chances of individuals finding employment, such as the number, nature and types of vacancies available in each locality. In the presence of internal validity threats it is unwise to infer that an observed effect is due to an imposed treatment.

Campbell and Stanley (1963) list a number of sources of internal invalidity, including selection, maturation and attrition. As far as selection is concerned, the validity of research findings can be called into question when an observed effect is considered to be due not to the treatment or intervention but to differences in the kinds of individuals or cases in the different experimental groups. Maturation is another example of a situation in which an observed effect is due to something other than the treatment received. In this case experimental results obtained in the pre-test and post-test stages may reflect changes taking place over time which would have occurred even if treatment had been withheld. For example, the evaluation of a new reading scheme for primary school children needs to take into account the fact that improvement is likely to take place as part of a natural process of cognitive development. It is also possible that treatment groups may become dissimilar as time passes because they mature at different rates. Attrition poses a threat to internal validity insofar as the loss of subjects from the experimental group, rather than the treatment itself, produces an observed effect.

Clearly, an important task facing the evaluator is the identification and control of those factors that may give rise to alternative explanations for an observed treatment effect. The idea is to promote internal validity and thus avoid making spurious causal inferences. This is perhaps best achieved by adopting random assignment procedures. As noted by Mark and Cook 'the value of random assignment is that it

	Pre-test		Post-test
Experimental group	R O	X	O
Control group	R O		O

FIGURE 2.1   *Pre-test, post-test, control group design*

creates treatment groups that, at the beginning of the experiment, do not differ from each other *on the average'* (1984: 82). In other words, prior to the introduction of the treatment the groups are on the average comparable and all known external confounding influences are eliminated as random assignment assumes that potentially confounding factors are equally distributed between the experimental and control conditions. Consequently fair comparisons between the outcomes of the two conditions are possible. This guarantee of equivalence of the experimental and control groups is one of the two virtues of random assignment. The second virtue is that the evaluator's confidence in the results obtained from a randomized experiment can be stated in statistical terms (Boruch, 1987). Randomized controlled trials are a particularly well-established experimental research design for assessing the effectiveness of drug treatments or other clinical or health care interventions (Newell, 1992).

There is more than one experimental design to choose from. The two designs which sometimes incorporate random assignment are the pre-test, post-test, control group design and the post-test only, control group design. These designs can be expressed using the notation adopted by Campbell and Stanley (1963) where X indicates the exposure of a group to the experimental condition or treatment (e.g. the new programme or policy initiative), O refers to an observation (e.g. the measurement of an outcome) and R signifies random assignment. The pre-test, post-test, control group design is presented in Figure 2.1. Symbols appearing on a given line refer to the same specific individuals, groups or cases, whereas those on parallel lines represent equivalent or matched controls. In the example in Figure 2.1 there are two groups, one experimental group and one control group. Both are measured prior to the experimental group receiving a treatment and both are measured following the treatment. This is the classic experimental design in which group equivalence is obtained by random assignment of individual cases to the experimental and control groups. The extent of the effectiveness of a programme is indicated by the size of the difference in the outcome measures of the two groups. Various statistical procedures can be used to ascertain the significance that may be attached to any observed difference.

The above example is of a two-group design used to examine the impact of one type of programme or intervention. However, it is not unusual for an evaluator to be faced with the problem of assessing a number of similar programmes, or variants of a single programme,

Post-test

Experimental group	R	X	O
Control group	R		O

FIGURE 2.2 *Post-test only, control group design*

simultaneously. By adding experimental groups, the pre-test, post-test, control group design can enable the evaluator to obtain some measure of the relative efficiency of the different programmes.

The second of the two experimental designs to use random assignment is the post-test only, control group design as described in Figure 2.2. This is similar to the classic experimental design with group equivalence being maintained. The difference lies in the fact that no pre-test measures are taken.

There is no guarantee that invoking a randomized experimental design will inevitably result in a successful summative evaluation. Although randomized experiments, as conducted by laboratory-based researchers, are of proven scientific merit, problems can often be encountered when attempting to introduce this research design into natural settings. Mark and Cook (1984) provide a comprehensive discussion of some of these problems, and consider how they might be tackled. They draw attention to the fact that ethical concerns may cause programme planners and staff to object to randomization as a method of assigning individuals to treatment and non-treatment groups. Those involved in the provision of personal social services or health care, in particular, may feel that it is wrong in principle for any treatment deemed to be beneficial to clients or patients to be withheld in the interests of scientific experimentation. Even if they accept that some form of allocation is necessary they may consider individual need a more appropriate criterion for allocation.

Ethical considerations can therefore undermine the commitment of programme staff to random assignment and form a potential threat to the ultimate scientific integrity of the experimental design. It is important that the random assignment is implemented as originally intended. Although it is the evaluator who decides the method of assignment it is usually the staff employed by the organization in which the evaluation is taking place who are responsible for implementing the chosen procedure and assigning individuals to treatment and control groups. This creates the possibility that staff may 'deviate from random assignment to satisfy their personal conception of how selection should take place, or merely to satisfy "difficult" applicants who are particularly vocal in their desire to receive a certain treatment' (Mark and Cook, 1984: 86–7). Although their actions are well meaning they nevertheless result in the unique qualities of the true experiment being undermined (Berk and Sherman, 1988).

In the first place the onus is on the evaluator to identify the cause of the initial resistance to randomization procedures and respond accordingly. It may be necessary for the evaluator to adopt the role of teacher and explain why random allocation is considered necessary within the context of a specific study. Attempts to undermine random allocation can be guarded against by adopting certain systems of randomization (Reicken and Boruch, 1974).

Even when random allocation procedures are successfully implemented there is no guarantee that the comparability assumed between the groups at the outset will be maintained throughout the course of the evaluation study. Non-random processes can threaten group equivalence particularly in the case of longitudinal research designs. Individuals may refuse to accept the proposed treatment at the start of an evaluation experiment, or having initially co-operated they may drop out of the programme at a later date. It is possible that differential rates of attrition may lead to differences between the treatment and control groups (Rossi and Freeman, 1993). This makes it no longer possible for the evaluator to argue that the groups are probabilistically equivalent on all characteristics, apart from the treatment received by the experimental group(s).

A further problem besetting the implementation of a randomized controlled experiment is its potential for creating inequities between groups. Individuals cannot be prevented from making comparisons between the way they are treated and the treatment they see others receiving. Reactions to perceived differential treatment may serve to obscure true treatment effects. Four types of reaction are identified in the literature: treatment diffusion, compensatory equalization, compensatory rivalry and resentful demoralization (Cook and Campbell, 1979; Mark and Cook, 1984). Treatment diffusion occurs when participants in an evaluation study who are assigned to a non-treatment group come into contact with the treatment. This can happen if programme personnel fail to observe the experimental protocol and allow control group members access to the treatment or service under evaluation. Compensatory equalization refers to a form of diffusion of treatment, whereby programme staff may distribute resources in such a way as to reduce the differences between treatment groups with respect to the nature and quality of treatment received or compensate the control group in order to establish what they perceive to be a more equitable state of affairs. Both these responses undermine the ideal of group comparability, which is the defining characteristic of random assignment.

Compensatory rivalry and resentful demoralization can occur when individuals acquire knowledge about the different treatment conditions being investigated. The former takes place when control group members become aware that they do not have access to a treatment or treatments enjoyed by others. This can sometimes lead to them attempting to perform better than those singled out for special treatment. However, perceived inequality of treatment may promote feelings of relative deprivation and produce resentment rather than increased motivation, resulting in deterioration in the performance of the control group. The difference in the post-test results, between the experimental and control groups, could therefore be attributable to the increasingly poor performance of the controls rather than simply a consequence of the positive effects of the treatment. As Mark and Cook (1984) observe, these four reactions cannot be eliminated by random assignment, unlike the threats to internal validity, and separate measures are required to deal with them.

Supporters of the use of experimental methods claim that randomized experiments, by providing the highest levels of causal inference, enable firm conclusions to be drawn regarding the impact of social programmes and policy interventions. At the same time, they acknowledge that these designs present serious implementation problems and are costly and time-consuming to conduct (Campbell and Boruch, 1975). However, it is also noted that a failure to experiment may prove costly for in the absence of reliable evidence resources may be wasted in supporting ineffective programmes while more efficient and cost-effective alternatives go unrecognized (Berk et al., 1985). The issue has become one of when such methods should be invoked. Some evaluators have outlined the conditions which should prevail before a true experiment is attempted (Dennis and Boruch, 1989), as well as recommending that such designs should only be used for evaluating major policy interventions (Dennis, 1990).

Quasi-experimental designs

Randomized field experiments are regarded by many quantitatively-oriented evaluators as a gold standard in producing systematic and robust evidence about the impact of a project or programme (Boruch, 1987). However, unlike the laboratory-based scientist, the social scientist working in natural field settings is not always able to exercise full experimental control. As previously noted practical or ethical considerations may preclude random assignment. The researcher may be brought in to evaluate a social programme after the individuals or groups have been assigned to treatment and non-treatment conditions. For ethical reasons a treatment may have been made available to all who display the appropriate eligibility criteria, thus making it impossible to construct a conventional control group. If for these or other reasons the evaluator is unable to introduce random assignment, as required by the true experiment, then a quasi-experimental research design is often recommended (Campbell and Stanley, 1963).

As Rossi and Freeman (1993) assert quasi-experiments are the best alternative to randomized experiments and are undertaken more often

Post-test

Experimental group   X   O

FIGURE 2.3   *One-group, post-test only design*

than true experiments. Indeed they encourage all evaluators adopting a true experimental model to give careful consideration, early on in the research design process, to the possibility of having to switch to a quasi-experimental design:

> It should be emphasized that if there is any chance that a true experiment may have to be treated as a quasi-experiment, perhaps because randomization might break down, it is wise for the evaluator to think through his or her effort as a quasi-experiment as well as a true experiment. (Rossi and Freeman, 1993: 299)

By taking such precautionary measures, the evaluator can ensure that if the implementation difficulties encountered when conducting a true experiment cause the researcher to abandon the research design, the evaluation exercise itself does not necessarily have to be curtailed. The study can be continued using a quasi-experimental design.

A distinction can be made between weak and strong quasi-experimental designs (Taylor, 1994: 267). The weak designs are also known as pre-experimental designs, three of which have been identified: the one-shot case study, the one-group, pre-test and post-test design and the static group comparison (Campbell and Stanley, 1963). The first of these, alternatively called the one-group, post-test only design, as illustrated in Figure 2.3, is the weakest of the three. Observations are made only after the individual or group has been exposed to the programme under evaluation. No control group is used. Consequently it is not possible to measure the impact of the programme by comparing 'before and after' measures as there are only data relating to the 'after' condition. Coupled with the fact that there is no comparable control group it is difficult to ascertain to what extent an observed effect is due to the experimental treatment. Although there are a limited number of special circumstances under which this design permits causal inferences to be drawn, these are rarely encountered in evaluation research and this design is best restricted to exploratory and descriptive research (Mark and Cook, 1984).

Figure 2.4 shows the second of the three pre-experimental designs, the one-group, pre-test and post-test design which is also referred to as the before and after study. As with the one-shot case study the only individuals or groups which are measured are those which receive the programme; there is no non-treatment or control group. This design, however, does allow the evaluator to measure change objectively by

	Pre-test	Post-test
Experimental group	O	X O

FIGURE 2.4   *One-group, pre-test, post-test design*

	Post-test
Experimental group	X O
Control group	O

FIGURE 2.5   *Post-test only, non-equivalent groups design*

taking measurements from the same group both before and after their involvement in a programme. Unfortunately, it does not give the evaluator any idea what results might have been obtained had the programme not been available. For example, the observed effects may be caused by factors operating at the same time as the programme but not related to it. This is only one of a number of weaknesses associated with this design (Campbell and Stanley, 1963).

Finally, the static-group comparison or post-test only, non-equivalent groups design (Mark and Cook, 1984), is a design which compares two groups, only one of which is exposed to the programme being evaluated. As shown in Figure 2.5 there are no measures taken from either the treatment or non-treatment groups prior to the implementation of the programme. In this respect, this design resembles the post-test only, control group experimental design described earlier. Clearly the difference in the notation is the absence of R which indicates that random assignment is not a feature of this design. Although measures are taken following the exposure of one of the two groups to the programme, because randomized assignment procedures are not followed it cannot be assumed that the two groups are comparable, apart from the fact that one experiences a specific programme and the other does not. It follows that differences in the way the two groups are selected may account for any observed differences in outcome measures. This design does not support the making of causal inferences.

Similarly, the pre-test and post-test quasi-experimental design with non-equivalent control group (shown in Figure 2.6) is like the classic experimental design described in Figure 2.1 above, except that the experimental and control groups are not formed by random assignment. Weak quasi-experimental designs clearly have their limitations. Some of these designs make use of a control or comparison group but, in the absence of random assignment, there is very little attempt to make the control group(s) comparable to the experimental group(s). In contrast, strong quasi-experimental designs are characterized by attempts to

	Pre-test	Post-test
Experimental group	O	X O
Control group	O	O

FIGURE 2.6 *Pre-test, post-test, quasi-experimental design*

make the control and experimental groups more comparable to each other. This is achieved by constructing the control or comparison groups either before or after the start of the programme to give what Rossi and Freeman (1993: 301) refer to as *ex ante* and *ex post* quasi-experiments respectively.

What distinguishes one quasi-experimental design from another is the method by which comparison groups are chosen. On this basis Rossi and Freeman (1993) identify four major types of quasi-experimental designs: matched controls, statistical controls, regression-discontinuity designs and generic controls.

Constructing a matched control group involves the evaluator choosing non-recipients of an intervention or programme who are similar in many important ways to those exposed to an intervention or programme. Matching can take one of two forms, individual or aggregate. In the case of the former, for each unit in the treatment group there is a matched control in the non-treatment group. This is the method of matched-pairs. With aggregate control there is no one-for-one matching. Instead an attempt is made to ensure that the experimental and control groups are equivalent when it comes to the overall distribution of a number of relevant variables. Rossi and Freeman (1993) note that increasingly sophisticated statistical procedures are now replacing matching in the construction of control groups. Nevertheless, the matched-pairs method is still useful especially when conducting small-scale, localized evaluations (Fitz-Gibbon and Morris, 1987).

Regression-discontinuity designs are among the most powerful non-randomized designs available and can be the basis for making causal inferences (Campbell, 1969). 'Evaluations that are based on regression-discontinuity designs come closest to the randomized experiments in ability to produce unbiased estimates of net effects' (Rossi and Freeman, 1993: 247). For these designs to work, cases need to be easily located on a quantitative dimension and the selection procedures which determine whether or not a case receives a designated treatment must follow a clearly specified formula and be uniformly enforced. It should be possible to identify a clear cut-off point on the quantitative dimension, which separates those units destined to receive a particular treatment from those considered ineligible. Given the implementation problems associated with this design it has had limited application (Trochim, 1984).

When a conventional control group is unavailable evaluators may turn to generic controls to provide some idea as to what might have happened if the programme treatment had not been provided. In other words generic controls are supposed to provide an estimate of the likely performance of untreated units or the typical response that could be expected from the population from which the experimental groups are drawn. In this way generic controls, based on perceived normative standards, provide a benchmark against which the performance of treatment groups can be judged. However, as Rossi and Freeman (1993) state generic controls lack depth and detail and therefore should be used as a last resort.

The basic logic behind the randomized experiment is replicated in the quasi-experimental design with the exception that, in the case of the latter, the experimental and comparison groups are not equivalent. In strong quasi-experimental designs attempts are made to guard against selection bias and create equivalent groups. As described above, constructed control designs can be created using one of four selection procedures. Other research designs are also available, such as, interrupted time series and cross-sectional designs. For more information about the methodological issues surrounding quasi-experimental designs see Campbell and Stanley (1963), Cook and Campbell (1979) and Cook (1983).

There is much controversy surrounding the legitimacy of the quantitative-experimental paradigm in evaluation research. Criticism comes not only from advocates of the alternative qualitative paradigm but also from those who make extensive use of experimental research designs and quantitative methods. For example, despite Campbell's stated preference for experimental methods he recognizes their weaknesses and at the same time acknowledges the important contribution of qualitative approaches (Campbell, 1979). In general, it is the methodological requirements of experimental design that have attracted the attention of critics. The need to establish and maintain controlled conditions through experimental manipulation can be a problem in more ways than one. Conflict can arise between the experimentalist evaluator and programme staff over the way in which a programme is managed over time. The evaluator is highly conscious of the fact that any change in programme structure or delivery during the experimental period can invalidate the experiment and he or she may therefore attempt to influence any decisions taken by management in this respect (Gruel, 1975). This focus on the programme as initially implemented illustrates another limiting feature of experimental designs, often cited by those who advocate the use of qualitative approaches, that is, that experimental models of evaluation rely almost entirely on intended outcomes or goals (Deutscher, 1977). What is to be measured is determined at the start of the evaluation with the result that in many instances the unintended programme outcomes or effects are overlooked. Early critics have also drawn attention to the fact that when experimental designs are used they invariably lead researchers to the conclusion that, by and large, the majority of evaluated programmes are ineffective (Guba, 1972; Weiss, 1972). It has also been claimed that the more stringent the research design, the greater the likelihood that no positive programme effects will be observed (Gilbert et al., 1975).

A realist critique of experimental designs

Of course there are many reasons why a particular programme may be found to be ineffective. For example, a programme may fail because it is poorly designed or not implemented as originally intended. Alternatively the observed inability of a programme to produce the desired effects may be a consequence of an inappropriate choice of evaluation methods rather than an accurate reflection of the impact of the programme. Pawson and Tilley (1994) describe in some detail how the failure of evaluation research to meet the expectations of policy-makers and service providers is partly attributable to methodological failure. They question the uncritical enthusiasm with which many evaluators have embraced the traditional experimental paradigm and adopted quasi-experimental designs. According to Pawson and Tilley the conventional experimental approach, although technically sound, is not suitable for universal application:

> It is high time for an end to the domination of the *quasi-experimental* (or OXO) model of evaluation. Such an approach is a fine strategy for evaluating the relative performances of washing powders or crop fertilizers, but is a lousy means of expressing the nature of causality and change going on within social programmes. (Pawson and Tilley, 1994: 292)

The basis of their attack on experimental evaluation is not its quantitative orientation but the very logic on which it is based.

As previously described the principal purpose of experimental research designs is to establish causality. The aim is to ensure that experimental and control groups are similar apart from the fact that one receives the programme and the other does not. The random allocation of subjects to treatment and non-treatment conditions is supposed to ensure that any observed differences in outcomes can be attributed to the effects of the treatment received and not to any differences in the composition of the two groups. This pre-test, post-test experimental design produces a black box type of evaluation (Bickman, 1987). Change is measured by simply taking account of inputs and outputs while simultaneously controlling for extraneous and intervening variables. However, the experimental logic incorporated in this design is thought to be seriously flawed, resulting in black box evaluations being unable to provide any real insight into the underlying causal mechanisms that produce treatment effects. What is at issue is the nature of causality.

Pawson and Tilley assert that the experimental paradigm is characterized by a successionist conceptualization of causality (Harré, 1972). The researcher makes causal inferences on the basis of observations that reveal regularities in the patterning and occurrence of events. As such, causes are not directly observed but inferred from the observation of events. As long as it is assumed that the treatment and control groups are identical, apart from the fact that the former receives the programme, any change observed in the treatment group is seen as being caused by the programme. Pawson and Tilley claim that a successionist perception of causality has little place in evaluation research, as it does not contribute to our understanding of how a programme works. To illustrate the point they use the case of neighbourhood watch schemes designed with the intention of reducing crime. Whether or not such initiatives achieve their primary objective can be easily ascertained by means of a simple before-and-after research design. However, this would reveal little if anything about the mechanisms by which an observed reduction in crime was achieved. Schemes may lead to a reduction in crime for many reasons, for example, increased awareness of crime may encourage residents to take active steps to protect their property; potential criminals may be deterred by the increased risk of detection. As Pawson and Tilley maintain, 'the point is to stress that neighbourhood watch schemes are a complex network of activities and decisions, and it is these interactions between people and not the "schemes", as such which (may) reduce crime' (1993: 4).

By exerting stringent experimental controls in order to ensure group equivalence the evaluator appears to be attempting to discover whether a programme is effective without paying any attention to the characteristics of those who are subjected to it. As Pawson and Tilley remark, 'This is splendid epistemology but lousy ontology, *since social programmes never work in this manner*' (1993: 8). Programmes should not be conceived as externally imposed forces which simply elicit responses from subjects, rather programmes become effective '*if subjects choose to make them work and are placed in the right conditions to enable them to do so*' (Pawson and Tilley, 1994: 294). Levels of involvement in and commitment to particular programmes will vary among subjects. Consequently if individuals or groups with characteristics likely to lead to successful outcomes are randomly assigned to experimental and control groups a finding of 'no effect' is likely to be observed. In short, following an experimental design serves to prevent the examination of the very factors relevant to understanding why a particular programme works. In the opinion of Pawson and Tilley to attempt to control for the influence of extraneous factors by random assignment is absurd as it prevents the evaluator from commenting on conditions favourable to the success of a programme and thereby providing policy-makers with useful information.

The way forward for Pawson and Tilley is not to abandon experimental methods altogether but to introduce a scientific realist strategy into evaluation methodology. The primary distinguishing characteristic of the realist approach is its position regarding the question of causality (Pawson, 1989). It rejects the successionist interpretation described above in favour of what has been termed the generative approach (Harré, 1972). According to this view, 'there is a real connection between causes and their effects, in the form of some "natural necessity" which links the two. In short it posits that there is a more basic level of reality than the event, namely the process or mechanism' (Pawson, 1989: 128). Within the context of evaluation research this encourages the evaluator to explore what takes place between the programme and the outcome by recognizing that 'it is not actual programmes which "work" but the reasoning and opportunities of the people experiencing the programmes which make them work' (Pawson and Tilley, 1993: 2).

Realists are critical of positivist approaches to scientific explanations because although they allow for predictions regarding the likely occurrence of future events, they do not explain why particular events happen (Keat and Urry, 1975). For them, adequate causal explanations cannot be achieved by merely observing the relations between phenomena. The researcher needs to look beyond those initial events that produce change, in order to explain the very process of change itself. As Pawson and Tilley observe, when applied to evaluation research this reasoning requires that attention be given to the notions of mechanism and context:

> Thus for a realist evaluator, outcomes are understood and investigated by bringing to the centre of investigation certain hypotheses about the mechanisms through which a programme seeks to bring about change, as well as considering the contextual conditions which are most conducive to that change. (Pawson and Tilley, 1994: 300)

This has important implications for the role of the evaluator as experimentalist. Clearly, something more than a simple input/output design is called for. Realist experimental procedure assumes that the evaluator has some theory as to the causal mechanisms behind a particular programme. By way of experimental manipulation the evaluator endeavours to create a context which the theory identifies as being favourable to the drawing out of the causal mechanism. Consequently, whereas the classic experimental approach to evaluation can be described as methods-driven, the realist approach can best be described as theory-driven.

The qualitative approach

Early critics of the use of experimental research designs and quantitative techniques to evaluate social programmes were quick to point out that while such traditional methods may make it possible, under certain conditions, to determine whether or not a particular programme has had an impact, they offer little insight into the social processes which actually account for the changes observed. Conventional approaches are capable of showing 'the extent to which a consistent programme has reached its goals, but rarely *why* the observed results occur [and] what processes intervene between the input and output' (Weiss, 1970: 59). A simplistic experimental design or black box type of evaluation concentrates on the relationship between inputs and outputs to such an extent that other important aspects are ignored (Chen and Rossi, 1983). For example, concentrating on measuring intended outcomes can lead to the unintended effects of programme initiatives being overlooked (Deutscher, 1977).

Education evaluators were among the first to challenge the dominance of the conventional paradigm and advocate the use of qualitative methods and methodologies (Guba, 1972; Stake, 1975; Parlett and Hamilton, 1976). They were disillusioned with those methodological strategies based on experimental designs and quantitative methods, which they believed, had consistently failed to meet the needs of educators and policy-makers. For Guba (1972), scientific techniques became discredited when they continually produced results that contradicted the experiential observations of practitioners by suggesting that many educational programmes had no demonstrable effects. Parlett and Hamilton (1976) have also drawn attention to the fact that it is often not possible to achieve the required degree of experimental control when evaluating educational programmes. For example, they observe how difficult it is to ensure that the integrity of a before-and-after research design is maintained throughout the course of an evaluation. Indeed they question such practice as it can prevent a programme from adapting to changing circumstances.

A characteristic feature of early attempts to find an alternative approach to evaluation is the change of focus from attempting to identify objective outcome measures to exploring actual programme activities. This change in emphasis is clearly evident in Parlett and Hamilton's definition of 'illuminative evaluation':

> illuminative evaluation takes account of the wider contexts in which educational programs function. Its primary concern is with description and interpretation rather than measurement and prediction. It stands unambiguously within the alternative anthropological paradigm. (Parlett and Hamilton, 1976: 144)

From their point of view an evaluation should describe the perceptions and experiences of those individuals and groups involved in a particular programme. In order to understand the internal dynamics of a programme it is considered necessary for the evaluator to employ a variety of qualitative methods including in-depth interviews with pro-gramme participants and direct observations of programme activities.

Stake (1975) provides another example of an educational evaluator who has a preference for qualitative methods, particularly case studies. He distinguishes between what he terms a preordinate approach and a responsive approach to evaluation work (Stake, 1980: 75). Preordinate evaluation makes extensive use of traditional quantitative methods. Following the precepts of the conventional or scientific paradigm it encourages evaluators to identify predetermined objective indicators of success, use standardized measuring instruments and adopt formal methods of data analysis.

In contrast, in responsive evaluation less importance is attached to issues such as measurement precision; instead emphasis is placed on the advantages to be gained from allowing an evaluation to emerge from a careful observation of the programme. As Stake asserts, 'An educational evaluation is *responsive evaluation* . . . if it orients more directly to program activities than to program intents [and] responds to audience requirements for information' (1980: 77). He is critical of conventional approaches for encouraging evaluators to dictate the form and conduct of evaluations, as they do, for example, when they con-centrate on the testing of a priori hypotheses. Stake firmly believes that it is the interests of the stakeholders that should be reflected in the research design. Whereas the preordinate model exhorts the evaluator to adopt the objective, external stance of the scientific investigator, the responsive approach favours a more involved role, encouraging the evaluator to develop a close working relationship with programme staff and participants.

Stake is readily identified as a pioneering figure in qualitative evaluation, primarily because of his support for the use of case study methods (Shadish et al., 1991). He not only raised the profile of quali-tative methods in evaluation research, but his responsive approach also had a strong influence on those evaluators who were seeking to establish the interpretivist or naturalistic paradigm as a viable alternative to the scientific paradigm (Guba and Lincoln, 1981). The fundamental methodological-philosophical arguments surrounding these two diver-gent paradigms have been outlined above. What remains to be discussed are the implications the interpretivist paradigm has for evaluation practice.

Interpretivist evaluation

As previously noted, the quantitative versus qualitative debate is not unique to the field of evaluation, but has long been established within the social sciences. For example, within sociology, perspectives which pose a direct challenge to the basic philosophical assumptions underlying the positivist paradigm have been around for a number of years (Schwandt, 1994). A common feature of these perspectives is the emphasis placed upon 'naturalism'. In its broadest sense naturalism rejects the view that the social world can be understood by employing those scientific modes of inquiry which have proved so successful in the physical sciences. Social phenomena are clearly distinct from natural phenomena and therefore need to be dealt with differently. The researcher must respect the nature of the social world, and endeavour, at all times, to be 'true to the phenomenon under study' (Matza, 1969: 5). This entails studying social interaction in natural surroundings with a view to discovering the social meanings that such interactions have for participants.

Interpretive interactionism is one perspective which adheres to the philosophical logic of naturalistic inquiry (Denzin, 1989). Its potential contribution to evaluation research centres around the emphasis it places on the importance of understanding lived experience.

> In social life, there is only interpretation. That is, everyday life revolves around persons interpreting and making judgements about their own and others' behaviours and experiences. Many times these interpretations and judgements are based on faulty, or incorrect, understandings. Persons, for instance, mistake their own experiences for the experiences of others. These interpretations are then formulated into social programs that are intended to alter and shape the lives of troubled people, for example, community services for the mentally ill or the homeless, treatment centres for alcoholics, medical services for AIDS patients. But often the understandings that these programs are based upon bear little relationship to the meanings, interpretations, and experiences of the persons they are intended to serve. (Denzin, 1989: 11)

Denzin points to the possibility that a failure on the part of programme planners to understand the subjective experiences of intended programme recipients can lead to the formulation of inappropriately designed programmes. He advocates that when conducting an interpretive evaluation primary consideration should be given to the point of view of those experiencing the problem the programme is designed to alleviate. Given the very nature of social phenomena, and the existence of multiple realities, all social researchers take sides and evaluators are no exception. Interpretive evaluation invariably involves taking the side of 'the underdog for whom policymakers make policies' (Denzin, 1989: 22).

The idea of the naturalistic paradigm as a viable alternative to the conventional positivist paradigm is developed in the writings of Guba (1978), Guba and Lincoln (1981) and Lincoln and Guba (1985). In their early work they claim that their primary motive was not to undermine the scientific paradigm and render it untenable, but to establish the fact that two competing paradigms exist. They describe the basic assumptions on which the two contrasting paradigms are founded. However, as Guba (1986) notes it would be wrong to assume that this implies there is a consensus within the evaluation community as to what actually constitutes naturalistic evaluation. The lack of an agreed definition can be attributed to the tendency to confuse method with methodology.

As Guba maintains there is the world of difference between using naturalistic or qualitative methods of data collection and analysis to supplement quantitative techniques within the framework of a positivist paradigm, and adopting a naturalistic methodology. In the case of the latter,

> the evaluator conceptualizes the study around what we call 'thinking naturalistically'. That is, the evaluator approaches reality as a multi-layered, interactive, shared social experience that can be studied by first learning what participants consider important. (Biklen and Bogdan, 1986: 95)

It is the methodological decision to think naturalistically which 'requires a paradigm shift of revolutionary proportions' and has major implications for the conducting of evaluations (Guba, 1986: 26).

Constructivist evaluation

Although Lincoln and Guba (1985) originally referred to their approach as 'naturalistic inquiry' they have since taken to calling their paradigmatic stance 'constructivist' (Guba and Lincoln, 1989). This does not represent a major change in philosophical outlook, as on their own admission, there are many similarities between the constructivist, interpretive and naturalistic positions. For example, all three viewpoints recognize the existence of multiple social realities and the need for the researcher to explore how individuals interpret and make sense of their social experiences.

Constructivists lay specific emphasis on the part played by the human mind in accounting for the nature and acquisition of knowledge. According to constructivist epistemology, the claim by positivists that it is possible, indeed desirable, to separate the observer from the observed is firmly rejected. Knowledge or truth is not discovered by detached scientific observation, but is a construction in the minds of individuals. These constructions 'do not exist outside of the persons who create and hold them; they are not part of some "objective" world that exists apart from their constructors' (Guba and Lincoln, 1989: 143).

Given the philosophical premises associated with naturalism and constructivism it is not surprising that 'there is no single philosophical logic of justification universally embraced by qualitative evaluators' (Greene, 1994: 536). However, it does not follow that there are no general principles or procedural guidelines to inform the prospective qualitatively-oriented programme evaluator. Lincoln and Guba (1985) and Patton (1987) provide an informative insight into the principles that evaluators need to keep in mind when actually conducting an evaluation.

From a constructivist standpoint a social programme can only be properly understood within its natural setting. Therefore, the evaluator needs to experience the context within which a programme operates and discover how the programme is experienced by policy-makers, programme staff and clients. This has implications for the research process. Commitment to the concept of multiple and constructed realities rules out the possibility of formulating a research design beforehand. It is unrealistic to expect the evaluator to know enough in advance about the circumstances surrounding the different perceptions of reality to be able to recommend a particular research design. They approach the research context as open-minded, willing learners, making no claims to know what the relevant questions are. In this respect they differ from their positivist counterparts: 'Whereas positivists begin an inquiry knowing (in principle) what they don't know, naturalists typically face the prospect of not knowing what they don't know' (Guba and Lincoln, 1988: 105). Consequently, in naturalistic or constructivist inquiry the research design is allowed to emerge or unfold as the research progresses.

It is not only the research design that is seen as part of an emergent process; theory is also considered to unfold as data are collected. This is in marked contrast to the traditional scientific paradigm in which existing theory guides the data collection process. As far as qualitative evaluation is concerned, inductive data analysis ensures that theory is generated from, or grounded in, the data. Glaser and Strauss (1967) were the first to advance the idea of 'grounded theory'. It is an approach in which, 'One does not begin with a theory, then prove it. Rather, one begins with an area of study and what is relevant to that area is allowed to emerge' (Strauss and Corbin, 1990: 23). It is not difficult to appreciate the attraction this approach holds for the naturalistically inclined evaluator, especially when given the fact that the unstructured complexity of multiple realities renders a priori theorizing impractical.

A paradigm of choices

As Patton (1986) notes, the merits and demerits of the scientific and naturalistic paradigms have been fiercely debated. Expressed in their pure forms the paradigms are logically incompatible. Not only are they based on fundamentally different philosophical premises, but also they are presented as representing mutually exclusive ontological and epistemological positions. Consider, for example, the assumptions made concerning the conception of reality. Whereas the scientific paradigm views reality as 'singular, convergent and fragmentable', the naturalistic paradigm subscribes to the opposing view that reality is 'multiple, divergent and inter-related' (Guba and Lincoln, 1981: 57). Given the perceived nature of the differences between the two paradigmatic stances, the possibility of a synthesis is strenuously rejected. As Guba and Lincoln assert, 'a call to blend or accommodate them is logically equivalent to calling for a compromise between the view that the world is flat and the view that the world is round' (1989: 93).

A belief in the irreconcilable nature of the two investigative paradigms is a recurrent theme in the methodological writings of Guba and Lincoln. They consider any attempt to integrate the two paradigms to be a futile and misconceived exercise:

> Like water and oil, they will not mix; indeed, to put them together is to adulterate each with the other. Like similar magnetic poles, they repel one another; to hold them in contact requires force, and when the force is released the methodologies fly apart. (Guba and Lincoln, 1988: 111)

Notwithstanding the fact that there are differences between quantitative and qualitative approaches, particularly with regard to the kinds of data collected and the types of analytical procedures employed, some social scientists have challenged the assumption that the two approaches are intrinsically associated with diametrically opposed philosophical positions (Cook and Reichardt, 1979; Bryman, 1988).

From the point of view of evaluation practice, it is important that an attempt is made to separate the debate over two clearly distinguishable and conflicting inquiry paradigms from the debate about the relative advantages and disadvantages of two distinct research methodologies. Pursuing the debate solely at the paradigm level creates the risk of producing a polarization between quantitatively- and qualitatively-oriented programme evaluators; this could ultimately lead to a failure to develop appropriate multi-method research designs in specific evaluation contexts (Péladeau and Mercier, 1993). Individual evaluators may be of the opinion that one paradigm is superior to another; however, it does not necessarily follow that they will reject outright those research methods favoured by the opposing paradigm. Indeed, Guba and Lincoln 'urge the use of quantitative techniques whenever they seem appropriate to the enquiry being conducted' (1981: 66).

Although Guba and Lincoln accept that there can be some mixing of methods in evaluation research designs, with naturalistic evaluators utilizing quantitative methods and quantitative evaluators adopting qualitative methods 'without prejudice' (1988: 105), they firmly reject any notion that there can be a mixing of paradigms. Integration is not possible; the evaluator must choose between the two paradigms. For them, 'Paradigms do imply methodologies, and methodologies are simply meaningless congeries of mindless choice and procedures unless they are rooted in the paradigms' (1988: 114). It would appear that while they condone a mixing of methods this is seen as being of limited value and can only be taken so far, given the fact that methods and paradigms are intrinsically linked. As Lincoln (1992) asserts methods can only be used to their full potential when applied within the context of the appropriate paradigm. Consequently, it is held that 'a shift in inquiry paradigm logically accompanies the desire to shift methods' (1992: 378). What has given rise to controversy is not so much the support for specific methods of evaluation per se, but the expressed belief in the ultimate superiority of a particular paradigmatic stance (Lincoln, 1991; Sechrest, 1992).

There is a danger that presenting the two paradigms as contrasting ideal-types conjures up an image of evaluation research as a dichotomous enterprise, in which prior affiliation to a singular paradigm effectively determines subsequent methodological decisions. Those who adopt such a position may be labelled 'purists' (Rossman and Wilson, 1985). For them the paradigms debate takes on an 'either-or' quality insofar as evaluators are seen as having to choose between what are perceived as two mutually exclusive paradigms (Smith, 1983). The epistemologic and ontologic assumptions underlying the two divergent perspectives preclude the possibility of combining paradigms in the interest of methodological pluralism. As Guba categorically asserts, 'we are dealing with an either-or proposition, in which one must pledge allegiance to one paradigm or the other' (1985: 80).

In depicting two methodologically distinct paradigms founded upon incompatible philosophical axioms, purists run the risk of emphasizing the differences between qualitative and quantitative techniques to such a degree that multi-method research designs are actively discouraged. There is a tendency for some researchers, when debating the paradigms issue, to ignore any similarities between the two positions and present them as polar opposites. For example, at one extreme, supporters of the scientific paradigm argue that quantitative methods are capable of producing 'hard' objective data that are amenable to rigorous statistical analysis, whereas, by comparison, qualitative techniques generate 'soft' data that are subjective. This categorization has its uses, but as Zelditch notes it can pose a dilemma for researchers: 'if you prefer "hard" data you are for quantification and if you prefer "real, deep" data you are for qualitative participant observation. What to do if you prefer data that are real, deep, *and* hard is not immediately apparent' (1962: 566).

The purists believe that there is a correspondence between paradigm and method: methods choices are determined by the intellectual and philosophical predilections of a particular paradigmatic stance. However, this is not a view that attracts universal support. Cook and Reichardt (1979) argue that the debate over paradigms has been overstated. They do not deny the importance of paradigms, nor do they reject the existence of a linkage between paradigm and method. However, they do question the assumption that the two paradigms are so fixed and rigid as to offer the researcher no real option other than to choose one or the other. Furthermore, they question the validity of the assumption that allegiance to a particular paradigm is the key determinant when it comes to making methods decisions.

Cook and Reichardt were among the first to recognize that the methodological parochialism exemplified in the paradigms debate had the potential to stifle creativity and innovation in evaluation research designs. They urged evaluators to adopt a 'flexible and adaptive' paradigmatic stance (1979: 19).

> There is no need to choose a research method on the basis of a traditional paradigmatic stance. Nor is there any reason to pick between two polar-opposite paradigms. Thus, there is no need for a dichotomy between the method-types and there is every reason (at least in logic) to use them together to satisfy the demands of evaluation research in the most efficacious manner possible. (Cook and Reichardt, 1979: 27)

Evaluators are exhorted to use whatever methods appear to be best suited given the nature and context of the evaluation situation.

Patton also recommends a practical approach with his 'paradigm of choices' which 'rejects methodological orthodoxy in favour of methodological appropriateness as the primary criterion for judging methodological quality' (1990: 38). Although he agrees with Guba and Lincoln, that paradigms are more than a mere collection of methods and in fact represent contrasting and competing conceptions of the nature of reality, he disagrees with the view that this has any practical significance when it comes to conducting evaluation research. For Patton, attempts to resolve the paradigms debate by establishing the supremacy of one of the paradigms is a futile exercise. He maintains that the evaluator needs to be situationally responsive and methodologically flexible. This entails moving between different paradigmatic stances as and when the need arises. Consequently, evaluators need to be well versed in both qualitative and quantitative techniques. As Patton asserts, 'the paradigm of choices recognizes that different methods are appropriate for different situations' (1986: 215). This is a pragmatic approach that allows for the integration of methods in a single evaluation study.

Summary

There is a view that the 'grand debate' over inquiry paradigms is a metaphysical exercise which merely serves to distract evaluators from practical work (Miles and Huberman, 1988). However, as we have discussed in this chapter, there are a number of compelling reasons why evaluators need to be aware of the philosophical principles which direct procedures for comprehending social phenomena. First, in order to make informed decisions concerning methods choices it is essential that evaluators understand the characteristic features of the major methodological paradigms. Second, there is a move towards methodological pluralism in evaluation research and an increasing use of mixed-methods research designs. Indeed, there are examples of attempts to achieve some accommodation among the different paradigms (Firestone, 1990). Third, increasingly programme evaluators are coming to see evaluation as more than simply the application of a diverse set of methods of data collection and analysis. There are those like Chen (1990), who feel that for too long evaluation research has been methods-driven and believe that the time has come to develop a theoretically-based body of knowledge unique to programme evaluation. Finally, evaluators need to have some insight into the philosophical assumptions behind their working practices if they are to meet the challenges of their critics. Marsland (1993) notes that the evaluator needs more than technical ability to ensure the production of sound, competent evaluation studies. He warns that concentrating on technical competence and ignoring the philosophical assumptions 'is precisely what opens the way to subversive critiques of the evaluation enterprise as a whole' (1993: 11). In short, the paradigm debate has implications for the choice of methods; therefore, knowledge of the differences between the various paradigmatic stances makes for more informed methods decisions.

3   Methods of Data Collection

A wide range of data collection methods and research techniques are available to the evaluator wishing to undertake a systematic evaluation of a social programme or assess the impact of a particular policy initiative. There is a widely held view that the methods used in evaluative studies are ones which have become established in applied social science (Cordray and Lipsey, 1986; Doig and Littlewood, 1992; Robson, 1993). Indeed, as Rossi and Freeman assert, 'one of the distinguishing characteristics of program evaluation is that its methods cover the gamut of prevailing social research paradigms' (1993: 6). According to this view, the practice of evaluation is heavily dependent upon the methods developed by social scientists for the collection of valid and reliable data. For Rossi and Freeman, the commitment to the 'rules' of social research is a fundamental feature of the evaluation enterprise. However, there are those who are critical of the tendency to treat evaluation as a specialist area of social science; they consider evaluation to be a discipline in its own right (Scriven, 1991a). Despite the controversy surrounding the intellectual origins of evaluation, social research methods occupy a prominent place in the repertoire of methods available to the evaluator.

It is not the purpose of this chapter to provide a detailed critique of the full range of methods at the evaluator's disposal. The aim is to describe briefly the characteristic features of some of the most commonly used methods, while drawing attention to their major strengths and weaknesses and highlighting the factors which are taken into account when making methods choices. For as Patton claims, evaluators need to 'be sophisticated about matching research methods to the nuances of particular evaluation questions . . . [and] have a large repertoire of research methods and techniques available to use on a variety of problems' (1997: 297). In general, data collection for evaluation entails identifying which variables to measure, choosing or devising appropriate research instruments that are both reliable and valid, and administering the instruments in accordance with general methodological guidelines.

The choice of methods is strongly influenced by the situation and context in which an evaluation is conducted. The task facing the evaluator is to provide 'the most accurate information practically possible in an evenhanded manner' (Berk and Rossi, 1990: 9). As Patton declares:

There are no rigid rules that can be provided for making data collection and methods decisions in evaluation. The art of evaluation involves creating a design and gathering information that is appropriate for a specific situation and particular policymaking context. (1987: 9)

Thus, the purposes and circumstances of an evaluation exercise will ultimately determine methods choices.

There are not only methodological and theoretical issues surrounding the nature and complexity of the evaluation questions which have to be taken into account at the research design stage, but consideration also needs to be given to the practicalities of conducting this type of study. Sometimes circumstances may preclude the use of certain research design strategies or prevent the adoption of specific data collection techniques. For instance, it is readily acknowledged that 'evaluation typically occurs under time and resource constraints that require difficult trade-offs' (Shadish et al., 1991: 476). In certain situations the evaluator may find that pragmatic concerns outweigh theoretical considerations when it comes to selecting methods. Given the wide variety of social and political contexts in which evaluations take place it is little wonder that situational responsiveness, methodological flexibility and creativity are seen as essential to successful evaluation practice (Patton, 1981).

Types of data

The evaluation enterprise is characterized by plurality and diversity, as witnessed by the broad range of data-gathering devices which evaluators have at their disposal. However, before we describe some of the more commonly used methods, brief consideration will be given to the broad categorization of different types of data. A particularly important distinction is the one made between quantitative and qualitative data. As described in the previous chapter, the terms quantitative and qualitative are often associated with two divergent epistemological positions that not only embody contrasting assumptions about the nature of reality, but also carry direct methodological implications. In the main, quantitative methods generate data that can be presented numerically and subjected to various types of statistical analysis, whereas qualitative techniques produce data that are not so readily open to statistical interpretation. As Miles and Huberman (1984) note, a major distinction between the two approaches is that one deals in numbers while the other is concerned with words.

The conventional image of the researcher working within the quantitative tradition is one of a detached investigator using standardized measurement techniques specifically designed for the purpose of gathering objective factual data that are not only replicable, but also amenable to statistical analysis. In contrast, in the case of qualitative research the researcher is the main instrument of data collection: maintaining a distance from the data is not an option. Qualitative data are used to obtain details of the subjective experiences of programme planners and participants in process-oriented evaluations. Given the inherent properties of these two types of data they are sometimes referred to by the labels 'hard' and 'soft' or 'objective' and 'subjective', terms that can carry connotations of superiority and inferiority, especially when used to categorize actual methods of data collection. This practice gives the impression that one method can be judged to be better or worse than another, purely on the basis of its intrinsic qualities. This, in itself, betrays a fundamental methodological principle in social research, namely, that 'methods must be selected according to purposes' (Hammersley and Atkinson, 1983: x). An assessment of the superiority of one method over another can only be made when we know the details of the context in which the method is to be applied. Ultimately, the evaluation problem or question should be the determining factor when making methods choices. To echo Berk and Rossi, 'our message is pragmatic; research tools should be chosen for the particular job at hand' (1990: 11).

Bulmer (1986) notes that methods have been caught in the cross-fire in the paradigms debate, with the result that some of the criticisms levelled at the contrasting paradigms have been inappropriately directed at methods. He suggests that it 'is much more fruitful . . . to consider the merits of different methods for the study of particular types of problem, and the possibilities of combining different methods in the study of the same problem' (1986: 187). Methods and evaluation problems require careful matching. As Daly and McDonald (1992) state, ineffective evaluation of health care is not always attributable to 'weak' methods. Strict adherence to a method deemed to be 'strong' may result in the wrong problems becoming the focus of the evaluation purely because the right problems are not amenable to analysis by the preferred method. Clearly, the evaluator needs to be aware of the array of methods choices available, as well as being able to identify opportunities for mixing methods. Some of the theoretical, methodological, philosophical and practical issues involved in integrating quantitative and qualitative approaches in multi-method research designs are discussed in Brannen (1995).

Data can be distinguished not only by means of their intrinsic characteristics but also according to how they are acquired. Conventionally, a distinction is drawn between primary and secondary data. Collecting primary data involves the use of research instruments, for example, questionnaires and interview schedules that have been constructed for the purposes of a specific study. As such, they are designed to produce data considered by the evaluator to be essential in order to address the evaluation issues generated by a particular policy or programme. Secondary data refers to those data collected by other researchers, organizations or government departments for their own purposes. These can provide a useful source of information for the evaluator. Official statistics on health, education and crime obtained from administrative returns or large-scale sample surveys, can provide important trend data against which the impact of policy initiatives can be evaluated. At the level of the organization, use can be made of routine monitoring devices set up prior to the involvement of the evaluator. Thus, whereas in the case of primary data the evaluator not only initiates the data collection process but also plays an important part in gathering the data, with secondary data the evaluator is confined to critically examining and analysing data produced by others. Both primary and secondary data can come in quantitative or qualitative forms.

It is also possible to distinguish between structured and unstructured data. A questionnaire in which respondents are asked to complete a series of standardized assessment schedules or attitudinal scales imposes a structure on the data at the point of collection. The predetermined nature of the response categories affords respondents little opportunity to express their individual feelings. In contrast, informal interviews or open-ended questionnaire items provide scope for individuals to respond in their own terms, thus producing a wealth of unstructured data.

The primary purpose in selecting a method or research technique is to gather data that will help to provide answers to the evaluation questions formulated during the conceptualization stage in the evaluation process. However, the evaluator would do well not only to bear in mind the fallibility of all evaluative methods but also to pay attention to the circumstances in which data are generated and gathered. With regard to the latter point, it needs to be acknowledged that data are the product of the procedures applied in their collection. It follows from this that data are only understandable within the context of these procedures, which are themselves determined by the purposes of the evaluation. Consequently, it is important that both evaluation practitioners and users of evaluation findings have a clear insight into the characteristic features of the various data collection techniques available.

Methods of collecting data

It is rare to find an evaluation study based on only one method of data collection. Normally a range of techniques form the core of an overall research strategy, thus ensuring that the information acquired has the depth and detail necessary to enable the evaluator to produce a report from which conclusions can be drawn with a certain degree of confidence. The methods described below are some of the ones most commonly used in process and outcome evaluations. As previously stated, the purpose of this chapter is not to provide a full-blown critique of these data collection techniques, but merely to identify some of their salient features and raise some issues surrounding their selection and application.

Questionnaires

The questionnaire is one of the most frequently used methods of data collection in evaluation research. It can be used to provide the main source of data in a study, as in the case of consumer satisfaction surveys of service users, or it can be a useful source of supplementary data, for example, when used to collect information from individuals participating in randomized control trials. The questionnaire is a major tool for collecting primary data.

As Hoinville et al. note, 'Questionnaires come in many shapes and sizes, from postcards to be filled in by respondents to multi-page documents to be filled in by interviewers' (1987: 27). However, no matter what their shape or size, all questionnaires are concerned with description and measurement. They can be used to provide a wealth of descriptive data pertaining to individuals or groups. Basic socio-biographical information covering age, sex, income, educational background, membership of professional organizations and the like can be obtained relatively easily and inexpensively by administering a suitably designed questionnaire. The type of information gathered will be determined by the aims of the evaluation. For example, in a study of community-based welfare provision, respondents may be asked factual questions about the nature and frequency of their use of certain services provided by local organizations or community groups.

In addition to containing factual questions, questionnaires can include assessment schedules, sociometric tests and attitude rating scales designed to measure a variety of social and psychological variables. Instruments such as these can be administered before and after the implementation of a policy or programme to determine if a planned intervention has had a positive effect on individuals. The evaluator can make use of existing scales and schedules covering a vast array of topics. There are psychometric tests for assessing personality and intelligence, social psychological scales for measuring concepts like self-esteem and group cohesiveness, as well as scales to estimate levels of social well-being, general attitudes towards the community and the fear of being the victim of a crime. Initially, the task facing the evaluator is one of locating a suitable existing scale. There are useful sourcebooks which describe some of the more commonly used scales and provide details on their use and interpretation (Miller, 1991). Adopting a scale previously used by others has the advantage that it will have been subjected to testing in terms of validity and reliability. If a suitable existing scale cannot be found the evaluator may have no alternative but to construct a new scale. Henerson et al. (1987) provide a useful introduction to developing and testing instruments for measuring attitudes.

Questionnaires are capable of producing large quantities of highly structured, standardized data. The quality of the information they provide is largely dependent upon the design of the questionnaire. Therefore, it is imperative that the evaluator considers not only the content of the questionnaire but also the issues surrounding its construction and administration. As acknowledged by de Vaus, 'Good questionnaires do not just happen: they involve careful thinking, numerous drafts, thorough evaluation and extensive testing' (1996: 105). What questions are asked will be determined by the aims of the evaluation, and these obviously differ from study to study. However, there are general guidelines that apply to the construction of all types of questionnaires. These will be briefly discussed in this section. Those readers requiring further information are advised to consult one of the many specialist texts which cover the methodological, technical and practical aspects of the design, implementation and analysis of survey questionnaires (Moser and Kalton, 1983; Fowler, 1988; Nichols, 1991; Oppenheim, 1992; de Vaus, 1996).

As May observes, 'the questionnaire is an instrument for measuring the ideas that go into its design. For this reason, the questions not only reflect the survey's aims, but also must be understood by respondents in a clear and unambiguous way' (1993: 75). While there is an opportunity for the researcher to clarify any ambiguities stemming from the wording of questions in situations where a questionnaire is administered by means of a face-to-face interview or telephone interview, there is no such opportunity in the case of self-administered questionnaires. Poorly framed questions or badly structured questionnaires can easily discourage respondents and lead to low response rates. Furthermore, any uncertainty surrounding the interpretation of certain questions can cast doubt on the validity of the data that are obtained.

In order to encourage respondent co-operation and increase the likelihood of eliciting accurate responses, it is essential that certain basic principles are followed when using questionnaires to collect data. First, the questionnaire should be delivered with a covering letter explaining the purpose of the research. Second, it is important that the document itself looks attractive and that all instructions are easy to follow. Third, questionnaires should not be too long; where possible filter or contingency questions should be used to enable the respondent to bypass items or sections that are not directly applicable to them. Arrows and instruction boxes can be provided to guide the respondent through the questionnaire. Fourth, the order in which questions are asked is important; questions should follow a logical sequence. Finally, question wording should be clear and unambiguous.

In the interests of clarity and precision great care needs to be taken over the phrasing of questions irrespective of whether these are of a closed or open format. Closed questions are ones which require the respondent to select one or more responses from a predetermined list of possible answers. Generally, individuals are not given an opportunity to explain the reasons for their choice or qualify their responses. Forced-choice questions are quick to answer which makes them a popular choice for inclusion in self-completion questionnaires. For some closed questions the response set may be a simple 'yes' or 'no'. However, rating scales, attitudinal statements and checklists offer more detailed verbal or diagrammatic response formats. A respondent may be asked to indicate how strongly they agree or disagree with an attitudinal statement in a number of ways. They may be asked to choose a number between one and ten on a continuum from strongly agree to strongly disagree, mark a point on a line from plus one to minus one, where zero is taken to indicate neither agreement nor disagreement, or select from a list of verbal categories the one which best describes their strength of feeling. The responses are pre-coded which speeds up the process of transferring the data to a computer for analysis.

Closed questions clearly have their advantages but care needs to be exercised in their construction. The respondent should be offered a full range of responses to eliminate the possibility of bias which can arise when respondents have a limited number of options from which to choose. As May (1993) notes, answers should meet two conditions: they should be exhaustive and mutually exclusive. To help comply with these conditions the researcher can undertake some exploratory interviews prior to designing the questionnaire in order to identify a range of likely responses. Once the questionnaire has been constructed it can be subjected to a pilot test, following which any necessary amendments can be made before the questionnaire is used. No matter how thoroughly this preparatory work is undertaken it always pays to expect the unexpected and include a category of 'other, please specify' in a fixed response set.

Open-ended questions allow respondents to answer in their own words, rather than being restricted to choosing from a list of pre-coded categories. They have the advantage of giving respondents leeway to elaborate on their answers. However, they also have their disadvantages, particularly when used in self-completion questionnaires. Whereas closed questions require the respondent to place a tick in the appropriate box, open questions call for greater deliberation and a written response. This can increase the amount of time the individual needs to devote to the exercise and may deter some potential respondents. Also, open-ended questions can generate a wide range of responses, some of which can prove difficult to categorize. In self-completion questionnaires it is advisable to keep open questions to a minimum; if they are used they are best placed towards the end of the questionnaire.

Whatever the format a question takes, the researcher must pay careful attention to how the question is phrased. When writing questions a number of points need to be borne in mind. First, use language appropriate to the target audience. Keep questions clear, straightforward and jargon-free; avoid the use of vague words and ambiguous or unfamiliar phrases. It may be appropriate to use technical terminology when surveying specialist groups, such as medical consultants, but not when sampling a general patient population. Second, avoid leading questions; do not begin questions with phrases like, 'Do you prefer . . .?' or 'Don't you agree that . . .?'. Third, do not use double-barrelled questions; these ask two questions in one, as illustrated in the following example: 'Do you feel that the new administrative arrangements are helping care workers and their clients?'. Fourth, always make sure that the frame of reference for a question is clearly stated, otherwise the question may be interpreted differently by different respondents, producing a wide range of responses which cannot be easily reduced to a manageable number of categories for the purpose of analysis. For example, when asking respondents about the frequency of an event or activity a list of responses should be provided which specify a suitable time frame, such as 'less than one a week', 'one a week', 'more than one a week'. These are just some of the guidelines for writing questions: additional pointers can be found in de Vaus (1996: 83–6) and May (1993: 81–2).

Design issues are of fundamental importance, because a badly designed questionnaire will generate inadequate data thus effectively reducing the chances a piece of evaluation research has of producing valid findings. A good questionnaire is one designed with the nature of the respondents in mind. The success of a questionnaire depends, in part, upon the ability of individuals to answer questions (Moser and Kalton, 1983). Not only must they be seen to have the knowledge required to provide adequate responses, but also the questions must be presented in a style and format commensurate with their cognitive and linguistic abilities. When dealing with young children, adults with learning difficulties or severely chronically impaired individuals, signs, symbols and pictures can replace words to identify different response categories. Where self-completion questionnaires are impractical, face-to-face interviews can be conducted by appropriately trained interviewers.

In summary, as a research instrument the questionnaire is a useful source of both quantitative and qualitative data. Although it has its limitations, and is not necessarily suitable for use in all evaluation contexts, many of its shortcomings can be overcome by careful planning and rigorous pilot testing.

Interviews

Interviewing is another research method widely used by evaluators. It is particularly popular with qualitative researchers and is considered by Guba and Lincoln to be the very 'backbone of field and naturalistic research and evaluation' (1981: 154). However, as a means of obtaining information it is not restricted to use with a particular research methodology. As Patton notes:

becoming a skilled interviewer will serve the evaluator well beyond field-work. Evaluators need interviewing skills to find out what stakeholders want from an evaluation, to gather information for use in designing a study, and to understand the context for an evaluation. Thus even evaluators who use only or primarily quantitative and experimental methods can benefit from improving their interviewing skills. (1987: 108)

During the early stages of an evaluation the evaluator may obtain information by talking to various individuals. It is largely through interviews with programme planners, administrators and providers that the evaluator acquires a full understanding of the nature of the programme, its principal objectives and the theory behind its design and implementation. This is an essential step in formulating the research design. The nature of the evaluation questions, and the context in which the study is undertaken, will largely determine whether or not interviews will be used as a method of data collection. Interviews can generate qualitative and quantitative data capable of addressing both process and outcome issues.

Dexter describes the interview as a 'conversation with a purpose' (1970: 136), while Lofland and Lofland refer to it as 'a guided conversation' (1984: 12). In general terms, a broad distinction is made between three basic types of interview format: the structured or standardized interview, the semi-structured or semi-standardized interview and the unstructured or unstandardized interview (Denzin, 1978). A structured interview, also referred to as a formal interview, relies on a questionnaire or interview schedule as the instrument for collecting data. Questions are asked of each interviewee in a systematic and consistent order. Interviewers are given detailed instructions on how to ask the questions and how to respond to any unanticipated responses or requests from the interviewee for further clarification of a question. The rationale behind this approach is that by enforcing a uniform structure on the interview, each respondent is effectively exposed to the same stimulus, thus ensuring that the responses are comparable. This type of interview is only used when the evaluator has a good idea what the relevant questions are.

A semi-structured interview follows a less rigid format. Although standardized questions, covering socio-biographical details like, age, sex, educational qualifications and the like, are included there are also open-ended questions designed to elicit more qualitative information. It is not essential that the questions adhere to a predetermined sequence. The interviewer has some control over how the research instrument is implemented and can vary the order and phrasing of questions should this prove necessary within the context of an individual interview. Also the interviewer is expected to probe for more information by encouraging respondents to digress and expand upon their answers.

The unstructured, unstandardized or focused interview is also known as the intensive interview (Lofland and Lofland, 1984) or the informal conversational interview (Patton, 1987). It is a purely qualitative interviewing strategy in which questions and follow-up probes are generated during the interview itself. The unstructured interview is completely open-ended in character and differs from the other approaches in allowing the interviewee to give their definition of a situation, thereby facilitating a greater understanding of the subject's point of view (May, 1993). As Patton states, 'The purpose of qualitative interviewing in evaluation is to understand how people in a program view the program, learn their terminology and judgements, and to capture the complexities of their individual perceptions and experiences' (1987: 115). This type of interviewing is particularly useful at the beginning of an evaluation study as it enables the evaluator to get a feel for the programme and become acquainted with programme staff and participants. The information obtained will provide valuable insights which will help the evaluator in choosing an appropriate evaluation design and constructing more formal interview schedules, questionnaires or evaluation sheets.

As far as methods choices go with regard to primary data collection the evaluator needs to decide whether to use a self-completion questionnaire or an interview technique, or indeed a combination of the two. In some evaluation situations both approaches may be equally appropriate on methodological and technical grounds and the evaluator may decide in favour of self-completion questionnaires on the basis of cost alone. However, it is often the case that there are strong reasons for opting for one or other of the two broad approaches. The nature of the evaluation question, the type of information sought, the characteristics of the programme recipients, the ease of access to data sources and the resources available will all have an influence on methods choices at one time or another. Questionnaires are generally preferred where the evaluator is seeking routine information from a large sample of individuals drawn from a wide geographical area. An interview is more likely to be the chosen method where smaller numbers are involved, the data required relate to individual experiences and the evaluator wishes to explore in some depth the opinions, expectations and actions of individuals.

There is no one right way of conducting an interview. As Guba and Lincoln assert, interviewing is 'highly individualistic and does not involve a set of techniques', there are no '"cookbook" techniques or sure-fire recipes' for success (1981: 158). The personal characteristics of the interviewer, the context of the evaluation and the interviewee's needs and expertise will all influence how well an interview is accomplished. Although there is no fixed formula governing interviewing, general advice can be offered concerning constructing interview schedules or guides, formulating questions and managing the interview.

An interview schedule is a highly structured research instrument used in standardized interviews. The process of developing a schedule of questions begins with the evaluator drawing up a preliminary list of categories deemed to be relevant given the evaluation situation. Ideas for categories come from a variety of sources, including information gleaned from programme literature and related documentary materials, data collected from unstructured, exploratory interviews with principal stakeholders, and knowledge acquired from similar evaluative studies undertaken elsewhere. Once the major categories have been identified, the evaluator proceeds to generate lists of questions relevant to each category.

Interview guides, as featured in focused or unstructured interviews, are considerably less structured. A guide or an agenda can consist of nothing more than a short list of topics which acts as an aide-mémoire to ensure that the interviewer addresses the same themes in all interviews (Burgess, 1984: 108). Lofland and Lofland (1984) provide some useful practical advice on how to prepare an interview guide for use in intensive interviewing.

Some guidelines for formulating questions have already been mentioned in the discussion of questionnaire design in the preceding section. The framing and construction of questions is also an important issue in unstructured interviewing. As Patton observes, 'The way a question is worded is one of the most important elements in determining how the interviewee will respond' (1987: 122). He maintains that from the point of view of qualitative evaluation, questions should be, at the very least, 'open-ended, neutral, sensitive and clear' (1987: 122). With reference to the first of these criteria, he draws attention to the importance of phrasing when he considers the qualities of a truly open-ended question. He notes that simply removing the response categories from a closed question does not automatically make it an open question, as the following example illustrates.

A typical closed question in a self-completion questionnaire might read: How satisfied would you say you are with this programme? (a) very satisfied, (b) somewhat satisfied, (c) not too satisfied, (d) not at all satisfied. Patton asserts that, as 'the desired dimension of response is identified in the wording of the question', simply asking the same question without the predetermined response categories does not make the question truly open-ended (1987: 123). The response categories may no longer be explicit, but the very phrasing of the question ensures that they remain implicit. If the aim is to allow individual interviewees to express, in their own terms, what they regard as relevant, then the question needs to be reworded. For example, the interviewer could ask: 'How do you feel about the programme?' This constitutes a truly open question.

A good question is one that is worded clearly and precisely so that the respondent has a good understanding of its meaning and what is expected by way of a response. No matter how clearly a question is phrased there is always the possibility that the interviewee may either inadvertently or deliberately give an untruthful or misleading response.

Therefore, it is advisable, when constructing an interview schedule or guide, to include questions that will reveal any inconsistency in responses (Denzin, 1970: 129). If the interviewee is suspected of lying then the interviewer may have to ask fairly directive and specific questions (Hammersley and Atkinson, 1983: 114).

Interviewing is not simply about asking the right type of questions in the most appropriate way; the interviewer needs to assume and maintain control over the interview. Initially, this may be easier with some interviewing strategies than others. For example, with structured interviews the interview schedule, with its carefully worded questions, prompts, probes and other instructions for the interviewer, imposes a format on the interview. The task facing the interviewer is to collect information by guiding the interviewee through a series of predetermined questions. In contrast, an unstructured interview is not scripted in the same way; the encounter between the interviewer and interviewee is much less formal and resembles a natural conversation. The primary purpose is to obtain data that provide an insight into how interviewees define and account for particular situations and circumstances. The interviewer does not attempt to prejudge what the relevant issues might be. Thus, in this approach the person being interviewed has some involvement in directing the course of the interview.

Regardless of whether the interview is structured or unstructured, successful management of the process is partly dependent upon the interviewer being an active listener and being able to establish a rapport with the interviewee. For Corimer and Corimer (1979), active listening is the very foundation on which good interviewing is based. Similarly, Guba and Lincoln (1981) profess that the 'skill of listening' is of paramount importance. Active listening is a prerequisite of effective communication. It is by careful listening to what is said that the interviewer is able to formulate meaningful questions, use prompts and probes effectively and generally respond in a manner which stimulates the flow of talk and encourages the continued co-operation of the interviewee.

There is no doubt that interviews are extremely powerful research tools in the social sciences; however, there is an established body of evidence suggesting that characteristics such as the age, sex, race, religion, demeanour, attitudes, expectations and appearance of the interviewer can have an influence on the quality and validity of response data (Rice, 1929; Hyman et al., 1954; Sudman and Bradburn, 1974). In addition to taking these factors into account, and possibly matching interviewers and respondents according to certain characteristics, the evaluator also needs to be aware of the special problems encountered when using the interview method in an evaluation context.

In most research situations there are only two groups with a vested interest in the interview: the researchers and the researched. In the case of evaluation, there is a third party to be considered, namely those responsible for organizing and delivering the programme which is under investigation (Weiss, 1975). The evaluator must gain their trust and confidence. Programme personnel, be they professional practitioners or administrators, will want to be reassured that any interviewing by independent evaluators does not disrupt the day-to-day running of the programme or jeopardize the relationship between programme staff and their clients. There is of course the question of using programme staff to conduct interviews; this can help to keep costs down as well as having other potential advantages. For example, as staff will be known to programme recipients they should experience little difficulty in gaining the co-operation of respondents and establishing a good rapport in the interview.

However, the use of internal interviewers also has its disadvantages. Weiss (1975) refers to how programme staff can find it difficult to keep the roles of service provider and research interviewer separate. She concludes that the disadvantages far outweigh the advantages and recommends that evaluation interviews are best conducted by external interviewers who are responsible directly to the evaluator. In this context, consideration also needs to be given to where the interview is held. The setting and location can have a significant influence on the success of the interview. As Hammersley and Atkinson observe, 'Different settings are likely to induce and constrain talk of particular kinds' (1983: 125). Interviewing a programme participant in the programme director's office may produce a different response than if the interview were conducted on neutral ground.

The problem of interview error is not confined to evaluation research. Nevertheless, there is a sense in which evaluation studies are more susceptible to threats to response validity resulting from bias and inaccuracy. This is largely attributable to the fact that evaluation research is distinguished from other research strategies by the assumption that there is a 'right' answer (Weiss, 1975). In outcome evaluations the principal objective is usually to ascertain whether or not a programme 'works'. Consequently, interviewees may feel they know the 'right' answers and respond accordingly. Responses may very well reflect the vested interests of respondents. If there is a feeling among programme staff that future funding is contingent upon positive evaluation findings, they may play down certain issues in the interview and emphasize those points which they consider show the programme in a favourable light.

It is impossible to completely eliminate interview error; the most the evaluator can do is take precautionary measures to deal with potential sources of error and thus reduce their impact. This requires that all aspects of the interview are carefully planned. As previously mentioned, although there is no one correct way of interviewing, there are many texts which offer general guidelines for conducting interviews (Lincoln and Guba, 1985; Patton, 1987).

So far the discussion of unstandardized interviews has concentrated on situations where there is a one-to-one relationship between the interviewer and the interviewee. However, recent years have witnessed a growth in the use of group interviews or what have become more popularly known as 'focus groups' (Merton and Kendall, 1946). This technique provides a relatively inexpensive and efficient way of collecting data particularly when the investigator is primarily concerned with obtaining an insight into the attitudes and opinions of groups, rather than acquiring specific information about individuals. According to Powell and Single, a focus group is 'a group of individuals selected and assembled by researchers to discuss and comment on, from personal experience, the topic that is the subject of the research' (1996: 499). The growing number of books describing how to conduct focus groups is testimony to the increasing popularity of this method of data collection (Goldman and McDonald, 1988; Stewart and Shamdasani, 1990; Morgan, 1993, 1997; Krueger, 1994).

There is no fixed size for a focus group interview, but the group must not be too large as this may inhibit some members from joining in the discussion. A typical focus group involves around six to twelve people who are brought together by the researcher for the purpose of answering a number of questions. A group moderator or facilitator encourages participants to respond in their own terms, while simultaneously ensuring that the focus of the group is maintained. The group setting allows participants to qualify their original responses in the light of comments made by other group members. By and large, when used in programme evaluation, focus group interviews have several advantages over self-completion questionnaires and structured interviews with individuals. On the practical side they can generate a lot of qualitative data fairly quickly; normally a focus group session lasts one to two hours. Also, they are relatively inexpensive to run and therefore a popular choice when financial resources are limited.

From a methodological point of view, focus groups have the advantage over questionnaires and structured interview schedules of allowing participants the freedom to raise issues that are important to them, rather than merely respond to a set of predetermined questions. They also provide the evaluator with an opportunity to directly observe the social processes and dynamics of group interaction. Depending on the composition of the group it is possible to develop a valuable insight into process issues, for example, programme administrators, practitioners and clients can be brought together to form a single focus group. Group interviews also introduce an element of quality control into the data collection process. As Patton notes, 'participants tend to provide checks and balances on each other which weed out false or extreme views' (1987: 135).

The focus group approach does have some disadvantages. Individuals may suppress or modify their true feelings when in the presence of others. There is not the same cloak of confidentiality as applies in the individual interview. Individuals may feel particularly inhibited when in a group where participants not only know one another, but also have to work alongside each other. There is also the question of the status of individual participants. Junior programme staff may be reluctant to openly criticize their senior professional colleagues, while service users may feel constrained by the nature of the professional–client relationship. Herein lies a fundamental methodological question: are the perceptions of a programme produced by this technique an accurate portrayal of what participants actually believe or are they an artefact of the focus group method (Krueger, 1994).

In spite of these shortcomings the focus group interview is a versatile research tool capable of meeting a wide range of evaluation needs and suitable for use at any stage in the evaluation process (Patton, 1987). Focus groups can be conducted to generate ideas to facilitate the initial planning or development of a programme of activities (Race et al., 1994). During the preliminary stages of an evaluation they can help identify what participants see as the key issues. They can also be held at critical stages in the implementation of a programme to obtain feedback from participants as to what problems are encountered and how they are resolved. It is also feasible to use the group interview method at the end of a programme to obtain participants' perceptions of the impact and overall effectiveness of the programme.

The purpose of qualitative interviewing, whether individual or group focused, is to capture the experiences, perspectives and understandings of the interviewees. The quality of the final analysis will be partly contingent upon the accuracy with which the data are recorded. When conducting lengthy, complex, unstructured interviews it is advisable to use a tape-recorder, with the interviewee's permission of course, so that a full text of the interview can be reproduced for the purpose of detailed analysis (Gorden, 1980). Unencumbered by the need to take copious notes the interviewer is free to concentrate on what is being said. However, it is recommended that sparse notes are taken to help the interviewer keep track of the direction and content of the interview (Lofland and Lofland, 1984).

Transcribing a taped interview can be a laborious, time-consuming and costly undertaking. The researcher needs to evaluate the advantages and disadvantages of tape-recording interviews in each evaluation setting. There are those who advocate restricting the use of the tape-recorder, claiming that in most circumstances a verbatim transcription is unnecessary and diligent, yet selective, note-taking is capable of generating sufficient data (Cheetham et al., 1992). Alternatives to producing a full transcription, such as, performing the analysis directly from the tape by replaying the interview and taking notes, are questioned on the grounds that time would have been saved by dispensing with the tape-recorder and taking notes in the first place (Fuller and Petch, 1995). These critics do recognize the existence of exceptional circumstances in which tape-recording is advantageous, as for example, when conducting in-depth interviews with senior policy-makers or where a detailed contextual analysis of the data is to be performed.

Observation

It is possible to distinguish between different uses of the term observation when referring to evaluation practice. In a general sense, evaluators make use of observational skills irrespective of the data collection methods they employ. Whether administering questionnaires, conducting interviews or visiting programme sites, evaluators are sensitive to the various ways people behave and how they interact in different physical settings. These observations are not systematic, but occur spontaneously in the course of conducting an evaluation. In a more specific sense, specially designed observational studies, using secondary data, can be undertaken. For example, in the field of health care evaluation, Woodward (1992) describes how the increasing availability of computerized databases have made it possible to conduct large-scale cross-sectional or longitudinal observational studies of the use and impact of new technology on health care delivery. A further use of observation is in the context of experimental or quasi-experimental evaluation research designs, where the evaluator subjects any observed differences between the experimental and control or comparison groups to statistical analysis.

In this section the focus will be on the use of systematic observation as a direct method of collecting primary qualitative data. The term 'systematic observation' applies when 'observation and recording are done according to explicit procedures which permit replication and . . . rules are followed which permit the use of the logic of scientific inference' (Reiss, 1971: 4). As such, observational fieldwork involves much more than the looking and listening that is part of everyday life. Evaluators require disciplined training and careful preparation before they become skilled observers and competent analysts of observational data (Patton, 1987).

A characteristic feature of this approach is that the evaluator becomes the main instrument of data collection, adopting, at any one time, a fieldwork role approximating to one of four basic types outlined by Gold (1969). These roles are differentiated from one another according to the degree to which the observer participates in the group or organization which is the subject of study. Gold labels the four roles as follows: complete participant, participant-as-observer, observer-as-participant and complete observer. The first two are examples of participant observation and the second two are examples of non-participant observation. As Burgess (1982) notes, the four roles are ideal typical constructs, and within the context of a single study the researcher may, from time to time, move between roles.

Participant observation, as a fieldwork strategy, involves the evaluator entering the social world of those engaged in programme activities in order to provide a full and detailed account of the programme. In the case of the *complete participant*, the role adopted by the researcher is a covert or secret one; those people under observation are unaware of the true identity or intentions of the observer. Researchers may sometimes find it necessary to take action to preserve their anonymity if they are to continue their work in the field. As observation and interviewing are concurrent activities in qualitative approaches, there is the possibility that covert participants may feel constrained from asking questions in field settings for fear of appearing unnaturally inquisitive, thereby running the risk of being exposed. When the chosen role is that of *participant-as-observer*, the reasons for the researcher's presence are made explicit, consequently, there is no threat of exposure. Overt observers might have the advantage of being able to freely question informants, but the fact that they are seen as researchers may influence how informants behave and respond to their questioning.

Vass (1984, 1990) describes how he used participant observation to study 'process' issues in the implementation and administration of community service orders. In the course of the fieldwork he completed 220 hours of community service with a group of sentenced offenders under the supervision of the probation service. As he recalls, 'I was treated as an "offender". As I was instructed to carry out particular duties, my attendance and performance, with a few exceptions, were monitored, evaluated and hours were credited by supervising officers as though I was under a real court order' (1990: 116).

The field roles of *observer-as-participant* and *complete observer* are, in a general sense, non-participatory roles. With regard to the former, contact with informants is brief, and although the role is an overt one there is no attempt on the part of the researcher to develop relationships with informants. As Gold notes, this role 'is used in studies involving one-visit interviews' (1969: 36). In the case of the complete observer, there is no social interaction whatsoever between the observer and the informant during the course of data collection, as is the case with 'systematic eavesdropping' (1969: 37) or when the behaviour of subjects in laboratory-based experiments is observed through a one-way mirror (May, 1993).

Observational techniques provide an important source of evaluation data, particularly when the evaluator is a participant observer. Qualitative evaluators are quick to identify the advantages associated with an 'inductive, discovery-oriented approach' to data collection (Patton, 1987: 73). First and foremost, some observational fieldwork is essential if the evaluator is to provide a suitably descriptive account of the core features of any programme. When there is a strong emphasis on participation, personal experience becomes an important resource. Direct experience of programme activities enables the evaluator to draw on tacit, as well as propositional, knowledge, in order to describe a situation or series of events (Guba and Lincoln, 1981). A second advantage of observational methods is that in some situations they can succeed where other methods fail or prove infeasible. For example, as both Patton and Guba and Lincoln note, observational techniques, when systematically applied, can provide new insights by drawing attention to actions and behaviour normally taken for granted by those involved in programme activities and therefore not commented upon in interviews. Also, there are circumstances in which it may not be possible to conduct interviews, such as when subjects are unable to communicate, as is the case with very young children, severely mentally impaired adults and confused psycho-geriatric patients. Unwillingness to communicate can also be a problem; some individuals may display reticence or simply refuse to be interviewed. In these circumstances observation may be the only realistic choice facing the evaluator.

There are a number of drawbacks to the use of participant observation. On a practical level, gathering, recording and analysing field data are costly activities, both in terms of time and money. As regards methodological issues, there is concern about the reliability and validity of observational data. The direct involvement of the observer in the situation under investigation can be a potential source of bias on two counts. First, with overt observation there is always the possibility that individuals will consciously modify their behaviour if aware that they are under observation. This is especially true when there are vested interests at stake, such as when the continuation of a programme is contingent upon a positive evaluation report. In this context, the conceptual distinction Van Maanen (1983) draws in organizational ethnography between 'operational data' and 'presentational data' is significant: 'operational data deal with observed activity (behaviour per se) and presentational data deal with the appearances put forth by informants as these activities are talked about and otherwise symbolically projected within the research setting' (1983: 42). Presentational data reflect the image subjects want to portray to others; it is 'a manufactured image of idealized doing' (1983: 42). These kind of data can present a false picture by disguising the real nature of the way individuals negotiate and accomplish the routine activities of a programme on a day-to-day basis. In endeavouring to present themselves in a positive light individuals may give out deliberately misleading information. The analytic task facing the fieldworker is to separate the operational from the presentational and in the process uncover attempts to deceive.

A second count on which the method of participant observation can lead to bias is when the fieldworker gets so caught up in the activities under observation that it affects what is actually observed. Close identification with a group over a sustained period of fieldwork can lead to the observer embracing the values and taken for granted assumptions held by group members. As Burgess (1984) warns, the role of complete observer carries with it the risk of 'going native'. Where the researcher takes the participant-as-observer role there is the problem of 'over-rapport' (Hammersley and Atkinson, 1983). This has particular implications in evaluation settings, as there are often a number of different stakeholders. The evaluator needs to be careful not to appear to be developing too close a relationship with any one group as this can lead to accusations of impartiality.

Knowledge of the advantages and disadvantages of participant observation is essential if evaluators are to make informed methods choices. When deciding on participant observation they have at their disposal not a single method, but 'a characteristic blend or combination of methods and techniques' (McCall and Simmons, 1969: 1). The participant observer does not merely collect data by direct observation, but uses access to programme participants to conduct informal conversational interviews, set up formal interviews and collect documentary materials.

In deciding on an observational research strategy the evaluator will take into account a number of factors including the purposes of the evaluation, the nature of the programme or intervention, the characteristics of the target population and the theory underlying the programme. Having decided on the appropriateness of qualitative methods, the next step is to decide the degree to which the fieldworker will participate in the programme being investigated. Patton offers the following advice:

> The ideal is to negotiate and adopt that degree of participation that will yield the most meaningful data about the program given the characteristics of the participants, the nature of staff–participant interactions, and the socio-political context of the program. (Patton, 1990: 209)

Programme staff have legitimate concerns about the nature of the methods used in an evaluation. They may seek reassurances that data collection will not impinge upon programme activities, place extra demands on staff or have any detrimental effects on those people the programme is designed to benefit. The situation usually demands that the evaluator discuss with staff the degree to which fieldworkers will participate in the programme and who will be informed as to the identity of the observers and the purposes of the evaluation.

Each new evaluation study presents a unique set of circumstances requiring careful consideration. For example, in some programme contexts the age, sex, gender, race or ethnic background of the fieldworker can influence not only the success with which rapport is established but also the quality of the data obtained. The personal biographical characteristics of the evaluator, and the nature of the programme setting, will go some way towards limiting opportunities for engaging in participant observation.

Wherever participant observation is used there are ethical issues to consider. There is a long-running debate in social research about the ethics of using covert fieldwork methods. While Bulmer (1982) warns against over-simplifying the debate, he observes that two diametrically opposed positions can be identified. At one extreme there are those who take the view that not revealing one's identity as a researcher, or concealing the true purpose of a research study from informants, constitutes unethical conduct. At the other extreme there are researchers who eschew arguments about ethical principles and see covert methods of data collection as a legitimate way of getting at the truth. Many evaluators reject complete covert observation as undesirable. Patton recommends 'full and complete disclosure' on the grounds that not only is it almost impossible for the 'secret' evaluator to maintain the deception, but the possibility of detection bringing the evaluation to a close places the evaluator under a certain amount of stress (1990: 213). However, Patton admits that in some situations full disclosure might not be a prudent choice, for example, if programme funders suspect improper conduct they may favour a covert evaluation strategy. This is not an option Guba and Lincoln would endorse in the case of programmes supported by public funds. Indeed they categorically assert that, 'we cannot think of a single instance in which it might be appropriate for the inquirer to go "undercover" in the evaluation of a publicly funded program' (1981: 202).

As we have shown in this section observational fieldwork encompasses a wide range of activities. Methods of observation can be overt or covert, can include collecting structured or unstructured data in the form of audio-visual recordings, taped interviews, completed checklists or detailed fieldnotes and involve the researcher as a participant or non-participant observer. There are no universal rules governing the choice and application of observational techniques in evaluation research designs. As Patton observes, although it is possible to provide general guidelines for fieldwork, 'what one does depends on the situation, the nature of the evaluation, the nature of the program, and the skills, interests, needs, and point of view of the evaluator-observer' (1990: 274).

Documentary sources

A variety of documentary materials are available to the evaluator. In classifying documentary evidence, Burgess (1984) draws a distinction between primary and secondary sources, public and private documents and solicited and unsolicited documents. Primary sources refer to documents compiled by individuals who have firsthand experience of the events described; examples include minutes of meetings, office memoranda and personal diaries. Secondary source material consists of documents produced by individuals who do not possess personal knowledge of the situation. An example would be a written synopsis of a lengthy official report, produced for the purposes of disseminating information to key personnel within an organization.

The distinction between public and private documents raises the issue of accessibility (Scott, 1990). Not all documents classified as being in the public domain are open to scrutiny and not all private personal materials are difficult to access. Public documents include administrative records held by national and local governments, official statistics and reports of government select committees. Many of these documents are freely available; however, there is restricted access to some unpublished government papers under the 30-year rule. Other examples of public documents include newspaper articles, letters to the editor, editorials, press releases, community newsletters, professional journals, reports of official inspectors and regulators, annual reports and publications by bodies like the Equal Opportunities Commission, the Audit Commission and OFSTED.

Burgess also distinguishes between solicited and unsolicited documents. The former category includes those documents the individual is asked to produce by the researcher; hence the researcher can exercise some control with respect to what information is included and the manner in which it is recorded. For example, in the evaluation of a health care initiative or health promotion campaign, respondents could be asked to record, in a personal health diary, their physical symptoms and subjective feelings of well-being over a period of time following the programme intervention. This produces primary data. With unsolicited documents the researcher is unable to influence the kind of information that is collected and must make do with what is available. The information will have been originally collected for a purpose other than an evaluation study and is therefore referred to as secondary data.

Documentary material provides a valuable source of information about the formal goals and aims of a programme. Content analysis of the minutes of a steering group or co-ordinating committee can provide a useful record of any problems with regards to programme implementation or management. A perusal of correspondence, internal memoranda, file notes and progress reports can reveal the extent to which there are any differences of opinion over the structure, organization or delivery of the programme. The information contained on client record cards and the routine performance monitoring data compiled by programme staff can be used to measure outcomes.

Diaries are another type of document that the researcher can request programme participants to keep for a specified period during the course of an evaluation study. These may take a number of different forms. Diaries can be fairly unstructured documents, with respondents simply being asked to record their thoughts and feelings about their involvement in a project or programme. Alternatively, a more structured format can be used with programme participants keeping a detailed log of their daily activities and providing comments under a number of predetermined headings. Whether the recording interval is in days, weeks or months will to a large extent depend upon the nature of the intervention and the scope and focus of the evaluation. Irrespective of whether a structured or unstructured diary format is adopted the 'diary–diary interview method' can be used (Zimmerman and Wieder, 1977). This involves the person who has completed the diary being interviewed in some detail on aspects of its content.

While it is important for the evaluator to make use of data derived from documents, the limitations of these data need to be recognized. For example, individual case files are compiled by professionals as part of the routine recording of their work with clients and as such do not necessarily provide a reliable monitoring device for evaluation purposes. As Cheetham et al. note with respect to the information contained in case records kept by social workers, this is often 'incomplete, insufficient or inappropriate to the needs of the evaluative researcher' (1992: 43). Not only is it possible for there to be a variation in the style and content of the records kept by individuals, but case monitoring procedures may also vary from one team or organization to another. This can pose problems when a multi-site evaluation research design strategy is employed. The poor quality of the data available may prohibit a retrospective study, forcing the evaluator to adopt a prospective research design involving the construction and implementation of a standardized case monitoring form.

Documentary material requires careful handling. It should not be assumed that documents constitute independent, objective records of events or circumstances. As Scott asserts, 'Texts must be studied as socially situated products' (1990: 34). The evaluator must develop an understanding of both the process by which a document is produced and the social and political context in which it is embedded. Case notes are highly selective accounts with a strong subjective element. They may also be written with a specific audience in mind. For example, those responsible for constructing case records are conscious of the fact that the contents of the files may be referred to at a later date if they are required by their superiors to justify their actions. According to Fuller and Petch, 'The use of case records must therefore be treated with caution; it is a second-order analysis of data which is already a selected record of the incident or activity under scrutiny' (1995: 53). Indeed, as May notes, documents do not reflect a straightforward, objective description of social reality, but by presenting a particular interpretation of events they help to construct a version of social reality. What is recorded is influenced by social, political and ideological factors. Thus the evaluator should be aware that, 'Documents might then be interesting for what they leave out, as well as what they contain' (May, 1993: 138).

Mixing methods

Commenting, some years ago, on the apparent dichotomy created between quantitative and qualitative methods by some evaluators, Cook and Reichardt suggested that, 'It is time to stop building walls between the methods and start building bridges' (1979: 27). Since then there have been some moves in this direction. There is evidence that evaluators are increasingly adopting diverse methods in tackling evaluation problems. Mixed-methods research designs, in some cases integrating quantitative and qualitative methods, are now an established feature of programme evaluation research and policy evaluation studies. This reflects not only a growing realization among evaluators that methods of inquiry are not necessarily tied to a particular paradigmatic tradition, but also a recognition of the relevance of qualitative research techniques in evaluation contexts.

> This consensus about neutrality of methods, along with the widespread acceptance of qualitative methods, has afforded the evaluation community a vastly increased repertoire of methodological tools and has renewed interest in the time-honored methodological strategy of triangulation. (Greene and McClintock, 1985: 524)

The term 'triangulation' is borrowed from surveying or navigation, where it refers to the practice of establishing the exact position of a given object by taking readings or measurements from multiple viewpoints. Using more than one reference point enables greater accuracy of measurement.

Applying this logic to social research, Denzin (1970) identifies four different types of triangulation: data, investigator, theory and methodological. First, data triangulation involves the creation of multiple data sets by collecting data in a variety of contexts and settings at different points in time. This may involve using the same method on more than one occasion or using different methods at different times. Second, investigator triangulation occurs when more than one researcher or evaluator investigates the same situation. Using multiple investigators ensures that a number of different viewpoints are represented. The approach adopted by individual evaluators is largely influenced by their disciplinary roots, theoretical orientations and methodological preferences. In some contexts evaluators may require specialist knowledge in substantive areas in addition to their technical expertise in evaluation methodology. Where this is the case there are advantages to be gained from working together in multi-disciplinary evaluation teams. Third, there is theory triangulation, which entails making use of a number of alternative or competing theories in examining the data.

Finally, and perhaps most importantly given the focus of this chapter, there is methodological triangulation. Here Denzin (1970) distinguishes between two broad subtypes, the 'within-method' approach and the 'between-methods' or 'across-methods' approach. The former entails applying the same method on different occasions or using multiple techniques within a given method. Examples include administering the same questionnaire to respondents on separate occasions or attempting to address the same phenomena using a mixture of different scaling techniques, attitudinal measures and open-ended questions. In contrast, 'between-methods' triangulation refers to the actual mixing of methods in a single research design. For example, a questionnaire survey of programme participants can be combined with non-participant observation of programme activities and qualitative interviews with samples of recipients and key workers.

Triangulation of one sort or another is a strategy that can be found in many process or outcome evaluation research designs. McIvor (1992) used triangulation as part of a mixed-method design in her study of the implementation and administration of community service orders in Scotland. Data were extracted from official documentary sources, such as social enquiry reports and community service case files. Questionnaires and interviews were used to gather information from offenders participating in community service schemes. Information regarding the policy and practice of each scheme was obtained by means of staff questionnaires and interviews. Informal discussions were also held with staff during regular visits to the twelve schemes under study. As Cheetham et al. remark, 'In this way, the relationship between scheme policy and its implementation could be addressed and its impact upon the offenders ascertained through the triangulation of data obtained by the use of different research methods' (1992: 47). Hine (1997) reports the use of similar methods in an evaluation of community service orders using an inputs–process–outputs evaluation design.

Rhodes et al. (1991) describe how they used investigator, data and methodological triangulation in their evaluation of an HIV outreach health education intervention project based in Central London. Two investigators employed a combination of quantitative and qualitative methods to collect a variety of different types of data. Both outcome and process issues were addressed in the study. To ascertain the extent to which intermediate outcomes or goals were achieved the evaluators undertook a systematic monitoring of the project's detached outreach work. This involved collecting data by means of a specially designed client contact sheet, which was completed by outreach workers following their first meeting with a client. These sheets were used to record details of the nature, content and outcomes of initial outreach sessions. A second monitoring form was used for subsequent meetings between outreach workers and clients. These client re-contact sheets contained additional questions to ascertain the outcome of previous referrals and identify any changes in reported behaviour. Data from both monitoring forms were subjected to a statistical analysis.

Multiple qualitative data collection strategies were a feature of the process component of the evaluation. Documentary materials, such as minutes of meetings, policy statements and progress reports, were studied by the evaluators so as to enable them to describe the origins and development of the project. In order to provide an insight into the management and delivery of the programme, primary data were collected using a variety of qualitative methods. These included in-depth semi-structured interviews with outreach workers and members of the project steering group, non-participant observational fieldwork at weekly project meetings, fieldnotes based on informal discussions with members of the project team, and participant observation by one of the evaluators, who for a short time, worked on the project as a sessional worker involved in outreach activities.

One of the main advantages to be gained from using triangulation as part of a multi-method research design is that it allows the researcher to have greater confidence in the research findings than is the case when a single method is used. Given that each research method has its own strengths and weaknesses, advocates of triangulation maintain that, as the strengths of one method can be expected to compensate for the weaknesses of another, the overall quality of the research data will be improved by using more than one method. According to this view, employing multiple methods effectively reduces measurement error and helps to overcome problems of bias. Furthermore, methodological triangulation is presented as a way of guarding against threats to both reliability and validity. As Jick observes, '"within-method" triangulation essentially involves cross-checking for internal consistency or reliability while "between-method" triangulation tests the degree of external validity' (1983: 136–7).

While there are undoubtedly gains to be made from adopting triangulation as part of an overall research design strategy, there is a view that 'it is naive to assume that the use of several different methods necessarily ensures the validity of findings' (Fielding and Fielding, 1986: 31). Combining quantitative and qualitative data clearly has its attractions but it does not always follow that the different methods produce mutually reinforcing results. Indeed, 'it is in the spirit of the idea of triangulation that inconsistent results may emerge' (Bryman, 1988: 134). When this occurs it raises the problem of how to decide which results to accept. The solution is not to simply find a way of choosing one set of results over another, as divergent findings can lead to a re-focusing of the original research question and provide the impetus for exploring new areas of inquiry.

In discussing the nature of the interplay between different methods, Rossman and Wilson (1985) identify three broad approaches towards the question of mixing methods; they label these the purist, the situationalist and the pragmatist. As mentioned in the previous chapter, purists take the view that quantitative and qualitative methods are embedded in separate, conflicting and irreconcilable paradigmatic traditions. According to this view combining methods is not an option. In contrast, those who take a situationalist position recognize the potential contribution both quantitative and qualitative research methods can make as part of a single research design, and maintain that the nature of the situation is a major determinant of the choice of methods. Although the two broad types of methods have clearly recognizable differences, they are generally considered to be complementary. It is only the pragmatist stance that advocates the actual integration of different methods in a single study. Arguments for and against integration are at the very centre of the epistemological debate concerning the distinction between quantitative and qualitative approaches (Brannen, 1995).

For Rossman and Wilson (1985), integrating data by means of between-methods triangulation involves three separate analytic functions, namely, corroboration, elaboration and initiation. Corroboration describes an analytic posture whereby the evaluator examines quantitative and qualitative data for evidence of convergence; the findings obtained by one method are used to corroborate the results achieved from using a different method. This procedure serves as an assessment of convergent validity. As for elaboration, this is the analytic function that provides depth to our understanding of a problem. According to Rossman and Wilson, elaboration works in two directions. Not only can qualitative data enrich the conclusions drawn from the statistical analysis of quantitative data, but quantitative information can also improve the level of understanding acquired as a result of a qualitatively-based analysis. Finally, there is integration at the analytic level in the form of initiation. This involves focusing on instances where findings diverge in order to 'initiate interpretations and conclusions, suggest areas for further analysis, or recast the entire research question' (Rossman and Wilson, 1985: 633).

Both situationalists and pragmatists subscribe to the view that there is no one best method that will meet all evaluation needs. Multi-method evaluation designs, incorporating quantitative and qualitative approaches, are recommended in situations where the following conditions apply: combining methods offers the possibility of enhancing validity; a full description of the programme and ensuing evaluation is called for; there is a focus on both outcomes and processes and there is a feeling that a mixture of methods is necessary to meet the informational needs of the various stakeholder groups (Smith, 1986).

There is no doubt that evaluation research offers ample opportunities for mixing methods. Whether conducting a summative or formative evaluation, it is often desirable to achieve a good balance of quantitative and qualitative approaches. However, given the nature of the evaluation enterprise, there are no fixed rules for producing the perfect multi-method evaluation research design strategy. Evaluators often work under practical constraints, which means that in making methods choices they are compelled to consider such factors as the size of the research budget, the time available in which to complete the evaluation and the potential certain methods have for disrupting programme activities. There are also ethical and political considerations to contend with; these too have implications for methods choices. Thus, the final blend of methods is not decided on the basis of methodological criteria alone.

Method and theory

The topic of methods choices cannot be dealt with fully without reference to the part played by programme theory in evaluation research. Describing how traditional approaches to evaluation have neglected programme theory in favour of a methods-oriented approach, Chen (1990) draws a distinction between two broad types of evaluation, which he labels method-driven and theory-driven. In the case of the former, rigid adherence to a particular method, or collection of methods, determines the focus and scope of an evaluation. The image of evaluation research as a predominantly methods-focused activity has its origins in the intensive, long-running and antagonistic debate between ardent supporters of the two conflicting methodological paradigms. With the theory-driven approach the evaluation is theory-focused; the evaluator chooses those research methods deemed best suited for testing the particular theory in question.

'Realistic evaluation', as pioneered by Pawson and Tilley (1992, 1997), is one approach to evaluation that takes the view that data collection should be theory-driven. As previously described, they assert that programme evaluators need to differentiate between mechanisms, contexts and outcomes. An understanding of contexts and mechanisms is essential if the evaluator is to explain exactly what it is about a programme that makes it effective. By 'mechanisms', Pawson and Tilley mean the ways in which an intervention or programme can be thought to have an impact. The evaluator begins by examining the elements of a programme to uncover what it is about the proposed measures that might produce the desired outcomes. For example, in a study of the effect of closed circuit television (CCTV) on car crime, Tilley (1993) lists a number of mechanisms through which CCTV may lead to a reduction of crime in car parks. These include the following: by increasing the likelihood of detection potential offenders will be deterred; the presence of CCTV may encourage more people to use car parks, thus increasing natural surveillance which may, in turn, help to deter would-be offenders; evidence of CCTV equipment may remind drivers of the risks of car crime and encourage them to be more vigilant and take greater care over vehicle security. From a realist perspective mechanisms constitute hypotheses and should be treated accordingly.

For Pawson and Tilley, theory has a significant part to play in evaluation. According to their realist evaluation research design, if the evaluator is to successfully identify the relevant evaluation questions, make the appropriate methods choices and correctly apply the chosen method or methods, then it is essential that programme theory is incorporated into the evaluation process. As Pawson and Tilley assert, 'We believe that data collection priorities are set within theory' (1997: 159). It is by generating propositions explaining how mechanisms are triggered in specific contexts, to produce certain outcomes, that realist theories guide the data collection process.

Both 'dogmatic purists' and 'pragmatic pluralists' are taken to task for adopting an essentially data-driven approach to making methods decisions. According to Pawson and Tilley, they misunderstand the purpose of the interview as an instrument of data collection by assuming that there is no distinction to be made between the subject's ideas and the subject matter of the interview. For purists and pluralists alike, whether using formal structured interviews or informal unstructured interviews, the primary objective is seen as being one of obtaining as accurate a view as possible of how stakeholders feel about a variety of aspects of a programme. Pawson and Tilley propose an alternative, theory-driven approach to data collection based on the realist assumption that, '*the researcher's theory is the subject matter of the interview, and the subject (stakeholder) is there to confirm, to falsify and, above all, to refine that theory*' (1997: 155). To this end they recommend that the evaluator adopt a 'realist' interviewing strategy.

In one sense, conducting a realist interview is no different from undertaking any other type of social research interview. The evaluator follows the standard guidelines for establishing good interviewing practice when it comes to the practicalities of setting up interviews, formulating questions, recording responses and developing a rapport with the interviewee. What is different about the realist approach is the way the interview is used to construct and test theoretical propositions expressed in terms of a configuration or patterning of contexts, mechanisms and outcomes. Both interviewer and interviewee play an active role in this process. As Pawson and Tilley assert, the key feature of the realist interview 'is the creation of a situation in which the theoretical postulates and conceptual structures under investigation are open for inspection in a way that allows the respondent to make an informed and critical contribution to them' (1997: 182). The respondent may be a policy-maker, practitioner, programme participant or a member of any other group of stakeholders.

In this formulation of the interview process both the interviewer and the respondent can be seen to play a part in developing and refining theory. This is facilitated by the interview following a teacher–learner pattern, in which there is a two-way flow of information. Take for example the case of an interview with a programme practitioner. The evaluator explains to the interviewee the purpose of the interview and the kind of information being sought. In responding, the interviewee offers an insight into the thinking behind the various planned interventions; this ensures the evaluator 'learns' the type of programme theories operating at the practitioner level. Using interview prompts and probes the evaluator seeks to explore how contexts, mechanisms and outcomes feature in these initial theoretical formulations. This leads to a more detailed and formal expression of the practitioner's original theories, which are eventually placed before the interviewee for them to comment upon with a view to providing further refinement.

As indicated above, realistic evaluation is not confined to using any one particular research tool or specific combination of data collection methods. The realist evaluator is free to select from the full range of methods available. The mixing of qualitative and quantitative approaches is a key feature of this type of evaluation. However, as Pawson (1997) argues, it is a mistake to assume that realist argument is just another way of making a case for methodological pluralism. Realists may be pluralists when it comes to choosing methods, but there is much more to this type of evaluation than simply combining methods. 'Realism is a *logic of investigation*' in which theory plays a central role (1997: 164). A realist theory of how programmes work provides the context within which data collection decisions are made. As Pawson and Tilley note, 'Only when we know what precisely it is that we are studying can we reach into the toolkit for the appropriate instrument' (1997: 159).

Summary

As this chapter has shown, methods choices in evaluation studies are influenced by a variety of factors. These include the nature of the evaluation problem; the information needs of programme providers and planners; the context of the evaluation; the characteristics of the programme participants; the methodological orientation of the investigator and the nature of the programme theory under investigation. The evaluator has a wide range of research instruments from which to choose. This chapter has described the major strengths and weaknesses of some of the more commonly used quantitative and qualitative data-collection techniques and noted the plurality of methods in evaluation research. We believe that effective evaluation depends upon evaluators having the skills to be able to draw from the broadest possible range of methods and, where appropriate, successfully mix methods in a single research design. The challenge is choosing the right research methods for the evaluation task at hand.

4   Evaluating Criminal Justice and Crime Prevention Programmes

Evaluation research has an important contribution to make to the development of policies and practice in the criminal justice system. Policy-makers need to have information about the relative effectiveness of different policy initiatives in order to make decisions about the future of existing programmes and assess the merits of new proposals. Professional practitioners working with offenders to reduce offending behaviour need to be able to establish which types of treatment are best suited to which types of offenders. For example, McIvor states (1995) it is only by subjecting probation practice to a full and systematic evaluation of its effectiveness that we will acquire a better understanding of which methods produce the best results and thereby be able to design treatment programmes accordingly.

Evaluation techniques have been applied throughout the criminal justice system. For example, there have been numerous studies covering the efficacy of community policing programmes (Bennett, 1992); the effectiveness of probation practice (Raynor et al., 1994); the impact of community penalties (Mair, 1997); the performance of the Crown Prosecution Service (National Audit Office, 1989); the effect of crime prevention programmes (Pease, 1994); the impact of police-initiated attempts to reduce the levels of fear of crime (Bennett, 1991), and the implementation and effectiveness of policing strategies designed to combat specific types of crime, such as, domestic burglary (Stockdale and Gresham, 1995). In all these areas evaluators have encountered practical, technical, conceptual and methodological problems. This chapter will explore some of these issues with reference to two specific fields of study: evaluations of the effectiveness of non-custodial sanctions and the impact of community-based crime prevention projects. Examples will be used to illustrate some basic principles in the logic and method of evaluation research design. In the case of the evaluation of non-custodial penalties, particular attention will be given to the use of reconviction rates as a measure of success. The discussion of the evaluation of crime prevention schemes will be used to highlight the importance of issues of research validity and theoretical orientation in the formulation of evaluation research designs.

Assessing the effectiveness on non-custodial penalties

One of the major features of the criminal justice system since the late 1960s has been the increase in non-custodial sentencing options. Successive pieces of legislation in the United Kingdom have produced new community-based penal measures: suspended sentences were introduced following the Criminal Justice Act 1967 (Bottoms, 1981), while the Criminal Justice Act 1972 made provision for 'day training centres' (Smith, 1982) and community service orders (West, 1976; Varah, 1987). The 1982 Criminal Justice Act further promoted the development of alternatives to imprisonment by recommending that probation orders should impose additional requirements on offenders. This Act, along with subsequent Criminal Justice Acts in 1988 and 1991, also provided guidance on sentencing decision-making designed to encourage courts to make greater use of non-custodial penalties.

These various sentencing initiatives were originally referred to as 'alternatives to custody' and collectively defined as 'those penalties which, following conviction and sentence, allow an offender to spend part or all of his or her sentence in the community and outside prison establishments' (Vass, 1990: 2). However, in recent years, a marked shift in the politics of crime control policy has resulted in the rehabilitative ideal in community sentencing being challenged by a belief in 'punishment in the community'. As expressed in the White Paper entitled *Crime, Justice and Protecting the Public*:

> The Government believes that more offenders should be punished in the community. There seems to be an assumption that custody is the only 'real' punishment. This is reinforced sometimes by confusing references to other penalties as 'alternatives to custody'. No other penalty can place the same restrictions on liberty as a custodial sentence; if it did, it would be another form of custody: so there can in reality be no 'alternative' to it, only other ways of punishing. (Home Office, 1990a: 18)

Such has been the change in policy rhetoric that the term 'alternatives to custody' has been replaced by the phrase 'community penalties' when referring to non-custodial sentences.

It is not surprising that the proliferation of community-based criminal sanctions has led to a growth in evaluation research. According to Pease et al. (1975) when dealing with new penal measures two types of evaluation can be identified. The first is largely descriptive and concentrates on identifying the rationale behind a new programme or policy initiative. The emphasis is on describing the early stages in the implementation of the programme. The idea is that the knowledge gained may inform decision-making about possible future changes. This is in contrast to the second type of evaluation, whereby the researcher 'attempts to show whether a measure meets its primary aim, which in

to selected criteria. However, this also has its disadvantages. If one-to-one matching is chosen it may not be possible to accommodate unusual cases; this is particularly a problem when more than two groups have to be matched. This can lead to a number of cases having to be disregarded. The usefulness of this approach is further limited by the fact that there are some fundamental and systematic differences in the characteristics of offenders given different types of sentences (Lloyd et al., 1994).

Many of the difficulties associated with experimental and quasi-experimental methods can be avoided by using prediction techniques (Farrington and Tarling, 1985) to help determine the effectiveness of sentences. Lloyd et al. (1994) calculated 'expected' reconviction rates in their comparison of probation orders, probation orders with special conditions, community service orders and custody. This entailed estimating the expected reconviction rate for each group of offenders on the basis of characteristics such as the offenders' age, sex, previous convictions and nature of current offence. The expected rate was then compared with the actual rate. Consequently, where the actual rate is lower than the predicted rate in a sentence group, it can be concluded that this sentence is more successful than the others in reducing the likelihood of reconviction. The study found very little difference between actual and predicted reconviction rates. In other words, the rates for the four different sentences were very close to what was expected given the offenders' age, criminal record and pattern of offending behaviour.

While prediction techniques have a number of applications in criminology, one of their most important uses is in providing 'a sensible baseline for the evaluation of programme effectiveness' (Humphrey et al., 1992: 37). The Audit Commission (1989) recommended the use of prediction techniques to calculate expected rates of offending, which could then be compared to actual rates, in order to evaluate the success of probation initiatives. Meanwhile, Copas (1994) developed a national risk of reconviction predictor for the probation service, which was used by Raynor and Vanstone (1994) in their evaluation of the 'Straight Thinking on Probation' (STOP) programme run by the Mid Glamorgan Probation Service. Using prediction instruments to assess effectiveness creates the possibility of developing alternative measures of success. Rather than reconviction per se being the sole criterion of success, the evaluator can calculate the risk of reconviction both before and after the imposition of a sentence. If the risk of reconviction is appreciably lower on completion of a sentence this may be taken as an indication of a successful outcome (Lloyd et al., 1994).

Evaluating probation day centres

The fact that care needs to be taken when handling reconviction data is illustrated in Mair and Nee's (1992) evaluation of probation day centres.

These centres, first given statutory recognition in the 1982 Criminal Justice Act, were renamed probation centres following the 1991 Criminal Justice Act. According to the provisions laid down in the legislation, during a probation order an offender can be required to attend a centre for a period of up to 60 days. These orders came to be known as 4(B) orders after the relevant section in the 1982 Act. Consequently, two types of day centre came in to being: 'the more informal, voluntary kind which tends to cater for inadequates whether they are offenders or not; and the 4(B) kind which is generally seen as providing a "heavy-end" alternative to custody' (Mair, 1988: 2). It is the latter type of centre that formed the focus of the evaluation by Mair and Nee (1992).

Their study was based on the analysis of 966 cases drawn from a sample of 38 day centres in England and Wales. They found that 606 offenders were reconvicted of at least one offence within 24 months of receiving a 4(B) order. This gave an overall reconviction rate of 63 per cent. Further analysis revealed that age and the number of previous convictions were related to the likelihood of reconviction. Higher reconviction rates were recorded for those offenders in the younger age groups: 68 per cent of offenders under 21 years of age were reconvicted, compared with 49 per cent of those aged 36 years or above. Reconvictions were also higher for those offenders with more previous convictions. The reconviction rate was 56 per cent for offenders with only one or two previous convictions, and this rose to 76 per cent for those with 11 or more previous convictions. There was also evidence of wide variations in the reconviction rates reported for individual day centres; Mair and Nee recorded reconviction rates ranging from 95 per cent to 31 per cent.

How useful are these outcome measures in helping us to determine the effectiveness of day centres? As Mair and Nee rightly claim reconviction rates alone are of limited usefulness in the evaluation of criminal justice programmes; they need to be viewed in a wider context and not accepted at face-value. For example, it is noted that the type of offenders required to attend probation centres under a 4(B) order tend to possess those characteristics normally associated with repeated offending. The researchers quote research by Phillpotts and Lancucki (1979) which demonstrates that there is a greater likelihood of reconviction the younger an individual is, the longer the list of previous convictions and where a custodial sentence has been served. They point out that given that day centres target such a high-risk group in the first place, a high reconviction rate is to be expected.

Despite the fact that there are problems associated with using the reconviction rate as a measure of the effectiveness of court disposals it is unlikely to be replaced. This being the case, Mair and Nee argue that the limitations of reconviction rates need to be recognized and 'they must be used and interpreted carefully and critically' (1992: 331). In particular, care needs to be exercised when making comparisons either among probation centres or across different disposals. Evaluators should note that 'a valid comparison must compare like with like in terms of age, offence, previous convictions, and previous experiences of custody over the same follow-up period' (1992: 335). Differences in the rates of reconviction between centres was partially explained by differences in the characteristics of offenders. For example, as regards previous offences, those centres with high recidivism rates had a relatively high percentage of offenders who had six or more previous convictions and a low percentage of attenders with two or fewer convictions. It is not only variations in offender characteristics that need to be taken into account. Consideration also needs to be given to the variations between the centres themselves. There are important differences with respect to staffing levels, the use of volunteers and the relative emphasis placed on therapeutic programmes and practical activities, which may influence outcome measures (Mair, 1988). There is a danger that by concentrating on the aggregate reconviction rate the impact of these local differences on the likelihood of reconviction will be overlooked. Indeed as Lloyd et al. (1994) assert national level reconviction rates are probably more suited to providing an indication of performance rather than a measure of effectiveness.

Comparing the reconviction rates of different disposals can also be problematic. Mair and Nee's study was hampered by the lack of any recent comparable figures. Although some national data were available these did not provide information on previous convictions and was therefore of limited usefulness. However, the researchers were able to make comparisons between the reconviction rate recorded in their study and the rates reported in three other recent studies of non-custodial disposals for serious offenders (Maitland and Keegan, 1988; Knivett et al., 1989; Roberts, 1989). All in all the rates compared favourably, leading to the general conclusion that on the basis of a consideration of reconviction rates day centres were 'a qualified success' (Mair and Nee, 1992: 338).

Clearly there is more to the evaluation of probation day centres than simply comparing the reported reconviction rates for individual centres. An initial step in any comprehensive evaluation is the clarification of evaluation criteria. The evaluator needs to acquire information on the aims and objectives of day centres in order to develop appropriate outcome measures. As Mair (1988) notes not only is it possible for centres to have more than one aim, but they may also differ with regard to the priority they attach to specific aims. In his survey of centres he found the most commonly stated aim was to provide an alternative to custody: 'If two aims were stated, the reduction of reoffending was the most common secondary aim; and if there were three, it was development of the skills of the client' (Mair, 1988: 7). The fact that a court disposal can have more than one objective has important implications for the researcher planning an evaluation study.

First, there is the question as to whether or not the multiple aims are compatible. Take for example the two main aims of providing an alternative to custody and reducing recidivism. Attempts at achieving the former may increase the likelihood of failing to secure the latter. If centres are used to divert high-risk offenders from custodial sentences they may find it more difficult to reduce offending behaviour. Second, the recognition of multiple objectives leads to a call for the use of several outcome measures. In this respect Mair (1991) distinguishes between two levels of criteria of effectiveness, namely primary measures and secondary measures. Examples of the former include the number of offences committed during the period of attendance at the centre, the pattern of offending during the period of supervision following attendance and the extent to which offenders are diverted from custody. In contrast secondary measures deal with specific objectives associated with the formal and structured activities provided by the centres. Thus if centres provide literacy skills training, anger management courses, job search programmes and alcohol education groups, these can all be independently evaluated.

It is this multi-faceted approach to the definition and measurement of outcomes, which acknowledges the complex nature of the objectives of sentences. In any evaluation it is essential that the key criteria by which a sentence is to be judged are made explicit. Once the evaluation criteria have been identified there is the question of the relative significance which is to be attached to each outcome measure. As Mair (1991) notes the primary measures may not be of equal importance. It is important at the outset for the evaluator to clarify objectives and measures of effectiveness with the various stakeholders. During the planning stage of the evaluation the researcher needs to consult with staff responsible for designing and administering the programme in order to establish what is perceived to be the logical relationship between multiple goals. For Mair the adoption of a multi-dimensional approach represents 'a new generation of evaluations of penal initiatives' by encouraging the search for a more imaginative and creative approach to defining and measuring effectiveness (1991: 7).

'Nothing works'

The tendency for researchers to concentrate on recidivism as the sole determinant of the success of a penal measure has resulted in many negative research findings. An early review of 231 studies of correctional programmes, in both custodial and non-custodial settings, undertaken between 1945 and 1967, concluded that, 'With few and isolated exceptions the rehabilitative efforts that have been reported so far have had no appreciable effect on recidivism' (Martinson, 1974: 25). This reported lack of any positive evidence to suggest that penal treatments reduce reoffending (Lipton et al., 1975) is often cited as providing the foundation for the pessimistic 'nothing works' doctrine, despite Martinson's later clarification of the original conclusions and his rejection of the 'nothing works' tag applied by others to the findings of the review (Martinson, 1979).

The cumulative negative evidence about the rehabilitative effect of penal treatments, as indicated by reconviction rates, provided support for those wishing to advance the 'nothing works' thesis. The evaluation of intensive probation provides a good example. The IMPACT (Intensive Matched Probation and After-Care Treatment) experimental project was conducted in four probation areas in England in the early 1970s, with the aim of studying the relative effectiveness of different methods of treatment of offenders placed on probation (Folkard et al., 1974). One of the objectives of the evaluation was to determine if the intensive supervision of adult offenders reduced recidivism. In each area experimental and control groups were established by random allocation procedures. Those assigned to the control group received normal probation supervision, whereas those in the experimental group experienced a more intensive, task-oriented type of supervision. In this, probation officers were given reduced caseloads to enable them to spend more time addressing the situational difficulties their clients faced in relation to family relationships, work, financial circumstances and the like.

The IMPACT study is a very good example of a field experiment. According to the logic of this research design the researcher is not only able to observe whether a predicted outcome follows a particular treatment, but by exercising influence over the allocation of individuals to experimental and control groups the researcher can ensure that these groups are comparable in certain respects and thus rule out alternative explanations of any observed differences in outcomes. As noted in Chapter 2 the validity with which statements can be made about whether or not there is a causal relationship between treatment and effect is, in this case, referred to as internal validity.

If the evaluator is to argue that a difference in outcome measures between experimental and control groups is to be attributed to the treatment received, then it must be shown not only that differential treatment was proposed, but also that it was actually delivered. In other words, information on programme implementation is required. This is provided in the IMPACT experiment. The researchers record that the general feeling among probation officers working with offenders in the experimental group was that they were not trying out new forms of treatment, but merely using the extra time available to explore more traditional forms of probation practice. Consequently, the difference in methods of working between the two groups was perceived in terms of 'degree and emphasis' rather than content (Folkard et al., 1976: 7) and checks were conducted to make sure that the contrast between the two styles of working with offenders was maintained throughout the experimental period (Folkard et al., 1974: 36).

It is important to establish the comparability of groups in an experimental research design, as this will enable the evaluator to attribute any observed differences in outcome measures to the effectiveness of different types of treatment, rather than to differences in the original composition of the groups. As previously noted the IMPACT experiment randomly allocated individuals to groups. Following comparisons between groups based on social background characteristics and personality factors it was discovered that, 'the main experimental and control groups in each geographical area were closely matched on the majority of variables' (Folkard et al., 1976: 6).

All in all this was a carefully designed field experiment. Experimental and control groups were compared on a variety of outcome measures. Although the findings of the evaluation were not all negative, 'IMPACT did nothing to suggest that treatment delivered to offenders within the context of a probation order was particularly effective at reducing recidivism' (Whitehead, 1990: 14). In other words, when reconviction rates after one year were compared across the study sites there was no evidence to support the claim that experimental treatment had a positive effect. Indeed, in three out of the four probation areas studied the experimental group reported a higher percentage of probationers being reconvicted. Overall the researchers concluded that, 'the findings from the IMPACT experiment . . . are consistent with Martinson's conclusion that no general effect from treatment can be demonstrated' (Folkard et al., 1976: 2).

Other evaluation studies in the 1970s and 1980s that used reconviction as a measure of success also failed to yield positive results. In a study of community service orders in six experimental areas in England, Pease et al. (1977) found no evidence of any reduction in reoffending following community service. Of those offenders who were sentenced to community service 44.2 per cent were reconvicted within twelve months, the comparable figure for those who were initially recommended for community service but given another sentence was lower at 33.3 per cent. A later study of reconviction rates following community service reported 36 per cent of offenders reconvicted within one year of their original sentence, this rose to 51 per cent after two years (Home Office, 1983).

Findings such as this created pessimism about the effects of alternatives to custody on recidivism rates. Consequently as the 'nothing works' thesis gained support the idea of rehabilitation through treatment came to be viewed with increasing scepticism. In an official review of the criminal justice system in 1976 it was stated that:

> the assumption that the type of penal disposal given to a convicted offender would have some effect upon his likely recidivism has figured prominently in

justification of various alternatives to imprisonment and the treatment concept still underlies to some extent the current approach . . . This assumption is now under serious attack on the basis of the evidence. (Home Office, 1977: 9)

It was not only non-custodial interventions which were considered to be ineffective; results from studies of the rehabilitative impact of residential treatment were also disappointing (Cornish and Clarke, 1975). The accumulation of negative empirical evidence was one factor which brought about the virtual 'collapse of the rehabilitative ideal' (Preston, 1980).

It has been suggested that the general conclusion that 'nothing works' was something of an overstatement (Bottomley and Pease, 1986). There is a sense in which supporters of the 'nothing works' doctrine were highly selective in their choice and interpretation of evaluation findings, as witnessed by their tendency to ignore the tentative tones in which some of the conclusions were expressed. For example, in his original article Martinson not only acknowledged that there were some successes to report, albeit these were isolated examples, but he also suggested that poorly designed research studies could be failing to detect the fact that some treatment programmes were effective to some extent. Likewise Pease et al. (1977) drew attention to a number of factors which needed to be taken into account when interpreting the significance of their main finding that there was no reduction in reconviction rates following community service. First, there was the question of the experimental nature of the scheme under investigation. The community service order was a new sentence that had only been introduced in six areas on a trial basis. Some pilot schemes had experienced teething problems which it was felt could have had an impact on the results. As the researchers noted, 'the reconviction data from this period may be quite different from reconviction data for a period when the scheme is better established' (1977: 23). Second, Pease et al. maintain that the circumstances surrounding the introduction of the new scheme were such that it was not possible to adopt a controlled, randomized experimental research design. A quasi-experimental design was chosen. Those offenders sentenced to community service formed the treatment group and those offenders who had been recommended for community service, but given another sentence, were assigned to the comparison group. When the researchers examined the comparability of the two groups they found that the comparison group was significantly older than the community service treatment group. As they acknowledge, this is of particular importance when interpreting the relevance of relative reconviction rates, 'since increasing age is associated with decreasing likelihood of reconviction . . . the community service group should, other things being equal, have been more likely to be reconvicted' (1977: 15). This illustrates how it is important to have knowledge about the particular context of an evaluation study in order to be able to put the findings into perspective.

According to an early critic of Martinson's original thesis, by concentrating on what works for offenders as a whole, he effectively overlooks the 'degree of effectiveness' displayed by some research findings (Palmer, 1975). In Palmer's view there is much to be learned by identifying which methods appear to have an impact on which type of offenders, and under what conditions the methods are likely to produce positive outcomes. The possibility of differential treatment effects was recognized in the IMPACT study. Folkard et al. (1976) created a typology of offenders from probation officers' assessments of the 'criminal tendencies' of their clients and the self-reported 'personal problems' of probationers. When comparing offenders on the basis of reconviction rates after one year, they found that offenders who were considered to have moderate or high criminal tendencies and a relatively small number of personal problems did significantly worse under conditions of intensive supervision than under normal probation conditions. Furthermore, the data also revealed that offenders rated as having low criminal tendencies and many personal problems were more likely to produce a successful outcome when placed in the experimental treatment group. Given the small numbers involved this was not a statistically significant finding. Nevertheless, the IMPACT experiment did produce evidence of a differential treatment effect for different types of offender. As the researchers concluded, although their failure to discover a general treatment effect was consistent with Martinson's original position, there was some evidence to warrant further exploration of Palmer's contention that, for some offenders, some treatments may have a positive effect under certain conditions.

'Something works'

Despite the reservations expressed by some researchers the nothing works thesis gained widespread support throughout the criminal justice system. As a result professional practitioners came to view any form of intervention as potentially ineffective, and thus saw little to be gained from routinely monitoring outcome measures, such as reconviction rates. It was not until the late 1980s that the influence of the nothing works doctrine was seriously challenged and the view that 'something works' began to gain currency. As Blagg and Smith (1989) observe, some criminologists came to the realization that the pessimistic interpretation placed upon the findings of early evaluation studies was not necessarily justified. Consequently, a more optimistic view of the contribution of community-based programmes to the reduction of offenders' criminality emerged. This new found optimism was based partly on the conclusions drawn from meta-analytical studies of programmes for juvenile and adult offenders. Andrews et al. (1990) note that although the overall impact of a particular form of treatment may be minimal there is evidence of some positive effects. This conclusion is based on both the re-analysis of 50 studies of juvenile correctional programmes, which Whitehead and Lab (1989) had originally claimed showed that interventions had little positive impact on recidivism, as well as on the findings from 35 studies of the outcome of correctional treatment for adult offenders. Andrews et al. conclude that there is evidence that some programmes work with some offenders, especially when particular attention is given to the 'delivery of service to higher risk cases, targeting of criminogenic needs, and the use of styles and modes of treatment . . . that are matched with client need and learning styles' (1990: 369). Following another meta-analysis of the results of nearly 400 programmes aimed at reducing the recidivism rate among offenders under 21 years of age Lipsey (1992) reported positive, albeit modest, overall treatment effects. The message from these meta-analyses appears to be that certain types of intervention are successful at reducing reoffending when directed at particular types of offender.

Positive findings also began to emerge from evaluation studies of specific probation projects. In a study of the impact of intensive group work on young adults on probation, Raynor (1988) describes how their reconviction rates compared favourably with those of offenders released from custody. Offenders who received 'enhanced' probation treatment 'were reconvicted significantly less than young men with similar ages, similar criminal histories and similar current offences who received custodial sentences' (1988: 113). The best results were achieved with those offenders who had substantial criminal records. Roberts (1989), in comparing the reconviction rates of young adults given intensive community supervision, as part of a Young Offender Project, with those receiving custodial sentences concludes that, 'The only benefit of custody appeared to be a very short term incapacitation effect which was quickly negated by a higher level and frequency of reoffending when the young men were released back into the community' (1989: para 17.1). After a two-year period the reconviction rate for the project sample was 68 per cent, compared with a rate of 89 per cent for those offenders who were originally recommended for the Young Offender Project but subsequently sentenced to custody. Of those who took part in the Project, those offenders with a large number of previous convictions, previous experience of custody and a history of serious offences against property had the lowest reconviction rates. The evaluative evidence from these local studies appears to suggest that for certain types of offenders, particularly those considered to be at high-risk of receiving a custodial sentence, alternatives to custody can achieve levels of reconviction below what would normally be expected given knowledge of their criminal careers.

Where does all this leave the measurement of the effectiveness of court disposals? At its simplest level, 'effectiveness is related to an offender not committing further offences' (Sainsbury, 1985: 36). However, as described above, there are problems surrounding the use of the reconviction rate as the sole criterion of penal efficacy. Not only does the reconviction rate require careful interpretation, but in order to determine the success of a sentence it is necessary to take several outcome measures into account. As McIvor warns in her evaluative study of community service in Scotland: 'It is easy to fall prey to the allure of reconviction statistics and to over estimate their significance' (1992: 181). She notes how it is no longer sufficient for researchers simply to ask whether or not a sentence reduces the probability of recidivism. A more comprehensive approach is called for, based on a broader definition of effectiveness.

McIvor was the first to examine the relationship between the perceived value to offenders of their work experience on community service projects and their reconviction rates in the three-year period following sentence. She found that those offenders who felt that community service had been a worthwhile experience were, on the whole, less likely to be reconvicted; if reconvicted this was less likely to be for crimes involving dishonesty. The study was designed to assess the relative effectiveness of twelve community service schemes in achieving certain specified policy objectives. Consequently the reconviction rate represented only one outcome measure. Other measures were chosen to assess various aspects of community service practice. For example, in concentrating on differences in the implementation and administration of orders McIvor examined procedures for dealing with failure to comply with the requirements of an order. Failing to attend a work placement is one of the most common reasons for returning an offender to court. Absences are deemed as either acceptable or unacceptable by community service staff depending on individual circumstances. To determine whether or not there were differences between schemes in the extent to which offenders failed to meet the requirements of their orders the number of acceptable and unacceptable absences recorded were selected as an intermediate outcome measure. Mair et al. (1994) also make use of several outcome measures in their study of intensive probation. Alongside reconviction rates they include diversion from custody, financial costs and the attitudes and experiences of offenders.

While it is important to establish in the first place whether or not a particular penal sanction has an intended effect, it is also important to be able to explain the reasons why this is the case. In other words the task is not simply to demonstrate the effects of particular sentences but also to develop an understanding as to how the effects are achieved. This requires the evaluator to adopt a more analytic research strategy, identifying and investigating which elements of a programme have an impact upon offenders and explaining how the observed changes make offenders less likely to commit criminal acts.

The need for evaluative research to systematically address how specific types of treatments lead to specific outcomes has been recognized for some time. Clarke and Sinclair (1974) comment on how some researchers appear to adopt a medical analogy when studying the effectiveness of penal measures; offending behaviour constitutes an 'illness' for which penal measures provide a 'cure'. This conveys the misleading impression that it is possible to describe the characteristic features of particular penal sanctions with the same precision and accuracy that one could describe a surgical intervention or course of medication. According to Clarke and Sinclair, by adopting what they see as the 'medical myth' evaluators overlook the complexities of penal treatments and the importance of such factors as the nature and quality of the relationship between those providing treatment and those receiving it in determining treatment outcomes.

Writing in the early 1970s, Clarke and Sinclair (1974) observe two broad streams in penal research, one which they label evaluative and the other sociological. The former they describe as being preoccupied with comparing the effects of penal treatments yet neglecting to describe fully the content and context of the treatments. Whereas sociological studies displayed a tendency to concentrate on describing, as opposed to comparing, treatment programmes. They suggest that combining the two approaches will facilitate a closer analysis of the treatment process.

This emphasis on the need to understand how a treatment works has implications for the way evaluation research is carried out. Clarke and Sinclair do not rule out the use of formal experimental research designs. They merely claim that such procedures can only be effectively utilized once the evaluator has a clear understanding of the treatment situation. This is achieved by the researcher pursuing what they describe as a 'scavenging' and 'opportunistic' approach in the early stages of the research. Information is gathered from a variety of sources in a loosely structured and semi-formal fashion. A more structured approach emerges as the evaluator's knowledge and understanding of the programme develops.

Looking at how programme outcomes are actually produced is referred to as process evaluation (Patton, 1986). This is an integral element in any comprehensive evaluation strategy:

> Only by studying how a sentence or treatment programme has been put into practice, how well it is meeting its immediate objectives, how it functions in organizational terms can we begin to interpret the meaning of any outcome measures (such as the reconviction rate) which might be used. Such a *process* evaluation enables us to understand more clearly *why* a penal measure may be working successfully or – equally important – why it may be failing. (Mair, 1991: 6)

A process evaluation provides more than a description of a programme and its intended effects. It explores how a programme changes and develops following initial implementation, thus providing the context within which to interpret outcome measures. In this way outcome evaluation and process evaluation are complementary. They can be effectively combined within one research design as described by Mair et al. (1994) in their evaluation of intensive probation programmes.

Diversion from custody

Reducing the possibility of recidivism is not the only aim of community-based sentences. At periodic intervals since the mid-1960s new policy initiatives have attempted to limit the use of custody. Concern about the continually rising prison population and the increasing financial costs of imprisonment have, at various times, led to the promotion of alternatives to custody. These alternatives have appeared in the form of new sentencing options, as in the case of the introduction of the community service order (Young, 1979); or they have resulted from changes to existing non-custodial disposals, as exemplified by the provision of 'intensive probation' programmes for specially targeted groups of offenders (Home Office, 1988). A measure of the effectiveness of these alternatives is the extent to which they are successful in diverting offenders from custody.

Assessing the diversionary impact of alternatives to custody is not simply a matter of comparing trends in sentencing statistics. The idea that a continually escalating prison population is proof that non-custodial alternatives are not fulfilling their diversionary function is based on some dubious assumptions about the relationship between prison and alternatives. As Vass (1990) states, it could be argued that if the alternatives had not been available in the first place the prison population would have grown even more. Similarly, a temporary reduction in the rate of imprisonment cannot be automatically attributed to the diversionary effects of alternative penal measures as there are a variety of other factors capable of determining changes in the prison population (Vass and Weston, 1990: 190).

The effectiveness of community service orders in diverting offenders from custody has been well researched. When this sentencing option was introduced the intention was that it would only be imposed for imprisonable offences. A view that was reinforced in guidelines issued to sentencers by the Home Office during the early years of the operation of the sentence:

> The community service order was introduced with the primary purpose of providing a constructive alternative for those offenders who would otherwise have received a short custodial sentence. (Home Office, 1978: 21)

Despite these sentencing guidelines early studies of the use of community service by the courts questioned whether orders were in fact being imposed in lieu of custody. On the basis of a study of national data Willis (1977) concluded that orders appeared to be reserved for offences for which a custodial sentence would not normally be considered appropriate. Young (1979) also found evidence of orders being used for trivial offences, which were highly unlikely to attract a sentence of imprisonment.

Clearly the most accurate way of establishing the tariff position occupied by a particular alternative to custody would be to obtain from sentencers, at the point of passing sentence, an indication as to which court disposal the alternative sentence was replacing. Unfortunately such direct information is not readily available and researchers have to resort to a number of indirect methods in order to determine the diversionary effectiveness of alternatives to custody. The idea is to estimate the number of those sentenced to community service who would otherwise have been sent to prison. This enables a diversion rate to be calculated (Pease et al., 1977). One way this can be done is to examine the sentences received by those offenders who were in breach of the conditions of community service and had their orders revoked. The assumption being that should the court decide to terminate the order and impose a custodial penalty, this would indicate that the original order was intended as an alternative to imprisonment. This of course would not apply in cases where revocation resulted because the offender had committed further offences, as these would influence the new sentence. Studies suggest that around 50 per cent of offenders who have their orders prematurely terminated for non-compliance receive custodial sentences for the original offence (Pease et al., 1977; McIvor, 1992).

However, this is not an ideal way of estimating diversionary impact. As Pease et al. (1977) argue, it is not unreasonable to assume that courts, when revoking orders, may decide that a custodial disposal is appropriate, not because this is what they would have originally imposed, but because they see the offender's failure to comply with the conditions as evidence of the need for a custodial sentence. McIvor (1992) also shows that in her sample of offenders who were breached those who received custodial sentences had, on average, completed a smaller proportion of their orders than offenders who were given non-custodial sentences. The implication is that courts may deal less severely with offenders who have completed a substantial part of their original sentence. McIvor concludes that, 'it is impossible . . . to use the resentencing of offenders who have been breached or whose orders have been for some other reason revoked as a reliable benchmark against which the diversionary impact of the community service order might be assessed' (1992: 136–7).

A more accurate indirect method of measuring diversion from custody involves assessing the custody risk of offenders placed on community service and those referred unsuccessfully for a community service assessment. The classification of custody risk scheme used by

McIvor places offenders in a high, intermediate or low risk category on the basis of their previous sentencing history (McIvor, 1990). By calculating the percentage of unsuccessful referrals in each risk category who were given custodial sentences, and then extrapolating these figures to the group sentenced to community service, McIvor was able to estimate that overall nearly 45 per cent of offenders who received community service would have probably received a custodial sentence if community service had not been an available option.

This finding of a limited diversionary impact confirms many earlier evaluative studies. Pease et al. (1977) used four different methods of measuring displacement from custody, three of these produced displacement figures within a narrow range from 45 per cent to 50 per cent. On the basis of indirect measures of diversionary effectiveness there is a general consensus that community service orders are not in the main used as an alternative to custody but are indeed used as alternatives to other non-custodial sanctions (Vass, 1981; Pease 1985). Studies of the views of sentencers reveal that community service is not only sometimes imposed as an alternative to other non-custodial penalties but is also regarded as a sentence in its own right (Vass, 1984; Carnie, 1990).

Monitoring changes in sentencing decisions following the introduction of a new non-custodial disposal is only the first step in estimating diversionary efficacy. An observed increase in the use of non-custodial penal measures may not necessarily be an indication of the success of a policy to divert offenders from custody, especially when some of those offenders given community sentences do not have a high risk of custody in the first place. There is a view that providing alternatives to custody merely widens the net of social control and draws in offenders for whom custody was never an alternative option (Cohen, 1979, 1985; Vass, 1990). Thus the evaluator needs to determine whether or not non-custodial alternatives and custody occupy similar tariff positions. This involves comparing the profiles of offenders in different sentence groups. If non-custodial alternatives function as a genuine diversion from imprisonment, then it seems reasonable to expect offenders in this category to have a profile more in common with that of the incarcerated group than that of the group receiving a community disposal not intended as an alternative to custody, for example 'ordinary' probation.

Some evaluative studies of individual diversionary projects involving enhanced or intensive probation have produced positive findings. Reporting on the Afan Alternative project designed to provide an alternative to custodial sentences for young adult male offenders, Raynor notes that 'the evidence strongly favours the view that the project was successful in bringing about a significant reduction of custodial sentencing in the main target group and that its clients were on the whole people at serious risk of custodial sentences' (1988: 170). Those assigned to the project had criminal profiles more similar to those offenders placed in custody than those put on 'ordinary' probation.

Brownlee (1991) and Brownlee and Joanes' (1993) evaluation of the Leeds Young Offenders Project also demonstrates diversion from custodial sentencing. They used a basic evaluative research design common to studies of this kind involving three sample groups (Roberts, 1989). The first group, labelled the 'project group', was composed of those offenders given a probation order with a requirement to attend the project. The second and third groups were made up of offenders in the same target age range who received custodial sentences in the West Yorkshire district during the research period. One group was designated as 'Custody A' and the other as 'Custody B'. The former comprised all those offenders who were given a custodial sentence despite having a pre-sentence report from a probation officer recommending a project placement as part of a probation order. The latter group included a one-in-two sampling of those young offenders given custodial sentences during the research period but not recommended as suitable for a project order.

The groups were compared on a number of characteristics believed to be significant in influencing the likelihood of custody. These included: principal current offence, level of court at which sentenced, most serious previous offence, number of previous offences, risk of custody score, number of previous custodial sentences and whether on bail or remand at the time of sentence. From the analysis it was concluded that:

> The group receiving project orders were not statistically different from those who were sent to custody despite a recommendation for a project order, except in terms of court at which sentenced; they differed from a sample group of those going to custody without referral only in that they were less likely to have been convicted of violence; overall, it is reasonable to suggest that the Project was operating as a genuine replacement for custody. (Brownlee, 1991: 20)

Thus there was every indication from the indirect evidence of the Project's tariff position that the Project was successful in recruiting offenders from the target group who faced a substantial risk of imprisonment. For example, the researchers reveal that as regards the median values on the risk of custody score there was no significant difference between the 'Project' group and the 'Custody A' group. Indeed, the median score for the former was 95 per cent (Brownlee and Joanes, 1993: 226).

As the above studies illustrate, assessing the extent to which diversionary policies and projects are successful in achieving their primary objective is fraught with methodological difficulties. In the absence of any direct evidence evaluators have to use indirect methods to establish diversionary impact; some measures of diversionary effectiveness are more accurate than others.

Evaluating crime prevention initiatives

Crime prevention is a fundamental objective of crime policy. By way of conceptual clarification it is possible to distinguish three broad types of prevention strategies: primary, secondary and tertiary (Brantingham and Faust, 1976). Primary prevention is a feature of those programmes and interventions that aim to remove or reduce the opportunities available for committing crime. Secondary prevention strategies are directed at those who are considered to be 'pre-delinquent' and at risk of offending in the future. Whereas tertiary prevention refers to attempts to deter convicted offenders from reoffending. The emphasis in this section will be on the evaluation of primary prevention approaches.

As a result of the government's growing concern about the rise in levels of recorded crime in the 1980s primary crime prevention became a key issue on the criminal justice policy agenda (Laycock and Heal, 1989). This approach to crime reduction was dominated by what was labelled 'situational crime prevention' (Clarke, 1983). It emphasized the importance of reducing opportunities for crime by increasing formal and informal forms of surveillance and improving the security of property by means of 'target hardening'. Evaluations of small-scale primary prevention projects in a number of diverse settings showed the potential for reducing the incidence of crime. For example, surveillance techniques reduced theft from shops (Van Straelen, 1978) and parked cars (Poyner, 1991), and increased security precautions at chemists' premises led to a reduction in the number of burglaries (Laycock, 1984). On a much larger scale, the Safer Cities Programme launched in March 1988 covered 20 project areas, which together accounted for a wide variety of crime prevention schemes. From its inception the intention was that the whole Programme, as well as individual projects, would be subject to evaluation. However, the size and scope of the initiative meant that the evaluators faced a number of serious technical difficulties and methodological problems (Ekblom, 1992; Tilley, 1993).

One community crime prevention scheme that has been extensively evaluated is Neighbourhood Watch (NW). The idea originated in the United States of America in the early 1970s (Washnis, 1976) and was first introduced into the United Kingdom in 1982 at Mollington in Cheshire (Anderton, 1985). Support for NW grew quickly and the number of schemes in England and Wales increased dramatically during the mid-1980s; in 1987 there were around 29,000 schemes in operation (Hope, 1988). Recent estimates suggest that there are now over 150,000 NW schemes incorporating over five million households (Dowds and Mayhew, 1994). As a crime prevention strategy it is perceived as a joint venture between the local police service and members of the community. Consequently there may be variations in the nature, organization and operation of individual schemes that reflect local conditions (Forrester et al., 1988). However, all schemes have the common aim of reducing crime, particularly residential burglary. An integral feature of most schemes is that of 'watching' or surveillance. Participants in NW are encouraged to become the 'eyes and ears' of the police by reporting to them any suspicious activity they observe in their neighbourhood.

In general, evaluations of collective crime prevention programmes have been criticized for lacking methodological rigour. It has been claimed that the majority of studies conducted in the USA are

> characterized by weak designs, an underuse of statistical significance tests, a poor conceptualization and definition of treatments, the absence of a valid and reliable measurement of program implementation and outcomes, and a consistent failure to address competing explanations for observed effects. (Lurigio and Rosenbaum, 1986: 20)

A similar conclusion is reached by Bennett (1990) following his review of evaluations of NW effectiveness conducted by the police and independent researchers in both the USA and England. He notes that the existence of serious methodological weaknesses makes it impossible to reach a firm judgement concerning the success of NW as a means of preventing crime.

Both Lurigio and Rosenbaum (1986) and Bennett (1990) describe how important it is for the programme evaluator to have a clear understanding of issues of research validity when formulating evaluation research designs. They criticize many crime prevention evaluations for failing to consider issues of validity in their methodological formulations. A fourfold typology of research validity has been identified, incorporating internal, external, construct and statistical conclusion validity (Cook and Campbell, 1976, 1979).

Internal validity, which has already been discussed in Chapter 2, basically refers to the confidence with which the evaluator can establish a causal link between the treatment and outcome. Within the context of crime prevention evaluation the evaluator needs to establish an explicit causal connection between the implementation of NW (the 'treatment') and any observed changes in the crime rate (the outcome or dependent measure). A case for a programme having causal significance can only be made once alternative explanations for the changes in the level of crime have been effectively eliminated.

As far as data collection is concerned, impact evaluations aim at quantifying estimates of preventive effect by analysing crime figures. A favoured research design is the pre-test–post-test design, in which crime rates are monitored in a target area before and after the introduction of a crime prevention initiative. However, as Bennett (1990) notes, in a 'before-and-after' study without a control area for comparison, the researcher cannot simply assert that an observed fall in the crime rate is directly attributable to the intervention. Even when control areas are incorporated into the research design the evaluator still faces a number of problems when it comes to actually detecting changes in crime levels.

Ascertaining the impact of a crime prevention initiative is not a simple matter of comparing the difference in crime rates in target and control areas before and after the implementation of the programme. The evaluator needs to ensure that the observed crime rates are reliable and representative (Ekblom, 1989). For example, it is possible that the introduction of a crime prevention scheme may accidentally coincide with a seasonal or natural short-term fluctuation in the local crime rate. In these circumstances an increase or decrease in recorded crime will give a distorted impression of the preventive effect of the scheme. These fluctuations can also be a problem when monitoring crime levels in the after phase of an evaluative study. As Lurigio and Rosenbaum acknowledge, this can pose a threat to internal validity: 'If a community adopts a crime prevention project during a period of extraordinary high (low) crime, which is elevated (depressed) due to random variation, there is a great likelihood that subsequent crime totals will drift closer to their "true" mean or average levels despite the absence of any program effects' (1986: 36–7). It is the statistical regression to the mean that constitutes a threat to internal validity.

One way of dealing with this problem is to extend the before and after phases of data collection and build a long time-series of crime rates in order to identify patterns and trends which can then be taken into account when determining the actual impact of a preventive scheme. As Ekblom (1989) asserts establishing before and after crime rates is beset with uncertainty and the exercise invariably involves a trade-off between reliability and representativeness.

External validity is concerned with the generalizability of evaluation research findings. The central question is to what extent can the results of a particular study be generalized across different projects, places or times? For example, in the context of crime prevention policy it is important to know if a programme, which leads to a reduction in crime rates in an inner city district, is likely to have a similar positive impact on a suburban housing estate. According to Lurigio and Rosenbaum (1986), community crime prevention evaluations face two major threats to external validity. The first relates to what they refer to as the 'interaction of setting and treatment'. They cite evidence which suggests that efforts to combat crime that are based on citizen participation are more likely to produce positive results when initiated in neighbourhoods in which there is already a strong sense of community identity and a cohesive social network. Where such characteristics are absent, and social disorganization is evident, community-based initiatives are likely to produce less favourable outcomes. The second threat to external validity stems from the 'interaction of history and treatment'. During the course of an evaluation something may happen in a community which has a direct bearing on its crime prevention efforts. Ultimately this may serve to undermine the ability of the evaluator to specify accurately whether a causal relation is generalizable from one time period to another.

Construct validity concerns 'the extent to which specific outcome measures, treatments, samples and settings employed in the research represent the theoretical construct of interest' (Judd and Kenny, 1981: 21). To establish a high level of construct validity the researcher needs to be aware of the relationship between theory and practice when undertaking a programme evaluation. This entails first of all identifying the theoretical premises of a programme or intervention. The importance of theory in programme evaluation is recognized by Bennett when he asserts that, 'particular attention needs to be paid to the theory of NW and the crime preventing processes that the programmes are supposed to instigate' (1992: 282). Behind every planned intervention there is some notion as to how and why certain activities or efforts may be expected to produce desired outcomes. Once the causal mechanisms responsible for generating the treatment effects have been identified, the next step is to ascertain to what extent the planned treatment corresponds to the treatment actually delivered.

The two principal theoretical models which inform community crime prevention evaluation are informal social control and opportunity reduction (Rosenbaum, 1987). Briefly, the social control perspective sees the growth in crime as a product of a number of changes associated with increasing urbanization including, the erosion of traditional normative structures, the increasing social disorganization of community life and the declining influence of informal mechanisms of social control. It is postulated that NW schemes can improve social contact and interaction at the community level thereby improving social cohesion and strengthening informal social control. This is seen as not only leading to a reduction in crime but also to a reduction in the levels of fear of crime (Skogan and Maxfield, 1981). The opportunity reduction model or victimization perspective (Bennett, 1990: 27) is based on the idea that collective surveillance reduces the opportunity for criminal activity by signalling to potential offenders that there is an increased likelihood of detection. While the two major theoretical perspectives have their supporters, Bennett describes how elements of both feature in the theoretical formulation of NW and concludes that this leads to problems when it comes to trying to clarify exactly how NW is supposed to work.

The extent to which the theoretical formulation of a crime prevention programme is successfully translated into practice is at the heart of construct validity. One of the main causes of poor construct validity is related to the failure to provide detailed accounts of the kind of initiatives being evaluated, which in turn makes it difficult to operationalize the major elements of the programmes (Yin, 1977). As Bennett notes, 'The problem is exacerbated when the evaluation relates to a comprehensive programme comprising NW and additional crime prevention measures. It is often uncertain to what extent the studies are evaluations of one programme, or many types of programme' (1990: 47). The solution is for the evaluator to take steps to enhance construct validity, for which a number of options are available (Mark and Cook, 1984). Basically it is essential for the researcher to provide a full account of the nature of the programme under investigation. This involves a careful explication of the core constructs of the programme and an examination of the theoretical premises on which the programme is based.

The final type of research validity to be considered is statistical conclusion validity. According to Lurigio and Rosenbaum, this 'generally refers to limitations or errors in the *analysis* of data and in the *measurement* of variables that can lower the sensitivity of an evaluation to real program effects or can mislead an investigator to falsely infer the existence of program effects' (1986: 39). With regard to data analysis there are two issues which give cause for concern in this respect. First, some community crime prevention evaluations designed to monitor crime rates before and after the implementation of a crime reduction programme do not subject their findings to any tests of statistical significance. Second, the use of inappropriate statistical procedures and techniques can produce misleading results. A common error observed by Lurigio and Rosenbaum occurs when evaluators comparing differences in the crime rates in the treatment area and control area, before and after the implementation of a crime reduction effort, perform two separate and independent statistical operations on the crime data. For example, analyses may reveal that the treatment area experiences a significant fall in the level of crime, while the control area does not experience any significant change. However, this should not be taken as proof of the effectiveness of the programme for it fails to take into account possible pre-test differences between the two areas. A single statistical operation is required to detect the significance of differential changes over time.

Issues pertaining to research validity feature prominently in Bennett's evaluation of the impact of two NW schemes in the London Metropolitan Police District. A quasi-experimental research design was adopted; full details of which are described in Bennett (1990). The research design incorporated four areas, two of these were experimental areas in which NW schemes were soon to be established; one was in Wimbledon and the other in Acton. An area adjacent to the Wimbledon experimental area was selected as a 'displacement area' on account of the fact that at the time of the evaluation there was a view that crime prevention efforts did not reduce crime so much as merely shift it from one location to another. Including in the research design a displacement area, which did not have a NW scheme, would make it possible to detect if NW had any displacement effects. A fourth area, also without a NW programme, and situated some distance from the other three was chosen as a control area. An attempt was made to try and ensure that the displacement area was similar to its adjoining experimental or treatment area in terms of social profile, geographical composition and crime rate. These selection criteria were also taken into account when the control area was randomly chosen.

Data were collected by means of crime and public attitude surveys conducted in the four areas a few weeks before NW schemes were started in the two experimental areas. The surveys were repeated after the schemes had been in operation for about twelve months. Victim surveys were the preferred method of measuring outcomes rather than crimes recorded by the police, as the latter are sensitive to changes in reporting behaviour and one of the aims of NW schemes is to actually encourage the public to provide the police with information. Subsequent analysis of the survey data revealed that,

> In both experimental areas the incidence (the total number of offences reported) of both household and personal victimizations increased from the pre-test to the post-test surveys. In the displacement area the rate of both types of offence remained constant and in the control area the rate went down for household offences and up for offences against the person. (Bennett, 1988: 251)

Two key questions emerge from this general conclusion: to what extent can the findings be interpreted as an accurate reflection of the impact of NW, and can the findings be generalized to other crime prevention initiatives?

Bennett (1990) addresses both of these questions in some detail in his explanation of the results of the evaluation exercise. He discounts the idea of a direct causal relationship between the introduction of NW and the increase in criminal victimization in the two experimental areas, largely on the grounds of a lack of any empirical evidence from other research to support the view that criminals are actually attracted to areas which display signs of crime prevention activity. To account for the fact that the observed effects were in the opposite direction to that hypothesized on the basis of NW theory, Bennett considers the possibility that a number of threats to internal validity may have affected the evaluation results. The assumption here being that the increase in crime rates may be due to factors unconnected to the presence of the NW schemes. Bennett finds support for this view following a consideration of the differences in the history of the NW areas, the discovery of the fact that crime rates were unusually low in one of the experimental areas during the pre-test phase of the evaluation and the possibility of there being significant unmeasured differences between the samples of respondents in the pre-test and post-test stages of the study.

The question concerning the generalizability of the findings of the evaluation raises the issue of threats to external validity. Bennett points out that it is not possible to generalize the results of his study to other populations because the experimental areas were not initially chosen to be representative. A feature of the research design was that the schemes chosen for evaluation had to be felt to stand a very good chance of being successful. This was not merely to ensure that the schemes lasted the duration of the experimental period, but from a methodological point of view, if the most promising schemes were found to have a negligible impact on crime rates then it would appear safe to assume that less promising schemes would be unlikely to be successful. After considering a number of potential threats to external validity Bennett concludes that 'there is little support for the conclusion that the results can be generalized to other populations, across settings or across times' (1990: 168).

Changes in crime rates and levels of reported victimization are not the only factors to be taken into account when assessing the effects of NW schemes. Despite the fact that the two programmes studied by Bennett had no measured impact on the incidence of crime there was evidence from the attitudes survey of a decline in the fear of crime against the household in both experimental areas, although the decline was only statistically significant in one of the areas. Fear of victimization against the person also showed a decline between pre-test and post-test surveys, but this did not reach a level of statistical significance in either NW area. Questionnaire data also revealed that in one area residents reported increased levels of satisfaction with their area, as well as a heightened sense of social cohesion.

This illustrates how evaluation studies can provide mixed results. The task facing the evaluator is to reach some general conclusion concerning the overall success of a programme. As Bennett concludes the schemes had a limited impact. Although some improvements were detected, the primary aim of reducing crime was not achieved. To explain why NW did not produce the expected effects he follows Rosenbaum's (1986) example and considers the reasons under three headings: 'measurement failure', 'theory failure ' and 'programme failure'.

Measurement failure can be said to occur when an evaluation fails to detect an actual programme effect because of a weak research design or inappropriate use of statistical methods of data analysis. Theory failure is a possible explanation of the inability to detect evidence of the desired programme effects in cases where a programme has been satisfactorily implemented and a sound methodological approach adopted. Finally, a programme evaluation may be based on a sound theory and an appropriate research design but fail to show signs of success because of programme failure or implementation error. For example, a programme may deliver the wrong type of treatment or an insufficient amount of the right type of treatment. It is this last explanation which

Bennett favours when he asserts that, 'the programmes implemented were, in some ways, weak versions of NW, which failed to instigate fully the mechanisms implicit in the theoretical formulation' (1990: 176).

The extensive use of quasi-experimental research designs, coupled with a preference for easily quantifiable output measures, have attracted some critical comment. As already discussed in Chapter 2, Pawson and Tilley (1994) attribute much of the lack of certainty in evaluation research to methodological failure. By this they do not mean to imply that those researchers adopting a quasi-experimental approach lack the technical knowledge and statistical expertise required to implement such a research design. Their criticisms are levelled at the very nature of the design itself, which they feel is unsuitable for the evaluation of social programmes. Basically, the crux of their argument is that the quasi-experimental paradigm contains a preconceived set of ideas as to what programmes are and how they work.

Pawson and Tilley use Bennett's (1991) evaluation of a police patrol initiative to provide a basis for their methodological critique. The initiative, introduced in two experimental areas, involved establishing a continuous police presence and increasing contacts between police officers and local residents. The primary aim of the exercise was to determine if the programme reduced fear of crime; a secondary aim was to discover if there was any impact on the general quality of life in the community. Through focusing on programme mechanisms and programme context Pawson and Tilley describe some of the problems associated with using a quasi-experimental method in this type of evaluation. First, a preoccupation with establishing a number of quantifiable outcome measures, such as the frequency of contacts between residents and the police, can lead to a programme being perceived by those responsible for its administration as nothing more than a loose collection of mechanical procedures. Thus the evaluator can fail to grasp just what it is about the nature and character of the patrol contacts which might bring about an improved sense of community. Second, a particular crime prevention programme may be successful because of the special conditions pertaining in a community or neighbourhood. Communities differ from one another in a myriad of ways, for example, in terms of social structure, demographic profile, ethnic composition and cultural background. The quasi-experimental method proceeds by attempting to control for such differences in the research design. According to Pawson and Tilley, 'Quasi-experimentation's method of random allocation, or efforts to mimic it as closely as possible, represent an endeavour to cancel out differences, to find out whether a programme will work without the added advantage of special conditions liable to enable it to do so' (1994: 298). They recommend that a scientific realist approach is taken, in which due consideration is given both to the mechanisms through which it is felt the desired programme outcomes will be achieved and to the contextual factors considered most likely to produce programme success. According to Ekblom and Pease, 'The scientific realist approach is interesting and provocative and in our view is likely to prove an immensely valuable contribution to the literature' (1995: 630).

Clearly those engaged in planning and implementing crime prevention programmes need to know not only which forms of intervention are most likely to be successful, but also to what extent they are applicable in different contexts. A detailed understanding of the social processes underlying the formulation and implementation of crime prevention efforts is essential. There is a view that this cannot be achieved by the quantitatively-oriented approach characteristic of outcome evaluation, but requires the use of qualitative research techniques (Crawford and Jones, 1996). While acknowledging the importance of the emphasis placed on the identification and conceptualization of programme mechanisms in the scientific realist perspective, Crawford and Jones argue that Pawson and Tilley treat all mechanisms as outcome-oriented (that is, as causal mechanisms) and thereby fail to appreciate the significance of what they term 'processual mechanisms'. These are 'processes and social arrangements which involve the nature of decision-making, communication, conflict management and negotiation' (1996: 23). They quote 'community consultation' as an example of such a mechanism. This may constitute an integral feature of a crime prevention initiative, but it cannot be seen in isolation as being the cause of a particular outcome.

Qualitative methods are particularly useful in studying the complex social dynamics of multi-agency co-operation in tackling community crime problems. Over the years numerous policy documents have stressed the need for a co-ordinated approach to crime control involving collaboration and 'partnership' between state agencies, independent organizations and the public (Blagg et al., 1988; Home Office, 1990b). Research has identified how power differentials, vested interests and ideological commitments can be sources of potential tension and conflict in multi-agency programmes (Sampson et al., 1988; Pearson et al., 1992). While Crawford and Jones (1995) confirm the existence of overtly conflictual interactions between agencies, they draw attention to the need to consider how conflict is managed informally 'behind the scenes' and the implications this has for the nature of inter-organizational relations. Using qualitative methods, such as informal interviews with project participants, non-participant observation at agency meetings and observations of routine encounters between programme personnel, it is possible not only to detect the existence of conflict but also to monitor how it is dealt with.

Karabinas et al. (1996) use qualitative methods in their process evaluation of a youth diversion project. Their primary interest is in the ways in which the different agencies involved in multi-agency efforts have been seen to favour different crime prevention discourses (Gilling,

1993). From their data they suggest that it is not necessarily the case that a single professional discourse dominates in the collective effort to control crime. Within multi-agency settings it is possible that a 'hybrid discourse' may develop 'which subsumes and balances these differences in the professional languages used by the various contributors' (Karabinas et al. 1996: 116).

Qualitative methods can also be used in conjunction with quantitative approaches. Janet Foster describes how she used ethnographic observation, interviews and focus groups to study the process of change on two housing estates involved in the Priority Estates Project. The fieldwork period lasted for 18 months on one estate in London and 12 months on another estate in Hull (Foster and Hope, 1993: 98–100). A questionnaire survey was also undertaken on the experimental and control estates, both before and after the introduction of planned changes, to estimate the effect of the project. Analysis of both the qualitative ethnographic data and the quantitative survey data revealed that there had been a reduction in crime on the experimental estates. The researchers acknowledge that by studying only two estates it is difficult to generalize the findings to similar projects in other areas. However, they do point out that by using a multi-method approach, combining a quasi-experimental design and a qualitative research strategy, they increased the reliability of the research findings.

Summary

Clearly there is considerable scope for the use of social research techniques in evaluating policy and practice at various points in the criminal justice system. This chapter has focused on two areas: the impact and effectiveness of non-custodial penalties and the evaluation of crime prevention strategies. The aim has been to highlight some of the major conceptual issues and methodological difficulties researchers are likely to encounter when conducting evaluations in these areas. In the case of community-based sentences the emphasis has been on measurement issues, such as, deciding what constitutes a successful outcome and determining the extent to which the reconviction rate can be taken as a measure of effectiveness. As regards the evaluation of crime prevention schemes, it has been shown that programme evaluation is not an atheoretical activity. Programme theory is an integral element in the evaluation research process. It is only by specifying the theoretical premises of a programme that the evaluator is able to explore fully the causal mechanisms at work.

5   Evaluating Health Care

Since the middle of the 1970s there has been a growth in the use of evaluation research techniques to measure performance standards in public sector organizations. Following the restructuring of the National Health Service in the 1990s, amidst the application of market principles to the provision of health care in the form of competitive tendering, contractualism and consumer sovereignty, demand for information on the effectiveness, cost and quality of health care services has escalated. This chapter will explore some of the methodological issues and practical problems encountered by evaluators working in this area. Particular attention will be paid to ways of determining treatment effectiveness; problems of defining and measuring health outcomes; conceptual issues underlying economic approaches to evaluation and the part played by patient satisfaction surveys and audit in assessing the quality of services.

Dimensions of health care provision

Donabedian (1980) has identified three broad dimensions of health care provision that can provide a focus for evaluation, namely, structure, outcome and process. The first of these refers to the physical environment of care, taking into account the nature, amount and distribution of buildings, equipment and personnel. Outcome evaluation is centred on the end results of care with the prime objective being to measure the impact of health care services. An outcome is defined as any change in the health status of a patient that can be directly attributed to the treatment or care they have received. Finally, evaluation of process involves a consideration of what actually goes on between health service professionals and patients during the course of the delivery of health care.

The dimensions of outcome and process will be the main focus of the present chapter. The former is concerned with issues of effectiveness, that is, the extent to which a treatment or policy can be seen to work. The task facing the evaluator is to determine whether or not the stated goals and objectives of the treatment, programme or policy are actually achieved. As Coulter notes:

Health-care evaluation involves defining the objectives of care, monitoring health-care inputs, measuring the extent to which the expected outcomes have been achieved and assessing the extent of any unintended or harmful consequences of the intervention. (1991: 115)

Defining objectives can constitute the first major stumbling block in any evaluation, irrespective of whether the focus of study is a national policy initiative, a co-ordinated local health care programme involving co-operation between a number of different services or an isolated example of a planned change in the delivery of care within a single institution. As far as the NHS as a whole is concerned, its objectives are often stated in very general terms and as such can prove difficult to operationalize. Take, for example, two of the main objectives identified by the Royal Commission on the NHS (1979): to encourage and help individuals to remain healthy and to satisfy reasonable public expectations regarding health care. More recent attempts at specifying the aims of the Health Service have produced similar highly generalized statements. The NHS has been described as being primarily concerned with improving and promoting health (HM Treasury, 1989) and providing patients with better health care and greater choice of services (Department of Health, 1989).

Whatever the general context of an evaluation, if effectiveness is to be used as an evaluative criterion, it is essential that policy or programme objectives are made explicit and clearly specified at the outset (Palfrey et al., 1992). The evaluator needs to develop appropriate indicators to measure the extent to which these objectives are achieved. Some of the problems encountered in establishing outcome measures are discussed below.

Although effectiveness measures are used to determine the impact of a service or programme, they do not necessarily take into account the resources consumed in order to achieve the objectives. In measuring performance a conceptual distinction can be made between effectiveness, economy and efficiency (Henderson-Stewart, 1990). As described above, the evaluation of service effectiveness involves assessing the extent to which specified goals are achieved. Economy is concerned with the costs involved in producing programme outcomes. Service costs relate to resources or inputs such as equipment, personnel and buildings. Efficiency measurement goes further than simply establishing the actual costs incurred; it involves looking at the relationship between the costs of a service and its substantive outcomes. This involves the application of economic concepts to service evaluation or performance review in the form of cost-benefit, cost-utility and cost-effectiveness studies (Drummond et al., 1987).

The process dimension of health care can also be the subject of evaluation. This places the emphasis not on the results of the care received, but on aspects of the actual delivery of care including initial access, diagnosis, treatment and rehabilitation.

Evaluating the effectiveness of health care

Establishing the effectiveness of medical interventions is best achieved through carefully constructed clinical trials. The randomized controlled trial (RCT), which is the medical equivalent of the classic scientific experiment, is the first choice research design for determining the efficacy of medical therapies (Cochrane, 1972). As a research procedure, an RCT can be described as an experimental study, in which the effects of one or more interventions or treatments are assessed by dividing a research population, by means of random allocation, into one or more experimental and one or more control groups (Schwarz et al., 1980). The idea is to ensure that the experimental groups and control groups are similar in many respects; this will allow valid inferences to be drawn about the impact of a particular medical procedure or treatment regime on individuals in the experimental group. By adopting random allocation procedures investigators can assume that any patient characteristics likely to influence the response to treatment are evenly distributed between the various groups. In essence the control group is a comparison group and is not necessarily left untreated. For example, in an evaluation of a new pharmaceutical preparation, individuals assigned to the experimental group receive the new drug while patients in the comparison group receive the drug normally prescribed for their condition. By comparing appropriate outcome measures, the researcher is able to conclude whether or not the new drug provides a more effective treatment. A control or non-treatment group could be included to create a true comparative experimental research design which would not only enable the evaluator to identify the most effective treatment, but also measure the impact of intervention compared with non-intervention.

Whether evaluating a treatment for the first time, or trying to establish the comparative effectiveness of different ways of treating a specific medical condition, the evaluator needs to be aware of the possibility that observed outcomes may not be a direct result of the treatment received. It is possible that subjects in an RCT may be affected by the very fact that they are participating in a treatment study. There is a danger that outcome measures may be an artefact of the research process. In drug trials this is known as the 'placebo effect', because to guard against this eventuality, the control or 'no treatment' group is given a placebo, that is a chemically inert substance in the shape and form of the actual drug undergoing trials. As all subjects participating in the study are treated, any difference in outcomes between the experimental and placebo control groups can be interpreted as a genuine effect and not merely a psychological consequence of receiving treatment.

Using a placebo in order to enhance objectivity is one way of creating what is known as a blind trial. Basically there are three principal parties involved in the evaluation of a medical intervention: the patients, the professional staff providing the care and the researchers engaged in evaluating the effectiveness of the treatment. Any or all of these can be made 'blind' to some aspects of the study. If this is the case for representatives of only one of these groups then the RCT is referred to as a single-blind trial. In the evaluation of a new drug, the patients may be the only ones who are unable to identify those who have received a placebo and those who have been given the active drug. Where it is not possible to disguise active treatment by using a placebo, some of the researchers engaged in data collection or analysis may be the only ones unaware as to the identity of the treatment and control groups. This is a precautionary measure to guard against the possibility of experimenter bias.

A single blind RCT design was chosen by Frost et al. (1995) in their study of the effectiveness of an outpatient fitness programme for patients experiencing moderate disability as a result of chronic low back pain. Patients referred to the physiotherapy department by orthopaedic consultants were asked if they wished to take part in the study if they met the criteria for inclusion. The patients who consented were randomly allocated to the treatment group (fitness programme) or control group. Both groups received information and advice relating to back care and attended practical workshops to learn relaxation exercises. Only those patients in the treatment group attended the special exercises classes designed to improve their fitness. A single 'blind' observer carried out the assessments of patients before and after treatment.

It is possible to construct an experimental design in which more than one group is blinded to some aspect of the study. The most common form is the 'double-blind' trial where placebos are used to ensure that neither patients nor clinicians are aware of which particular type of treatment is being administered. A 'triple-blind' trial can be created when, in addition to the above, the data are coded to prevent those responsible for the final analysis from distinguishing between the treatment and control groups.

Mynors-Wallis et al. (1995) adopted a double-blind RCT in their study of the treatment of major depressive disorders in primary care. In order to evaluate the effectiveness of a psychologically-oriented problem solving treatment model, they set up controlled clinical trials to compare three treatment groups. Patients assigned to the psychological treatment group met with a trained therapist over a three-month period to identify and discuss their problems. Solving the patient's problems then became the major focus of the treatment. No medication was prescribed. Patients in the other two groups were given drug treatment; one group was given the antidepressant drug amitriptyline and the other received a placebo. Both patients and therapists were unable to distinguish the active drug from the placebo.

Randomly allocating patients to an experimental group or a control group is a way of making sure that factors likely to affect outcome measures are distributed identically across treatment and non-treatment groups. By and large this helps to prevent confusing the estimated treatment effects with the impact of other non-specified factors that may affect the outcome. This is because the groups in the experimental design are, on average, comparable before the medical intervention takes place. The RCT research design improves internal validity and offers the evaluator a methodologically sound way of demonstrating whether or not a treatment is more effective than chance in improving symptoms.

Working within the experimental paradigm, the evaluator aims to exclude extraneous variables, carefully control the nature and degree of the intervention and measure precisely the impact of the treatment. However, a number of practical problems and ethical dilemmas surround the implementation of RCTs.

Creating blind trials by using a placebo to eliminate bias and increase objectivity has its limitations. For example, the nature and type of treatment under investigation can be a key factor. It is only possible to mount double-blind trials in situations where the treatments can be successfully disguised and delivered in a similar manner. This is the case in drug trials where placebos are used which are identical in appearance to the active drug, thereby ensuring that neither patients nor health care workers can distinguish between the two. However, given the context of many health care evaluations it is not always possible to disguise the treatment. Take for example the evaluation of day-case surgery for hernias (Russell et al., 1977). This study was undertaken at a time when it was routine procedure for hernia patients to receive post-operative hospital care for a period of five days following surgery. The idea was to determine whether or not it was feasible for patients to be discharged on the same day as the operation, with formal home-based care provided by the district nurse. All patients in the study were exposed to the same surgical operation. Those in the experimental group were operated on early in the morning and discharged the same evening, whereas patients in the comparison or control group experienced the 'traditional' hospital stay of five days.

Thus randomized field experiments can be undertaken without conducting blind trials. For many evaluators, this experimental research design provides a benchmark against which alternative designs are often judged (Berk and Rossi, 1990). Indeed, within the field of medical practice the RCT is considered by many to be the single most scientifically valid method of evaluating the effectiveness of different clinical procedures or health care treatments (Bracken, 1987). However, it does not necessarily follow from such claims that the results of RCTs should necessarily be accepted at face value. As is the case with any type of research, empirical findings require interpretation. In order to know how much significance to attach to a set of results it is necessary to know something about the conditions under which the results are produced. This involves establishing the extent to which the experimental research protocol is adhered to throughout the study period. It is important that the experimental evaluator develops an awareness of some of the problems likely to be encountered when trying to replicate the 'true' experiment or control group design in health care settings.

First, random assignment itself can give rise to ethical objections on the grounds that individuals in the experimental and control groups receive differential treatment. Higginson and McCarthy (1989), in a study of palliative care, describe how general practitioners expressed concern about the random allocation of terminally ill patients which resulted in only those assigned to the treatment group receiving care from a domiciliary support team.

Evaluators may encounter resistance to randomization, especially when those responsible for providing health care services feel that their patients are being denied access to appropriate treatment. In a controlled intervention study designed to determine whether additional social support given to women during pregnancy produced beneficial results, Oakley (1992) describes how the midwives involved in the study, expressed concern over the random allocation of women to different care groups. They felt that this sometimes resulted in women they considered to be in need of additional support being allocated to the control condition, while others who were deemed to have sufficient social support were assigned to the intervention group to receive extra care. Oakley notes how the midwives tried various ways of influencing the randomization process. Some attempted to identify a pattern in the allocations so as to enable them to predict future assignment outcomes in order to ensure that the women under their care received the support the midwives felt they needed.

The standard RCT design can be modified to reduce the possibility of individuals who are clearly in need being denied access to a treatment or service on account of random allocation to a control or non-intervention group. Fitz-Gibbon and Morris (1987) recommend the borderline method of forming a true control group. Individuals considered to have the greatest need receive the benefits of the programme but do not take part in the evaluation study. Those who are designated as borderline cases are randomly assigned to either treatment or control conditions. While this overcomes the ethical problem of withholding treatment from deserving cases it does have its limitations. As Fitz-Gibbon and Morris acknowledge, the findings are only generalizable to borderline subjects; inferences cannot be drawn about the effects of the programme on those considered to be in greatest need. The borderline method is particularly appropriate for studies designed to determine whether or not there is any justification for expanding an existing programme.

A second problem encountered with RCTs is that many individual studies are based on very small numbers of patients, thus making it difficult to draw any definitive conclusions from the results. This is especially the case when there are only moderate differences in outcome between the various treatment and control groups. One solution is to undertake a meta-analysis of completed randomized trials. This is considered to be one of the most appropriate methodological strategies for systematically reviewing existing research evidence (Egger and Davey-Smith, 1995). The International Cochrane Collaboration, which was set up in 1992 to promote the collation and dissemination of evidence from RCTs, aims to create a register of all RCTs with a view to producing regular meta-analyses.

When conducting a meta-analysis it is essential that suitable precautionary measures are taken to reduce the possibility of bias. First and foremost, it is important that all or nearly all the relevant trials are included in the analysis (Clarke and Stewart, 1994). This can be difficult to achieve, irrespective of whether the meta-analysis is dealing with published or unpublished data. In the case of the former, there is the question of publication bias. Trials which produce positive results are far more likely to be reported in the literature than trials which reveal negative findings (Egger and Davey-Smith, 1995). Consequently, a meta-analysis that is heavily reliant upon published material is unlikely to reach a balanced conclusion regarding the efficacy of a particular treatment. Tracking down unpublished studies and gaining access to the data can also be a time-consuming exercise.

Meta-analyses of completed trials can be based on aggregate data or individual patient data. Clarke and Stewart (1994) outline the additional benefits to be gained by using individual level data when conducting a systematic review. Working with individual patient data makes it possible to check for errors in the randomization process which may threaten the scientific integrity of an experimental research design. If a study is to be included in a meta-analysis, the original researchers can be contacted and further information obtained. Also the ability to identify individual cases allows for the possibility of updating the analysis by including any previously missing information or follow-up data provided by the original researchers. However, probably the most important benefit individual data has over aggregate data is that it enables the researcher to calculate more accurately the timing of specific events. As Clarke and Stewart assert 'the time to event analyses contribute greater statistical power than is possible with the limited number of time points that would be available with aggregate data' (1994: 1009).

A third problem associated with using RCTs to measure treatment effectiveness concerns the fact that sometimes a prescribed treatment may produce an adverse reaction, sufficient to cause it to be discontinued and an alternative form of treatment administered. Bias can be introduced into the findings if the data relating to these cases are omitted. Patients who are withdrawn from a randomized trial because of the effects of the treatment, or crossover treatment groups in the experimental design must, for the purposes of analysis, be considered as belonging to the treatment group to which they were first allocated. This is referred to as 'analysis by intention to treat'.

Finally, there is the issue of the extent to which the results from controlled trials provide a basis for decision-making in clinical practice. No matter how methodologically sound and well conducted a trial may be, the results will be of limited value to the clinician if the subjects are atypical of the usual patient population. This can occur as a result of what has been termed 'pre-randomization bias'. Patients selected to participate in a clinical study are often drawn from a characteristically distinct subset of patients within a particular disease category. As research activity tends to concentrate on specialist clinics and treatment units, subjects tend to be representative of the more severe cases. Furthermore, patients can sometimes be excluded because they possess characteristics that are deemed to pose difficulties when it comes to the interpretation of the trial results. For example, researchers may decide to exclude those patients suffering from more than one illness.

Despite these limitations the experimental evaluation research design with randomly constituted concurrent controls is regarded as superior to all others, not least because it allows causal inferences to be made. It is particularly suited to evaluating the efficacy of medical interventions in circumstances where the treatment can be clearly defined, discrete variables can be identified and it is possible to exclude or control for extraneous variables and potentially confounding factors. When attempts are made to pursue the experimental ideal in the evaluation of multi-faceted health care programmes, initiatives and interventions, numerous practical difficulties are encountered.

The evaluator cannot assume that a programme will be implemented as originally intended by those responsible for its design. Indeed, it may prove difficult to determine the goals of a programme, as these may be perceived differently by policy-makers, programme administrators, health care practitioners and service recipients. Once a programme is in operation there is no guarantee that it will function unchanged throughout the evaluation period. The recruitment of new personnel midway through a study may lead to a change in working practices. With large-scale evaluations there is the added problem of ensuring that experimental protocol is adhered to and data collection methods are implemented in a uniform fashion across all the research sites.

There are many features of the social world of health care provision which militate against the use of experimental designs. Pursuit of the experimental ideal can be a source of tension between the evaluator and the professional practitioner or service provider (Illsey, 1980). The conditions imposed by an evaluator in an attempt to emulate the true experiment can cause administrative difficulties and ethical dilemmas for those responsible for programme implementation. The solution is not necessarily the total abandonment of experimental methods. Standard types of research designs are rarely used in programme evaluation without some kind of modification. As Chambers et al. comment, 'choices in regard to how research designs are constructed . . . should not be based on their conformity to abstract types of designs but on the particularities of the individual evaluation context' (1992: 224). They refer to this as the 'particularity principle'.

In certain circumstances practical problems and ethical concerns can preclude the setting up of randomized controlled designs in effectiveness studies. The evaluator may have to forgo the experimental ideal and adopt a quasi-experimental research design. A feature of this design is the use of non-random methods in the selection of concurrent comparison groups. A number of options are available to the evaluator. First, subjects can be allocated to treatment and non-treatment groups in a systematic fashion, for example, according to whether they were born on odd or even numbered days. Such allocation procedures appear simple to operate but they are open to abuse. Second, the evaluator can compare a group experiencing a programme intervention with a group in a different locality that does not have access to the programme. An attempt can be made to make the intervention group and comparison group as similar as possible with regard to a number of salient characteristics; a procedure referred to as matching.

Individual patients may be matched according to characteristics such as age, medical history and occupation. Where institutions are the focus of study, the number and status of health service personnel, the geographical location of the clinic or unit and the number of registered patients may constitute suitable matching criteria. Studies of the effectiveness of hospice care have made use of retrospective matching to create comparison groups (Parkes, 1985). However, this procedure has its difficulties. It is not always easy to know which are the most appropriate features to choose when matching study units. Also, as the number of chosen features increases, it becomes more difficult to achieve matched samples.

A further option available to the evaluator, in the absence of randomly allocated patients, is to make use of historical comparison groups. This involves consulting the records of past patients to identify those who have received the comparison treatment; they then form the historical control group. This procedure has attracted considerable criticism. Research shows that the conclusions drawn from studies employing this method of selection can be misleading (Cranberg, 1979; Diehl and Perry, 1986). Basically, the problem is that given the changes that have occurred over time in diagnostic practices, there is some doubt that historical controls and current patients constitute comparable groups for the purposes of investigating the effect of a new treatment.

In situations where experimental methods and quasi-experimental designs are impracticable the evaluator may have to resort to non-experimental techniques to evaluate the effectiveness of clinical interventions or the impact of programme initiatives. One of the most popular non-experimental designs in health care research is the case-control study (Schlesselman, 1982). Study units are selected on the basis of the presence or absence of the outcome that is the subject of the evaluation. Cohort studies are another type of non-experimental design. A cohort consists of a group of programme participants who are observed over a period of time to determine whether the programme has had an effect, and if so, how long this effect lasted. For purposes of comparison, a cohort similar in profile to that which underwent the programme, but was not itself exposed to the programme can be constructed. By their very nature, cohort studies are long-term exercises, which means they are not only costly to undertake but also susceptible to bias as a result of attrition (Fink, 1993).

The cross-institutional design has also been proposed as an alternative to the traditional experimental approach. Here the researcher does not aim to create experimental conditions by seeking to control aspects of a planned intervention prior to measuring its impact. A key feature of the cross-institutional design is that the researcher takes advantage of the existing diversity of practice within a particular field of service provision. This involves selecting a number of service delivery sites, identifying the characteristic features of the intervention strategy or treatment model each site operates, measuring the respective outcomes and determining the extent to which any observed differences can be attributed to differences in the type of treatment or service provided. Booth (1985) provides a good example of a cross-institutional design in a study of residential homes for elderly people in four local authority areas.

From a methodological point of view the cross-institutional design has its weaknesses. Noting that the successful implementation of the design rests upon there being recognizable differences in both process and outcome across the chosen research sites, Cheetham et al. warn that, 'apparent differences in outcome may, however, disappear when account is taken statistically of variations in intake to the sites' (1992: 28). Thus the researcher needs to attempt to control for those characteristics considered to be important determinants of the success of a programme.

Measuring outcomes: health status and the quality of life

A critical step in the successful evaluation of health care initiatives is the identification of appropriate outcome measures or indicators of health status. This applies whether the aim of the evaluation is to ascertain the efficacy of a new clinical procedure, assess the impact of a local or national health promotion campaign or establish, by conducting a health needs assessment, how best a community might use its health care resources to achieve maximum health benefits. Whatever the evaluation research question or favoured mode of inquiry the evaluator will encounter measurement problems.

A valid health outcome measure is one that gives an indication as to the health status of persons or populations. Any definition of health status must be based on a concept of health. However, sociological studies of comparative health beliefs reveal that health is a multifaceted, complex and abstract concept (Williams, 1983; d'Houtard and Field, 1984; Blaxter, 1990). Not only are there marked differences in lay people's definitions of health, but their perceptions do not always match those held by health professionals. Consequently, there is much controversy surrounding the conceptualization and measurement of health outcomes.

A general distinction can be made between negative and positive definitions of health (Calnan, 1987). Within the context of the scientific, biomedical or disease-based model, health is viewed in largely negative terms, as the absence of illness or disease. Ultimately, what in fact is being measured by many health status indicators is not health itself, but the lack of health. The converse of negative health status is positive health. This is a much broader concept as the following implies:

> Positive health could be described as the ability to cope with stressful situations, the maintenance of a strong social-support system, integration in the community, high morale and life satisfaction, psychological well-being, and even levels of physical fitness as well as physical health. (Bowling, 1991: 7)

Given the diverse nature of the constituent elements, and the need to ensure that the research instruments chosen to measure health meet the necessary criteria of reliability and validity, it is hardly surprising that measurement problems are commonplace.

Mortality rates and morbidity indices are among the most easily available objective measures used in health studies. However, their adoption as outcome measures requires careful consideration. For example, it has been shown that the apparent objectivity of these indicators cannot necessarily be taken for granted. As Prior (1985) notes, the information obtained from death certificates, which is used to compile official mortality statistics, is not of a consistent quality. Haynes (1988) also draws attention to some of the methodological issues surrounding the definition and measurement of mortality and morbidity.

In certain clinical circumstances, survival may be an appropriate way of assessing the value of a treatment. By means of clinical trials, the effects of medical or surgical interventions can be evaluated by comparing the case fatality rates over a five-year survival period. However, it does not always follow that death and survival represent the best way of determining success and failure, even when dealing with the treatment of chronic illnesses (Ebrahim, 1990). Other broader measures may be used to give an indication of successful outcomes in terms of improvement in personal health status. It is possible that an evaluation may reveal that some types of intervention may not produce any significant impact on survival rates, but may cause patients considerably less physical discomfort and emotional distress than alternative forms of treatment. Also, as Fitzpatrick (1994) observes, survival is not the only outcome; many surgical interventions or medical treatments are designed to have a positive impact on general aspects of a patient's well-being. He gives the example of joint replacement surgery which, by improving mobility and reducing physical discomfort, leads to a general improvement in the quality of life experienced by treated patients.

Clearly, there is both the quantity and quality of life to consider. As Patrick and Erikson argue, these are two 'distinct but related concepts used to evaluate the present and future state of an individual or group of people' (1993: 21). Whereas the former is relatively easy to measure objectively, as it is determined by the length of time a patient survives after undergoing a particular type of treatment, the latter, by comparison, encompasses a wide range of subjective indices spanning the physical, mental and social dimensions of health. These indices of personal health status and health-related quality of life are based on the subjective judgements of health professionals or patients. This form of subjective health assessment is not intended to replace the objective indicators used in clinical and medical measures. On the contrary, the idea is that it can be used in conjunction with conventional physical measurements and laboratory-based tests, to provide more detailed information from which conclusions can be drawn concerning the overall health status of an individual.

There is a voluminous literature dealing with the construction, implementation and analysis of standardized scales used in subjective health measurement questionnaires (McDowell and Newell, 1987; Bowling, 1991; Stewart and Ware, 1992; Wilkin et al., 1993; Streiner and Norman, 1995; Jenkinson and McGee, 1997). A discussion of these scales is beyond the scope of this chapter. The intention here is merely to identify the main types of health status instruments available, identify their potential as outcome measures in health care evaluations and highlight some of the methodological issues evaluators need to consider when choosing measuring instruments.

A large number of validated instruments are available for collecting data from patients about their state of health. These scales differ in terms of their scope and content. Some are designed to measure general health status, while others are disease-specific. An example of the former is the Nottingham Health Profile (Hunt et al., 1986), which comprises 38 questions covering the following categories: energy level, pain, emotional reactions, sleep, social isolation and physical abilities. The assumption is that these generic health scales can be used as primary measures of outcome across a variety of treatment conditions and with different patient populations (Patrick and Deyo, 1989). Applied before and after treatment they can be used to detect if there has been any net improvement in self-reported general health.

Generic scales are designed to cover a wide range of conditions; therefore it is more than likely that they will contain items which are not relevant when applied to patients with specific health problems. As the idea is to measure change in health status following treatment, it would seem sensible to adopt an instrument that is sensitive to the clinical intervention under investigation. Disease-specific scales are designed to target those areas considered most likely to be directly affected by the treatment given. A good example of such an instrument is the arthritis impact measurement scale (Meenan et al., 1980) which includes items on manual dexterity, functional mobility and experience of pain.

Subjective measures of health status have a number of different applications. In randomized clinical trials they 'provide a highly informative method of measuring appropriate outcomes' (Fitzpatrick, 1994: 35). Not only do they assist in monitoring the positive impact of particular treatments but they also help in detecting the unintended and harmful effects some interventions may have on the general well-being of patients. Self-report health status questionnaires can also be used to estimate changes in levels of health in populations as part of an evaluation of the effectiveness of health care programmes and initiatives.

The evaluator needs to take a number of factors into account when choosing an appropriate health status measure. Initially, there is the question as to whether to adopt a generic or disease-specific scale. One advantage of generic measures of health status is that by incorporating a much wider range of health-related issues, they increase the likelihood of detecting unexpected side-effects of a treatment or intervention. However, as mentioned above, some items may prove to be inappropriate for detecting changes within particular patient populations and a disease-specific measure may be preferred. The focus of the evaluation study will be one of the main factors influencing the choice of health status measures.

Once a decision has been reached regarding the type of scale to be used, the evaluator must then decide whether or not to employ an existing scale or develop an entirely new instrument. There are many well-established health inventories currently available and there are clear benefits to be gained from making use of them. For example, constructing a new scale can be an elaborate and time-consuming exercise that can be conveniently bypassed if a suitable instrument already exists.

Whether choosing or designing a scale, careful attention needs to be given to issues of reliability and validity. As regards reliability, a questionnaire instrument must be reproducible; in other words, it should be capable of producing the same or similar results, when completed on more than one occasion, by the same individuals, within a short time span. This is provided, of course, that it can be safely assumed that nothing occurred in the interim period likely to bring about a real change in health status. This is one measure of reliability and is referred to as test-retest reliability.

Health status instruments also need to be tested for validity. The evaluator must assess the items or health indices used in a questionnaire for content validity. This involves scrutinizing the component parts of a scale to establish if all the relevant aspects of the attribute being measured are in fact included. One form of content validity is known as face validity; this refers to whether items in a scale appear, on the surface, to make sense and look as though they are capable of measuring the variables they claim to measure. Streiner and Norman (1995) describe the various technical procedures involved in estimating the reliability and validity of health measurement scales.

It is not sufficient for a health status measure merely to meet the minimum criteria of reliability and validity; it must also be sensitive to change if it is to function adequately as an outcome measure. Indeed, a scale may give the impression of high reliability precisely because it is inefficient at detecting change. There is also evidence to suggest that instruments that are valid can be insensitive to change (Guyatt et al., 1992). Sensitivity to change, referred to as 'responsiveness' (Fitzpatrick et al., 1992), is recognized as 'an indispensable characteristic of any health status instrument' (Ziebland, 1994: 43). To be viable, an instrument needs to be able to detect any significant changes that occur in the health status of individuals and groups over time, even if the changes are small.

Technical and methodological issues aside, the evaluator also needs to consider the context in which a particular health questionnaire is to be used, as well as taking into account the characteristics of the patient group at whom it is aimed. As Ziebland et al. (1992) observe, misleading inferences can be drawn from patient responses if the circumstances in which the questionnaire is administered are ignored. The very experience of being in hospital may influence how patients respond to certain scale items. For example, standard measures of mobility, which contain items relating to a range of daily activities, may not be appropriate in hospital settings where the physical surroundings and ward regime impose restrictions on patients. The potential effects of hospitalization need to be borne in mind when comparing the results of health status questionnaires administered to the same set of patients twice, once during their stay in hospital and then again shortly after being discharged. A dramatic improvement in patient scores may not be an accurate reflection of the actual improvement in health status between the two periods. The same scale item may have a different meaning in different settings.

The items included in a scale not only need to be relevant to respondents, but also easily understood by them. For example, generic or disease-specific scales designed for use with adults of working age may contain questions about activities of daily living which are of little relevance to children and the elderly. In some cases, even when an appropriate scale has been identified, the patient may be in a mentally confused state or in such poor physical health that it is not feasible to administer a self-report questionnaire. In these circumstances those engaged in the day-to-day care of the patient, either as professional health workers or informal carers, can be enlisted as proxy respondents. Although there is evidence to suggest that there is some agreement between the subjective health assessments made by patients and their proxy respondents, this tends to occur when focusing on specific areas, such as, the performance of routine daily activities. Proxy respondents are less likely to agree with patients when asked about anxiety levels, emotional state, experience of pain and general discomfort, and changes in health status (Epstein et al., 1989).

If the evaluator has no alternative but to use proxy respondents then steps must be taken to keep threats to validity to a minimum and improve the accuracy of responses. According to Albrecht (1994), this can involve a number of actions on the part of the researcher. First, patients can be asked to nominate their own proxies, as there is evidence to suggest that patient-nominated proxies provide more accurate assessments. Second, it is essential that proxy respondents are made fully aware of the nature of the exercise and suitably prepared for the task. Third, they could also be asked to comment on how confident they feel about the accuracy of their own assessments.

Basically there are three broad categories of subjective health measures: those that establish health profiles of individuals by recording symptoms of illness, those that provide an assessment of the individual's ability to perform a range of normal daily tasks and those that attempt to measure general well-being. All three types of measure can be found in quality of life scales. Health status, functional status and social well-being are not the only dimensions of the quality of life identified by researchers. Quality of life is a broad, complex, multi-dimensional concept incorporating psychological, social psychological, economic, philosophical, social, cultural and spiritual dimensions. It is, therefore, not surprising to find considerable controversy surrounding its definition and measurement (Wiklund et al., 1992). The conceptual confusion is added to by what Bowling (1991) sees as a general tendency to assume that all non-clinical indicators are potential measures of the quality of life.

Patrick and Erikson offer a global definition which describes health-related quality of life as 'the value assigned by individuals, groups or society to the duration of survival as modified by impairments, functional states, perceptions, and social opportunities influenced by disease, injury, treatment, or policy' (1993: 76). Five core concepts feature in this definition: opportunity, health perceptions, functional status, impairment and death or duration of life. The first four concepts are subdivided into domains that represent behaviours, perceptions, attitudes and physical and emotional states. For example, functional status is a core concept that comprises eight different domains covering social, psychological and physical functioning. Four of these domains, namely, social role limitations, social integration, social contact and intimacy, when taken together constitute social functioning. Indicators are identified for each domain. For example, the frequency with which individuals visit friends or relatives is one possible measure of social contact.

The number of concepts, domains and indicators vary from measure to measure. For example, the instrument designed by Becker et al. (1993) to measure quality of life experienced by patients suffering from mental illness contains nine domains; the Medical Outcomes Study (Stewart and Ware, 1992) makes use of eight health concepts; the Index of Health Related Quality of Life (Rosser et al., 1992) contains over forty scales covering distress, disability and discomfort and the Schedule for the Evaluation of Individual Quality of Life (O'Boyle et al., 1992) requires respondents to nominate five areas of life which they consider important in determining their quality of life.

The multi-dimensional nature of the concept has not surprisingly given rise to an accumulation of instruments designed to measure the quality of life experienced by individuals. The use of multiple indicators ensures that a wealth of information is provided. However, problems can be encountered when trying to achieve a unified measure of quality of life for comparative purposes, particularly if improvements in one domain or dimension are associated with deterioration in another. Evaluating the overall impact of a treatment on the quality of life is not possible unless there is some way of establishing the relative value attached to each domain or dimension.

In general, health-related quality of life measures fall into two broad categories; those designed to measure quality of life experienced by an individual at a particular point in time and those which combine quality of life with quantity of life by including a measure of life expectancy. Over recent years health economists have displayed an increasing interest in the type of measures found in the second category. As described in the previous section, economic evaluation involves not only establishing the effectiveness of an intervention but also ascertaining the costs involved. In this context economic costs represent not merely the amount of resources used to support a particular programme or intervention, but also take into account the benefits that could have been obtained had the same resources been put to some other use.

The Quality of Well-being Scale (QWB) (Kaplan and Bush, 1982; Kaplan and Anderson, 1988) and the Quality Adjusted Life Year (QALY) (Williams, 1985, 1987; Williams and Kind, 1992) offer two ways of quantifying outcome measures so as to enable health economists to compare the relative benefits of different interventions or treatments.

While both instruments quantify health output in terms of life expectancy they also recognize the importance of making adjustments to reflect changes in the quality of life enjoyed by the patient following treatment.

The QWB scale measures the benefits of medical care in terms of 'well years'. A 'well year' represents a year of optimum quality, that is a year when the individual is in good health and free of illness. The scale uses a number of items on physical activity, social interaction, general mobility and capacity for self care to ascertain the level of social well-being. For example, if illness reduces an individual's quality of life by one half, one year of life will be deemed to be equivalent to 0.5 'well years'. Consequently, if as a result of medical intervention the patient's quality of life improves, say to 0.75, then the treatment will be considered to have produced 0.25 'well years'. Using data on life expectancy it is possible to calculate the total years of 'well life expectancy' for patient populations undergoing specific treatments. The idea is that this will enable those responsible for making resource allocation decisions to identify those treatments that are the most cost-effective.

Similarly, the QALY technique is based on a single number representing the quality of life: a score of 1 signifies a year without illness and a score of less than 1 a year of life of less than optimal health. For Williams (1985), quality of life is quantified by measuring it in two dimensions, namely, disability and distress. In the final calculation consideration is given to both the quantity and quality of life. Take for example the case of a seriously ill patient who, without medical intervention, has a life expectancy of one year, but can be expected to live for a further four years following treatment. The change in the duration of life (i.e. 'life year') is weighted by a factor deemed to represent the change in disability and distress (i.e. 'quality adjusted'). If the quality of life scores for the additional four years are 0.4, 0.3, 0.2 and 0.1, the typical benefit of the treatment is 1.0 QALY.

Although there is some variation in QALY methodology (Kaplan, 1995), a feature common to all approaches is that they depend on information about the costs associated with different treatments, as well as details of the benefits obtained in the way of health gains. Ultimately the aim is to compare different treatments in terms of health benefits as a ratio of costs. It is this combining of data on cost-effectiveness with perceptions of the quality of life following treatment which has made this technique attractive to economic evaluators. Different interventions can be compared according to the cost per quality life year gained. Take the hypothetical example of two operations, one with a QALY rating of 1 (0.4, 0.4 and 0.2) and one with a score of 2 (0.7, 0.6, 0.4 and 0.3). If the cost of the former was £200 and the latter was £100 then the second operation would represent a more efficient use of resources.

QALY methodology has attracted considerable critical comment. Mulkay et al. (1987) question what they see as the taken for granted background assumptions behind the measurement procedures adopted by Kind et al. (1982) to create a quality of life valuation matrix. Basically, 70 individuals, including doctors, nurses and patients, were asked to score the levels of disability and distress associated with a variety of health states. According to Mulkay et al., there are some highly contentious assumptions of correspondence, stability and quantification behind this research technique. First, they express doubt over the extent to which it can be assumed that the judgements elicited by such an artificial exercise actually correspond to the evaluations people make in normal everyday circumstances. Second, the assumption of stability is challenged, on the grounds that presupposing that the stated preferences of individuals are relatively stable effectively ignores the socially influenced character of their evaluative responses. As they assert, 'as we come to recognize the social character of the research process and the socially generated character of subjects' responses, the assumption that the social researcher is eliciting relatively stable and context-free evaluations becomes much less plausible' (Mulkay et al., 1987: 556). Finally, the assumption that the numerical assessments made by respondents in the research setting accurately reflect pre-existing numerical scales of preferences is open to question. The authors note that, 'Given the wholly artificial nature of the measurement procedure, it seems likely that the smooth distribution of scores produced in these attempts to measure quality of life is a result of respondents' recognition of a quantification already implicit in the analyst's pre-arranged categories' (1987: 556). Thus there is the possibility that quality of life measures may be an artefact produced by a measurement process constructed according to the preconceptions of the evaluator.

QALY methodology has attracted criticism from other quarters. Goodinson and Singleton (1989) question whether Williams' original sample of 70 'healthy' respondents was large enough and sufficiently representative of the general population to produce a valuation matrix suitable for universal application. Grimley Evans (1992) notes how elderly patients may be disadvantaged by the nature and content of some quality of life measures. This raises the question as to whose valuations should be taken into account when measuring the quality of life: those of the patients, the population at large or health care professionals? Indeed, research indicates there are differences in the value judgements made by different groups. In comparing healthy volunteers and patients, Sackett and Torrance (1978) found that the length of the illness was a significant factor in influencing the valuations of the latter. Studies of the quality of life of cancer patients report differences between the assessments made by doctors and patients (Spitzer et al., 1981; Slevin et al., 1988).

If the QALY technique is to be used to inform decision-making in health care management then it is essential that detailed data are available on the costs of different types of treatment and the actual impact they have on the quality of life. Unfortunately this outcome data is not readily available in a form which allows it to be easily included in QALY calculations. Furthermore, doubt has been expressed concerning the accuracy of some of the mortality and morbidity data used in QALY measurement (Drummond, 1989).

In recent years QALY measurement has become the subject of much debate, with emphasis being placed upon the methodological, technical, theoretical, philosophical and ethical issues surrounding the development and application of the QALY as an outcome measure in health care evaluations (Baldwin et al., 1994).

Evaluating efficiency

If policy-makers or service managers are to make decisions about whether or not to continue, extend or curtail a particular programme or policy then they not only need knowledge of the benefits it provides, but also information about the costs incurred. There has long been a recognition of the need to find ways of measuring efficiency in the NHS (HMSO, 1956). The search for resource efficiency measures was given added impetus by the organizational reforms and administrative changes introduced in the 1980s following the Financial Management Initiative (HMSO, 1982), the Griffiths Report (DHSS, 1983) and the introduction of resource management into the Health Service (British Medical Association, 1989). The Government also had in mind the controlling of public sector costs when designing the reforms contained in the NHS and Community Care Act 1990.

Performance indicator systems were originally introduced into public sector organizations in an attempt to provide managers with comprehensive statistical data to aid decision-making. The National Health Service was the first major public service to use performance indicators on a large scale. Initially around 140 indicators were identified (DHSS, 1983); these were composed mainly of resource efficiency measures such as the number of patients treated and the length of stay in hospital. A feature of the early performance indicator scheme was that it enabled comparisons to be made both within and between health authorities. The emphasis was placed on input, throughput and output, illustrating that the scheme was primarily designed for management purposes with the focus clearly on issues of efficiency and economy of service provision, rather than on the actual outcome or effectiveness of services (DHSS, 1985).

Efficiency analysis is the province of health economics. The two most widely used formal methods for estimating the efficiency of medical interventions or health care programmes are cost-effectiveness and cost-benefit analyses. These 'can be viewed both as conceptual perspectives and as sophisticated technical procedures' (Rossi and Freeman, 1993:

365). A detailed description of the various technical procedures is beyond the scope of this section, but the purpose here is merely to provide a general overview of the conceptual thinking behind economic approaches to evaluation and outline the basic steps involved in undertaking an economic evaluation. Readers wishing to find out more about the formal methods involved should consult a specialist text (for example, Warner and Luce, 1982; Drummond et al., 1987).

Establishing the economic efficiency of a health programme involves examining the relationship between its costs and the impact or effect it has on patients. Cost-effectiveness analysis calculates the financial cost incurred in achieving outcomes. A cost-effective programme or treatment is one which can either be shown to provide the maximum aggregate health gains for a given level of resources, or be seen to produce a given level of health benefits at the lowest cost. This type of analysis can be particularly useful for comparing the relative efficiency of different services or programmes which have a common goal or objective. The programme that records the least cost per unit of output, or displays the greatest impact per unit of cost, is deemed the most efficient.

Cost-effectiveness analysis is best applied when there is one clearly identifiable outcome measure to consider, such as the total number of life years saved by a particular treatment or the total number of patients treated over a specified period. Where health gain is measured on a number of different dimensions it becomes more difficult to interpret the results obtained from the application of cost-effectiveness techniques.

The limitations of this form of economic appraisal are not confined to situations where there are multiple outcome measures to consider. Cost-effectiveness analysis has a problem dealing with added life years, insofar as all years of life are treated as being of equal value, with no adjustment being made for changes in health status. It has been noted that quality of life factors are ignored: classified as 'intangibles', they are acknowledged but not quantified. Cost-utility analysis overcomes this problem by incorporating quantitative measures of the quality of added life years in its calculations. QALYs are calculated, as described in the previous section, by adjusting added life years by the utility value of the resulting health status to obtain a measure of the quality of life.

In contrast to cost-effectiveness analysis, cost-benefit analysis is an altogether more ambitious technique. Whereas the former measures benefits in terms of some standard indicator of clinical outcome, such as survival, or the number of years or months free from illness, the latter measures benefits in terms of their actual or estimated monetary value. Thus, costs and benefits are reduced to a common denominator, usually money. This enables comparisons to be made between programmes and policies that have entirely different outcomes. In the final analysis, cost-benefit results are presented in either the form of the ratio of costs to benefits, or by a figure representing the net benefit (or loss).

As Sloan (1995) observes, there is no consensus among economic evaluators as to the methods to be used when conducting a cost-benefit or cost-effectiveness study. Analysts choose from a variety of methods and individual analysts have their own preferences. However, it is possible to identify basic steps in the process of undertaking an economic evaluation. Sloan describes six stages, outlined below, which are derived from a publication by the United States Department of Health and Human Services (DHHS, 1992); in many respects these stages are broadly similar to the six distinct phases outlined by Phillips et al. (1994).

The six basic steps identified by Sloan are as follows. First, the evaluator needs to develop a clear understanding of the principal aims of an intervention or programme that is to be evaluated; identify the specific characteristics of the patient or client group at whom it is directed; acquire information about the intervention it is replacing; and identify alternative ways in which the programme objectives might be achieved.

The second step involves establishing the costs incurred by a particular treatment or intervention. This is not a case of simply estimating the direct financial costs resulting from the provision of a treatment or service, which in itself can be a complex exercise. The cost-benefit analyst perceives costs in a much wider context. For example, there are indirect costs to the patient to consider, such as the loss of earnings during the period of treatment and convalescence, as well as social costs in the form of state welfare payments to support the patient while they are unfit for work.

Third, the evaluator must identify the relevant benefits stemming from an intervention. Direct benefits will be in the form of improvements in the health status of the patient; however, when calculating net health benefits it is important that any adverse side-effects of the treatment are taken into account.

According to Rossi and Freeman (1993), correctly identifying the relevant costs and benefits of a programme or intervention is one of two major measurement problems facing the evaluator when using cost-benefit analysis techniques. The second measurement problem is in expressing both costs and benefits in monetary terms. Measuring costs and benefits constitute the fourth and fifth steps in the methodology of efficiency analyses.

If the results of cost-benefit analyses are to inform decision-making then it is essential that all costs and benefits are identified and accurately measured. One consequence of failing to include all costs in the calculations is that, in the final analysis, a programme intervention may give the appearance of being more efficient than it actually is. Similarly, the efficiency of a treatment or programme can be underestimated if some relevant benefits are omitted. Furthermore, accurately estimating costs and benefits can be a problematic exercise, especially when dealing with intervention programmes which do not produce an immediate effect but are expected to have an impact at some future date. Evaluators take into account the time factor by converting costs and benefits data into a common measure to allow for meaningful comparisons to be made; a technique referred to as discounting.

It is readily acknowledged that economic evaluation is a long way from being a precise science (Phillips et al., 1994). Indeed, there are numerous ways of conceptualizing and measuring costs and benefits; therefore it is important that the results of economic evaluations are treated with caution. This brings us to the sixth step in conducting an efficiency analysis, which is undertaking a sensitivity analysis. This involves making allowances for the existence of uncertainty in the measurement process by calculating how possible changes in costs and benefits might influence results. For example, the analyst may calculate the likely consequences of a fixed percentage increase or decrease in costs.

Performance evaluation: the quality of health care

As a result of the National Health Service reforms in the 1980s and 1990s the evaluation of the quality of health care became 'a mandatory part of service provision' (Ellis and Whittington, 1993: 18). District Health Authorities in England and Wales set up quality assurance committees whose primary function was to monitor standards of service. Patient satisfaction surveys and audits were adopted as two of the main methods of data collection in the process of quality performance evaluation.

Patient satisfaction surveys

Studies of patient satisfaction with the medical and nursing services they receive form an important component of health care evaluation research. However, 'Although the patient's distinctive viewpoint is now widely recognized to be a vital element in the evaluation of health services, there is still no consensus about optimal ways of capturing this perspective' (Fitzpatrick, 1997: 98). The initial interest in consumer opinion as a potential measure of the quality of health care provision pre-dates the introduction of medical audits and quality assurance initiatives in the 1980s (Morrell, 1970; Doll, 1973). There are many early examples of local and national studies of patient attitudes towards various forms of health care. For example, in a national study of general practice, Cartwright (1967) found that only 3 per cent of patients complained that the care they received was unsatisfactory. Although a later study drew more critical comments, the vast majority of patients claimed to be satisfied with the service provided by their general practitioner (Cartwright and

Anderson, 1981). During the same period there were studies of the extent to which recently discharged hospital patients were satisfied with the care received while in hospital (McGhee, 1961; Cartwright, 1964). Some studies also surveyed attitudes of patients attending outpatient clinics (OPCS, 1978).

The later growth in the popularity of patient satisfaction surveys, along with more systematic attempts at collecting data on consumer opinion, can be linked to the emergence of the consumerist ethos in the organization and management of public sector services which stresses patient choice, professional accountability and responsiveness to consumers' preferences. As the Griffith Report on the National Health Service noted, it is the responsibility of the management board to 'ascertain how well the service is being delivered at local level by obtaining the experience and perceptions of patients and the community' (DHSS, 1983: 9). The recommendation that performance should be monitored against users' views led to an increase in patient satisfaction surveys (McIver and Carr-Hill, 1989). The idea that the consumers' viewpoint should be taken into account when planning service provision was endorsed by the White Paper entitled 'Working for Patients' (Department of Health, 1989) which emphasized the importance of promoting patient choice.

Evidence from patient satisfaction surveys undertaken in different health care settings reveals that most patients, when asked to give an overall assessment of the care they have received, claim to be satisfied. In a sample survey in the South East of England, Williams and Calnan (1991) found general levels of consumer satisfaction to be very high. According to their data, obtained from a self-completion questionnaire, 97 per cent of respondents were satisfied with the dental care they received, 95 per cent expressed satisfaction with the service provided by their general practitioner and 83 per cent claimed to be generally satisfied with the hospital care they received as an inpatient.

Similar high levels of general patient satisfaction are a common feature of earlier surveys of consumer opinion (Locker and Dunt, 1978). However, when patients are asked direct and specific questions about their experiences of health care services they are more likely to express dissatisfaction. For example, when asked about their experiences of general practitioner consultations, 38 per cent of respondents in the Williams and Calnan (1991) study were unhappy about the length of time they had to wait in the surgery before seeing the doctor, 25 per cent felt that insufficient time was devoted to the consultation and 26 per cent felt that the doctor did not provide them with enough information. From this and other studies it would appear that patients' assessments of professional competence are only one predictor of consumer satisfaction. The nature and quality of the patient–professional relationship and the amount of information patients receive are also important sources of dissatisfaction (Ley, 1982; Kincey et al., 1975).

Indeed, according to some observers, patients are more likely to express dissatisfaction with the 'manner and means of the processes of health care delivery', than they are with the professional competencies displayed by health workers or the outcome of the care received (Kelman, 1976).

Given the current popularity and widespread use of patient satisfaction measures in quality assurance in the NHS (Dalley and Carr-Hill, 1991) and their general application in other areas of health care evaluation, it is important that the conceptual and methodological issues surrounding the definition and measurement of consumer satisfaction are understood. A number of writers have remarked on the fact that although patient satisfaction measures have been used in a wide variety of health care contexts there is some ambiguity surrounding the definition of the concept and its subsequent operationalization (Locker and Dunt, 1978; Fitzpatrick, 1990; Bond and Thomas, 1992). It has been referred to as an 'ungrounded concept' (Williams, 1994: 514).

In an early review of consumer satisfaction research, Locker and Dunt comment on the lack of clarification of what the concept means either to researchers who use it or respondents who express it. This lack of conceptual clarification is still an issue and is summed up by Fitzpatrick when he asserts that,

> Patient satisfaction is one of those concepts that has a common-sense meaning which is rarely subject to critical scrutiny. It is sometimes treated as an attitude or set of attitudes but is more usefully thought of as an evaluation or set of evaluations by the patient. (Fitzpatrick, 1990: 20)

Clearly, patient evaluations are important, but if the findings of satisfaction surveys are to be accurately interpreted and used to inform policy decision-making, we need to have both a clear idea as to what research instruments are actually measuring when applied to the construct of satisfaction and an understanding of how patients make their evaluations (Williams, 1994).

Self-completion questionnaires are the primary method of data collection in patient evaluation research (Jones et al., 1987). Questionnaires are relatively cheap and easy to administer and produce easily quantifiable data. There is no standardized format for such questionnaires and they tend to vary in scale and content from study to study. The simplest questionnaires ask respondents to give 'yes-no' answers to questions about aspects of their contact with the health care services. From the responses it is possible to calculate what percentage of respondents are satisfied or dissatisfied with a particular treatment or service.

One problem with this format is that it treats patient satisfaction as a categorical variable, thus ignoring the fact that people are capable of making finer judgements when it comes to evaluating service provision.

From the information obtained, the researcher is only able to comment on the extent to which patients are satisfied or dissatisfied, nothing can be said about the relative intensity with which the satisfaction and dissatisfaction is felt. As Locker and Dunt (1978) observe, a multi-dimensional rating scale provides a more sensitive instrument for measuring consumer opinion. Consequently, many studies employ scaling methods, such as adjectival rating scales, with discrete or continuous response sets, to measure patient satisfaction. A popular choice is the Likert Scale, in which the rater expresses an opinion by responding to a specific statement on a five-point scale ranging from 'strongly agree' to 'strongly disagree' (Streiner and Norman, 1995).

Scaling techniques can be applied to individual items or a number of items can be combined to provide a scale of satisfaction for a specific dimension of care, for example, the patient–professional relationship. Offering respondents more than two response categories allows them to be more discriminating in their responses. This makes it easier to detect differences between health care services and monitor changes in satisfaction levels over time.

The use of the questionnaire as a tool for measuring patient satisfaction has given rise to considerable critical comment on methodological grounds. First, there are doubts about the reliability of findings from patient surveys. As already indicated, most sample surveys record generally high levels of patient satisfaction. However, this may be indicative of a failure to develop a suitably discriminating measure of satisfaction (Carr-Hill, 1992). The level of satisfaction uncovered may, in part, be determined by how the questions are posed. It is in this context that Williams and Calnan refer to the divergence between the 'general' and the 'specific'. They assert that, 'whilst high levels of *general* consumer satisfaction are usually found, greater dissatisfaction is usually expressed in response to question (sic) of a more detailed and *specific* nature' (1991: 708). There is also evidence to suggest that open-ended or unstructured questions can produce different results from direct questions. By their very nature open-ended questions give respondents greater scope for displaying critical views and opinions (Calnan, 1988). However, patients may express satisfaction or dissatisfaction with a particular aspect of their care when questioned directly, but may not attach sufficient importance to this aspect to encourage them to offer any comments in response to an open-ended question (Locker and Dunt, 1978).

Second, patient surveys have been criticized on the grounds of scope and content, with some being dismissed as public relations exercises rather than being seen as serious attempts at gathering information for the purposes of policy-making (McIver and Carr-Hill, 1989). It has been claimed that some surveys have a distinctly 'managerial' or professional bias, insofar as the aspects of care on which patients are asked for their opinions reflect the interests and perspectives of the providers of care rather than those of the recipients themselves (Calnan, 1988). According to Evason and Whittington, some patient surveys concentrate on relatively superficial issues, such as the quality of waiting rooms, while ignoring 'the harder issues surrounding treatment priorities, quality of life and equity of access' (1991: 74).

Third, there are problems with establishing the validity of items or scales used in patient satisfaction questionnaires. A fundamental issue here is whether or not the answers given by respondents are a true reflection of their actual feelings. What Fitzpatrick (1990) terms 'normative effects' may have an impact upon the replies to standardized questions. Respondents may feel compelled to provide positive responses so as not to offend their carers (Halpern, 1985). Fitzpatrick and Hopkins (1983), interviewed patients attending neurological outpatient clinics and found that although a small number of patients were unhappy with some aspects of their first visit to the clinic they were reluctant to describe themselves as 'dissatisfied'. For example, some interviewees expressed the view that their negative experiences were an unavoidable consequence of the fact that the clinics had to deal with such a large number of patients. In the circumstances they felt it would be unreasonable to appear to be unappreciative of the efforts of the medical staff.

Clearly questionnaires have limitations when it comes to eliciting and measuring patients' perceptions of their care. A badly designed questionnaire can 'give misleading results, limit the opportunity of patients to express their concerns about different aspects of care, and encourage professionals to believe that patients are satisfied when they are in reality highly discontented' (Whitehead and Baker, 1992: 152). These limitations do not preclude the use of questionnaires, but underline the need for researchers to have an understanding of how patients arrive at judgements about their satisfaction with care in order to design research instruments which are capable of accurately ascertaining users' views.

The problem with many patient satisfaction questionnaires is that they are based on a number of questionable assumptions. First, there is the common-sense assumption that satisfaction with health care is primarily determined by the extent to which the actual experience meets prior expectations. Second, it is assumed that patients conceptualize and naturally evaluate their care in terms of a continuum of satisfaction. Furthermore, the actual level of satisfaction is seen as being ascertained by asking patients to respond to items on a rating scale, which uses verbal designations or numbers to differentiate between different levels of satisfaction. Third, one-shot structured surveys give the impression that patient evaluations are relatively fixed or stable generalized dispositions.

It is not unreasonable to assume that patients hold expectations about many different aspects of health care provision. In fact early research supports the idea of a direct relationship between expectations and satisfaction (Stimson and Webb, 1975; Larsen and Rootman, 1976). However, there is a growing research literature, which suggests that the relationship is not necessarily direct. Not only is there evidence that patients express satisfaction even when their expectations have not been fulfilled (Linder-Pelz, 1982; Moores and Thompson, 1986), but in some studies it has been found that patients do not necessarily know what to expect prior to treatment (Cartwright and Windsor, 1992).

Small-scale qualitative studies of patient satisfaction have been instrumental in questioning the nature of the link between expectations and satisfaction. From an analysis of interview data from patients attending a neurological outpatient clinic, Fitzpatrick and Hopkins concluded that 'there was little relationship found between expressed expectations and subsequent satisfaction' (1983: 304). On the whole, expectations were found to be 'fluid and emergent and were revised in the light of experience' (1983: 302). The researchers describe how patients' expectations were not determined solely by previous contacts with medical services but were also influenced by their views about their current illness.

It is the use of qualitative methodology which has established the existence of a disjunction between patients' own descriptions of their expectations and the assumptions about their expectations contained in much survey-oriented research. Qualitative studies recognize the dynamic nature of patient satisfaction and acknowledge that the criteria patients use when making evaluations change over time as they acquire more knowledge and information. Given the problematic nature of the concept of expectations some researchers have suggested an alternative approach to explaining the way patients evaluate health care. According to Calnan (1988) patient perceptions of care are influenced by four major factors: the patient's initial reasons or motives for seeking medical help; the level and nature of their experiences of the health care services; their perceptions of the socio-political ideologies underlying the provision of medical care and lay views of health which shape individual decisions regarding health care.

Audit

Although the introduction of quality assurance systems into health care settings is a fairly recent development, concern for the quality of care has existed ever since the practice of medicine or healing was deemed a specialist activity. Adopting an historical perspective, Ellis and Whittington (1993) identify three stages in the development of quality assurance in health care: the embryonic, emergent and mandatory stages.

The embryonic stage dates from the very earliest days of medicine when professional codes of conduct for practitioners were first formulated. Quality assurance was not a recognized concept but the fact that there were guidelines governing medical practice suggests there was a concern for the quality of care provided by physicians. The emergent stage refers to a much later period in the twentieth century when the notion of quality assurance began to establish itself, largely through the attempts of individual practitioners and professional associations to evaluate aspects of the delivery of care and monitor the standards of education, training and practice of health professionals. The mandatory stage emerged out of the major restructuring of health care provision following the implementation of the 1990 National Health Service and Community Care Act. This piece of legislation incorporated many of the policy proposals contained in the White Paper entitled *Working for Patients* (Department of Health, 1989). While the Conservative government sought ways to reduce costs and obtain value for money, it also stressed the importance of improving the quality of services available to patients. The issue of quality was further emphasized by the introduction of the Patient's Charter (Department of Health, 1991). Periodic audits were recommended as one way of evaluating the success with which health care organizations were meeting the principal policy objectives behind the reforms.

There is much confusion surrounding the definition of the term 'audit'. Norman and Redfern (1995) acknowledge that it is a term that has acquired many different meanings in the health care setting. While Lawrence maintains that it is 'such an unsatisfactory term that it is hard to understand how it ever became adopted by the medical profession' (1993: 3). Despite these definitional problems, audit is increasingly being adopted as a method of evaluation throughout the health service. A distinction is commonly made between medical audit and clinical audit. The former is defined as, 'the systematic, critical analysis of the quality of medical care, including the procedures used for diagnosis and treatment, the use of resources, and the resulting outcome and quality of life for the patient' (Department of Health, 1989, quoted in St Leger et al., 1992: 52). It is a technique which has come to be widely used in monitoring and assessing the quality of medical care provided by general practitioners (Royal College of General Practitioners, 1985) and hospital-based medical staff (Shaw, 1990). Generally, medical audits take the form of a confidential process of peer review by members of the medical profession. In contrast, clinical audit extends beyond the field of medical practice and involves other professional groups in assessing the quality of care they provide (St Leger et al., 1992: 53). For example, a number of audit systems have been designed to measure quality assurance in nursing (Bradshaw, 1987), while the therapy professions, such as clinical psychology, occupational therapy, physiotherapy and speech and language therapy, are also showing an increasing interest in developing clinical audit activities (Kober, 1995).

The distinction between medical and clinical audit is not always clear and can prove inappropriate in some settings, particularly where an integrated system of health care delivery operates. For example, as far as primary health care is concerned, the term 'medical audit' is used to refer to audit carried out by any member of the primary health care team, which includes doctors, nurses and administrative staff (Lawrence, 1993). Indeed, there is a possibility that in the future the distinction will cease to be of any significance. As the various health professions engage in audit there is an increasing likelihood that medical audit will eventually merge into multi-professional clinical audit (Kogan, Redfern and Kober, 1995).

Audit activities can be categorized in terms of the three quality dimensions (structure, process and outcome) identified by Donabedian (1980) and described at the beginning of this chapter. An audit of structure is primarily designed to describe the quality of the physical surroundings in which health care is delivered and assess the general structural aspects of care. It can include reference to the provision and layout of treatment rooms, the age and condition of specialist medical equipment, the level of staff training, the organization of medical teams and the ratio of staff to patients. Clearly, these structural characteristics are important and have some bearing on quality, particularly insofar as there are likely to be more opportunities for promoting and improving the quality of care if the appropriate medical equipment, diagnostic services and treatment facilities are readily available to health professionals. However, an audit of structure does not contain any reference to the actual performance of those involved in the delivery of care. This is covered by process and outcome audits.

A process audit concentrates on what health care workers actually do for their patients; the focus is on the interventions actually made. An audit of outcome looks at the results of interventions, such as whether there is an improvement or deterioration in the health of the patient. The distinction between structure, process and outcome criteria in the audit process can be illustrated by the example of the study of the care and treatment provided by the primary health care team for patients with risk factors for cardio-vascular disease (Farmer, 1993). An audit of structure would, for example, establish whether or not the medical practice had its own ECG machine, and review the procedures for recording information about patients to ascertain if those at risk from cardiovascular disease could be readily identified and if information about them was easily accessible for the purposes of the routine monitoring of their health.

Farmer mentions how the medical records of patients can provide the basis for a process audit of the detection of risk factors for cardio-vascular disease. Records can be scrutinized to determine which risk factors have been detected and what advice or treatment the patient received. For example, if the patient is a smoker, do the records show that they have been offered advice on how they might give up the habit? In the broadest sense, a process audit involves all that is done to and for patients; it covers the technical, clinical and humanistic aspects of prevention, diagnosis, treatment and rehabilitation.

An outcome audit concentrates on the results to the patient of health care intervention. In other words, outcomes describe the impact and effectiveness of treatment. However, as Donabedian (1988) notes, outcome is not simply a measure of health or well-being; he defines outcome in broader terms, as the changes in a patient's current and future status that can be attributed to antecedent health care. Thus, outcomes of care include not only measures of mortality, morbidity and general physical well-being, but also changes in the patient's level of social functioning.

Outcome measures are not always easy to identify, as many factors can influence a patient's condition, thus making it difficult to ascertain whether an observed improvement in health is a direct result of antecedent care or the consequence of other factors. A distinction is often made between intermediate outcomes and definitive outcomes. An intermediate outcome describes a measure that falls between process and final outcome. In the cardio-vascular example, a stroke or a heart attack can be considered to be a definitive outcome, whereas controlling blood pressure constitutes an intermediate outcome. The most useful intermediate outcome measures are those which predict definitive outcome.

Whether an audit focuses on structure, process or outcome will largely depend on which aspects of the quality of care are being investigated. For example, if the issue is one of equal opportunity of access to treatment and services for all those in equal need in the community, a combination of a process and outcome approach would be appropriate. An audit of process would establish if certain categories of patients were more likely to gain access to particular kinds of services and identify any evidence of differential treatment. An outcome-oriented approach would look for evidence of bias in treatment outcomes. In many cases, audits of the quality of health care involve a combination of structure, process and outcome. Maxwell (1992) provides a quality assessment framework for health care systems, which incorporates Donabedian's structure–process–outcome model.

Whatever the context or form an audit takes, the basic principles are the same. With reference to general practice, Hughes and Humphrey (1990) outline the key stages in the audit process as follows. First it is necessary to articulate what general practitioners are trying to achieve for their patients. Essentially this entails defining what constitutes good practice by identifying standards and setting targets against which actual performance can be measured. This is followed by a systematic collection of empirical data relating to various aspects of the treatment and care of patients. These data are then compared against the established standards of good practice in order to identify any deficiencies or shortcomings. If performance is revealed to be below what is considered an acceptable level, remedial action is taken and the effects of this action on the quality of care becomes the subject of further monitoring. Thus, audit can be viewed as a cyclical process, hence the term 'audit cycle' (Fowkes, 1982). As Roberts (1990) observes, if medical audit is to be effective it needs to be seen as a developing, rather than a static, process.

It is commonly assumed that it is the continuous movement through the sequence of stages in the cyclical process that helps to ensure that quality of health care is maintained and indeed improved. The notion of a cyclical sequence can be extended to the patient care cycle with its four main stages of assessment, planning, implementation and evaluation (Norman, 1995). However, Norman discusses the limitations of the cycle metaphor in this, and other contexts, and notes that in certain circumstances linear or spiral models may offer a more realistic representation of audit practice.

Those groups that have influence at various stages in the audit process will largely determine the scope, content and impact of an audit. In one sense, audit is seen as a bottom-up activity initiated by health care workers concerned with monitoring professional standards and improving the quality of the service they provide. The process becomes one of measuring professional activity through self-assessment or peer-evaluation. However, given the structural and organizational changes within the health service, managerial interest and involvement in clinical audit is on the increase; this has given rise to an alternative view of audit, as a top-down management-led activity (Packwood and Kober, 1995).

The primary purpose of audit is to bring about appropriate change in practice. Medical audit has the potential to change patterns of established practice by encouraging doctors to question existing arrangements and develop new ways of working. The information provided by regular systematic audits can be used to improve the planning and delivery of care in the pursuit of higher standards and greater clinical effectiveness. Clearly there are benefits to be gained. However, it is possible to overestimate the part audit plays in improving patient care (Baker, 1991; Hopkins, 1991). Medical audits are conducted by members of the medical profession; they constitute a form of peer review and their findings are confidential. The whole process is very much under the control of the medical profession. Decisions concerning the form and content of an audit are taken by medical personnel; there is little consultation with patients and other interested parties when deciding on the criteria against which performance is to be evaluated.

Summary

This chapter has highlighted some of the methodological issues, methods choices and measurement problems encountered by researchers engaged in outcome and process evaluations of the provision and delivery of health care services. It has not been the intention to provide a systematic review of the full range of approaches available to the would-be evaluator. The primary aim throughout has been to identify the basic strengths and weaknesses of some of the more popular evaluation methods and techniques used to study the effectiveness, efficiency and quality of health care.

6   Evaluating Schools: Inspection as Evaluation

A feature of the so-called 'rise of the evaluative state' (Neave, 1988) in the 1980s was the emergence of formal evaluation as a tool used by politicians and policy-makers to inform their decision-making and justify their actions. As House asserts, 'Evaluation serves important legitimation, information, and control functions for governments in advanced capitalist societies' (1993: 52). This is nowhere more apparent than in the field of state education where concern about the standards of schools and the introduction of new policy initiatives created a demand for a more systematic approach to evaluation. For example, the Government White Paper entitled Better Schools (HMSO, 1984) stressed the need for local education authorities to develop monitoring activities to evaluate the performance of schools in their areas. The introduction of policy initiatives, such as the local management of schools, created new evaluation opportunities (DES, 1988). In the last two decades the school has occupied a central position in educational evaluation. This chapter will outline some of the main approaches to evaluating school performance and discuss the specific role inspection plays in the evaluation process.

Educational evaluation

The focus of an evaluation will determine what kinds of information the evaluator needs to collect. Decisions as to what methods will be employed can only be made once the object of the evaluation has been identified. Any of the following may form the object of an evaluation: pupils, teachers, schools, colleges, curricula, educational programmes and policy initiatives. As regards school performance evaluation there are four major sources of information: research findings; performance indicators; self-evaluation and inspections.

Research

Since the late 1970s educational research in both the United Kingdom and the United States of America has made a useful contribution to our understanding of what factors help to make schools a success. In this context a broad distinction is normally made between school effectiveness research and school improvement research. While both provide a rich source of evaluative information they represent two distinct traditions in educational research.

School effectiveness research involves making judgements about what schools have achieved, and as such concentrates on finding ways of measuring the 'quality of the school' (Mortimore, 1991). The emphasis is on identifying exactly what it is that makes schools effective. Educational research in this tradition relies heavily on easily quantifiable outcome measures in the form of school test and public examination results. These kinds of data on pupil achievement are used for identifying differential effectiveness not only between different schools but also within a single school (Nuttall et al., 1989). In specific studies school effectiveness researchers may use questionnaires, classroom observations and other data collection techniques in order to explain any observed variation in the measures of effectiveness.

As Reynolds (1995) observes, the findings of large-scale school effectiveness research in recent years have gone some way to overthrowing the view prevalent among educational researchers in the 1960s and 1970s that schools can at best only have a minimal impact on children's development. He maintains that one of the major contributions of effectiveness research has been the creation of a 'known to be valid' knowledge base, which has the potential to inform policy-making and professional practice in education. A number of researchers have attempted to categorize the salient factors that make for effective schools. For example, Sammons et al. (1995) identify eleven different factors: professional leadership; shared vision and goals; a learning environment; concentration on teaching and learning; purposeful teaching; high expectations; positive reinforcement (clear and fair discipline); systematic monitoring of progress; pupil rights and responsibilities; home-school partnership and an image of the school as 'a learning organization'.

In contrast to school effectiveness research, school improvement concentrates more on process rather than outcomes. Formative evaluations of school improvement aim to understand the processes of planned educational change in a localized context and to this end many adopt a naturalistic mode of enquiry based on qualitative methods. However, this does not mean that outcome measures cannot be usefully employed in studies of school improvement (Fullan and Hargreaves, 1992). Not only is it possible for quantitative and qualitative methods to be combined in either effectiveness or improvement research but there are gains to be made from bridging the gap between the effectiveness and improvement perspectives. As Brown asserts, 'ultimately the credibility and value of school effectiveness evaluations must be judged by the formative contribution they make to the improvement of education'

(1994: 58). She maintains that the findings of large-scale surveys undertaken by school effectiveness researchers need to be viewed in conjunction with small-scale studies in order 'to establish any sort of understanding of what goes on in schools which are identified as "more" and "less" effective' (1994: 63).

Performance indicators

Under the educational reforms of the late 1980s local education authorities were required to evaluate on an on-going basis the effectiveness of the introduction of local management of schools in raising educational standards and improving the quality of teaching and learning in schools (DES, 1988). Local education authorities were required to set objectives for their schools, provide them with resources and monitor their performance. Among other things, this generated the need for more elaborate and systematic information systems for judging schools' performance. Performance indicators are a key feature of such management information systems. According to Fitz-Gibbon, a performance indicator is 'an item of information collected at regular intervals to track the performance of a system' (1996: 5).

In discussing performance evaluation in education, Wilcox draws a distinction between 'simple indicators' and 'performance indicators': 'Simple indicators correspond to what are usually understood as management statistics. A simple indicator may become a PI (performance indicator) when it is related to a specific management objective and a value judgement is involved' (Wilcox, 1992: 66). Performance indicators can be used to measure both processes and outcomes. However, considerable care needs to be taken when selecting, analysing and interpreting performance measures.

School performance outcomes refer to what a school actually achieves. There is a common assumption that summary measures of academic progress, in the form of school test scores and public examination results, provide readily available and easily quantifiable indicators of the effects of schooling. Furthermore, the results from national examinations are thought to provide a framework within which meaningful comparisons can be made between schools. For example, schools are sometimes compared on the basis of their pass rates or the proportion of pupils achieving above-average grades. However, assessing the relative performance of schools in this way has its limitations. Information on academic performance needs to be viewed within the wider context of the characteristics of the pupils concerned and these may vary markedly from one school to another. When using the results of public examinations for the purpose of assessing the effectiveness of secondary schools, knowledge of the intake characteristics of the relevant pupil cohorts is vital if valid comparisons are to be made between schools. It is important to try to establish the 'value added' by the school when measuring learning outcomes. This can only be achieved if schools have some indication of the abilities of individual pupils at the time they enter their new school. The SATs (Standardized Assessment Tasks) tests for the National Curriculum, which are taken by all pupils at ages 7, 11, 14 and 16, are of some help in this regard.

There is a growing literature on the development of performance indicator systems in educational evaluation (CIPFA, 1988; Hulme, 1989; Oakes, 1989; Fitz-Gibbon, 1990). The A-Level Information System (ALIS) and the Year Eleven Information System (YELLIS), described by Fitz-Gibbon (1996), are in use in state schools and colleges, while a number of independent schools have adopted Middle Years of Schooling (MYIS) (Spencer, 1996). ALIS, an information system pioneered in north-east England, provides participating institutions with A-level examination results, details of teaching and learning processes, information on students' aspirations and levels of satisfaction with their courses and data on their attitudes towards the subjects they studied. The system provides a useful source of evaluative information, in the form of performance indicators, for staff in the participating schools and colleges: Fitz-Gibbon refers to it as 'monitoring with feedback' (1996: 5). ALIS enables staff to view the performance of their own institution alongside that of similar institutions linked into the system. Confidentiality rules ensure that the participating schools and colleges cannot be identified by name.

Performance indicators designed to measure the effects of schooling are not restricted to examination results and test scores. For example, data can be collected to ascertain what proportion of pupils in a school are satisfied with the education they have received, what proportion are actively involved in various types of extra-curricular activities and how many hours of homework pupils are set each week. As Gray and Jesson (1990) assert, in order to produce publicly credible knowledge about schools' performance, high quality performance indicators are required. In their opinion performance indicators should be: capable of directly measuring or assessing schools' performance; central to the process of teaching and learning; capable of covering significant parts of schools' activities but not necessarily all or even most of them; chosen so as to reflect the existence of competing educational priorities; capable of being assessed; couched in terms which make it possible to determine whether or not changes in the level of performance indicate improvement or deterioration; and few in number (Gray and Jesson, 1990: 95–6).

If performance indicators are to be used as a way of demonstrating accountability, then it is imperative that those who are being held accountable have confidence in the information-gathering procedures and assessment tools used in this type of evaluation. As Gray and Jesson observe, evaluation is not only a technical process but it is also a social process and consequently the selection and construction of performance indicators calls for consultation and negotiation.

Clearly, performance indicators are potentially important evaluative tools and provide useful information for those engaged in the management, planning and delivery of education and training. However, performance indicators are insufficient on their own to provide an adequate system of evaluation. As Wilcox notes, 'PIs do not speak unambiguously for themselves' (1992: 72) but can only be really understood by drawing on information outside their frame of reference. As such he concludes that they 'are better seen as adjuncts to inspection and self-evaluation rather than substitutes for it' (1992: 75).

School self-evaluation

School self-evaluation is a form of internal evaluation sometimes referred to as 'school-based review' (Wilcox, 1992: 15). Ever since the educational reforms of the late 1980s schools have been required to undertake an annual review of their performance. This can take the form of a planning cycle in which priorities are identified, an action plan is formulated, development targets are clearly specified and outcomes determined. The process is referred to as self-evaluation as the assessment is conducted entirely by in-house staff. The subject of this type of evaluation need not necessarily be the whole school but could be an innovative teaching method, a specialist educational programme or a set of instructional materials.

The extent to which schools can embrace self-evaluation as a viable option depends largely upon the organizational realities of school life. Any evaluation exercise has time and resource implications. Given the daily pressures under which many teachers and other school personnel operate there is no spare time to devote to conducting full-blown evaluations. Furthermore, teachers do not have the technical research knowledge required to undertake certain types of evaluation. However, some of the skills necessary for evaluation work can be acquired through involvement in participatory evaluation. Basically, this form of evaluation involves trained evaluators and practice-based decision-makers (e.g. teaching staff) working in partnership (Cousins and Earl, 1995). In this way practitioners can learn something about the fundamental aspects of evaluation and develop the skills needed to conduct their own small-scale studies in the future.

Unlike the kind of research-based studies normally undertaken by professional evaluators and social researchers, the evaluations conducted by education advisers, school inspectors and teachers often have a short time span. Wilcox (1992) refers to the approach adopted by this diverse group of practitioners as 'time-constrained evaluation'.

Inspection

Educational inspection is a form of external evaluation. It involves the monitoring and evaluation of educational institutions, services and programmes. Despite some form of inspection having been in existence in British state schools since 1833, it 'has tended to be a somewhat shawdowy and ill-understood approach to the monitoring and evaluation of the public education system' (Wilcox, 1992: 9). One of the reasons for this is the fact that prior to 1983 the reports of inspections conducted by Her Majesty's Inspectorate (HMI) were not available to the public. However, since the 1992 Education Act introduced a new national system of inspection of schools by the Office for Standards in Education (OFSTED), inspection has been given a much higher profile and is now being carried out on a scale never attempted before (Brooks and Hirsch, 1995).

Inspections provide a useful source of information about the performance of schools and the workings of the education system. In broad terms, inspection has three major uses (Wilcox, 1993: 97). First, it provides individual institutions with an independent assessment of their strengths and weaknesses and thereby helps them to identify priorities for development. Second, the aggregate findings from a number of reports of institutions in the same category can provide policy-makers and planners at local education authority (LEA) level with a knowledge base to inform strategic planning. Finally, public dissemination of inspection findings, either by publication of inspectors' reports or media coverage of the contents of reports, serves to increase the public's general awareness and understanding of educational issues.

As a method, inspection has been described as 'a modified form of naturalistic enquiry' (Wilcox, 1993: 94). Inspectors can be likened to qualitative researchers entering natural field settings, such as schools, as non-participant observers. They collect evidence by means of classroom observations and informal interviews with teaching staff. Use is also made of quantitative information such as test results and pupil attendance records. The multi-faceted nature of the inspection is clearly evident in the approach adopted by OFSTED. OFSTED inspections have elements of the following: compliance monitoring (checking on statutory requirements like attendance and adherence to the National Curriculum); systems monitoring (assessing how teaching and learning are organized and managed); performance tracking (monitoring outcomes such as test and examination results); and auditing (the efficiency, effectiveness and propriety of financial management). In addition, inspectors also make judgements about the quality of the school, the quality of the learning experience and the grading of teachers.

The OFSTED inspection is the focus of attention in this chapter. The next section provides a brief description of the development of schools inspection in England and Wales and outlines the role of OFSTED inspectors. This is followed by a discussion of the extent to which the inspection process meets the standards required for effective evaluation.

Schools inspection

A brief history

There is a long history of school inspection in Britain. The first school inspectors appeared in 1833 when the government appointed four inspectors to oversee the establishment of schools for children who worked in the factories. Six years later Her Majesty's Inspectorate (HMI) was founded. Following the 1870 Education Act, which introduced compulsory elementary education, local school boards began to employ their own inspectors who operated alongside those appointed by HMI.

Since its inception the work of HMI has revolved around three core tasks: providing central government with information on educational matters; checking on how public funds are used in the educational sector; and giving advice on good practice to those charged with the responsibility of running educational institutions. The influence of HMI has fluctuated down the years (Lawton and Gordon, 1987). During the first two decades of the second half of the twentieth century, HMI experienced a decline in its fortunes. However, with the growing concern about standards in schools in the early 1970s the demand for school inspections increased. By the end of the decade HMI had produced two national inspection reports on primary and secondary education. These reports were critical of the standards of achievement demonstrated by pupils in the middle range of ability and recommended that national standards of attainment should be established for different age groups (Bolton, 1995). By the 1990s, the number of full school inspections undertaken by HM inspectors declined as they concentrated on responding to government requests for information on specific issues. HMI visits were comparatively rare events (Thomas, 1996). With the establishment of OFSTED in 1992 the number of HM inspectors was reduced from 480 to 175, with 40 of those remaining being assigned to monitoring OFSTED inspections (Bolton, 1995). Dunford (1998) describes the decimation of HMI by the 1992 Education Act as a needless act of destruction.

Education advisers employed by local education authorities have also played an important role in inspecting schools. The period 1980 to 1992 saw a marked growth in the involvement of local authority staff in this kind of activity, as inspection teams were formed out of what had formerly been advisory teams (Wilcox and Gray, 1996). However, as DuQuesnay notes, although these advisers were often called inspectors they 'were a long way from having a systematic strategy for monitoring, evaluating, improving and reporting on the quality and effectiveness of schools' (1995: 106).

In a similar vein, Wilcox et al. (1993) report that prior to 1988 local advisory and inspection staff were ambivalent about inspection. They spent less than 10 per cent of their time on it, and this meant that under 1 per cent of state schools were inspected annually. Following the Education Reform Act (1988), funding became available to develop coherent inspection policies and this generated a fairly prompt response, with over three-quarters of local education authorities claiming to be 'engaged in considerable amounts of inspection' (Wilcox et al., 1993: 216). The inspections varied in nature. They ranged from full school inspections, through subject-specific inspections across all schools in a single LEA, to single subject inspections within one school. All in all, the LEAs responded positively to this new policy initiative and developed some innovative strategies of inspection. However, the full inspection was the method they used the least of all. When a few years later the 1992 Education (Schools) Act presented 'full scale inspections as the ideal type' LEAs were taken somewhat by surprise (Wilcox and Gray, 1996: 31).

National inspection: OFSTED

As stated above, OFSTED was established in 1992 and commenced inspections of secondary schools in September 1993 and started inspecting primary schools a year later. The Chief Inspector of Schools (Head of OFSTED) is appointed by the Secretary of State for Education, and must 'have a regard to such aspects of government policy as the Secretary of State may direct' (Harris, 1995: 50). The Chief Inspector must provide information to the government about the functioning of the public education service. This entails paying particular attention to four major areas: the quality of the education provided; the educational standards achieved; the spiritual, moral, social and cultural development of pupils; and how well schools manage their financial resources (Harris, 1995). The overarching aim is that inspection should lead to improvement (Matthews, 1995).

OFSTED inspection teams consist of one team leader (the Registered Inspector) and a number of team inspectors (including at least one lay inspector). Inspectors are required to judge the success of schools and in so doing promote school improvement. In addition to this they must address issues of:

> accountability of the school and its governors to parents, pupils and the public; compliance with statutory requirements, regulations and duties; consumer choice, in terms of information necessary for open enrolment; improvement to help schools re-focus their priorities and also implement them and finally, value for money in terms of educational gains in relation to costs. (Matthews, 1995: 68)

Instructions for gathering this information are set out in the Framework for the Inspection of Schools (OFSTED 1992; 1994; 1995a). This framework incorporates topics such as evidence required, detailed specification of the criteria for judgement, principles and code of practice. While these documents draw on the experience of HMI and LEAs in conducting inspections, they do make the methodology of the inspection process more explicit (Bolton, 1995; Wilcox and Gray, 1996).

All OFSTED inspections follow a set format. A national sample of schools is drawn up by OFSTED; school governors complete a form with details of the school; OFSTED frames a specification for inspection and invites tenders. Registered Inspectors and their teams then submit tenders which are judged on a 'value for money' basis by OFSTED. The team then makes arrangements with the school, about when to carry out the inspection, and the school sends them information, including the 'Pre-inspection Context and School Indicator'. The school provides information on a number of basic performance indicators covering inputs, processes and outputs. These include examination and test results; pupil–teacher ratio; number of pupils with Special Educational Needs; number of teachers; average class size; teaching time per week at Key Stages; pupil exclusions; destinations of pupils where applicable; income; expenditure per pupil; attendance figures and the numbers of pupils in receipt of free school meals.

Before an inspection begins inspectors meet the governors, headteacher and parents. A questionnaire is usually sent to all parents. Inspections normally last for one week, although in some cases this can be extended to two weeks. During the course of an inspection inspectors undertake classroom observations and observe all activities that take place on the school premises. Standardized assessment sheets are completed and grades awarded under a number of headings. Teachers are asked to submit samples of pupils' work representing three broad categories: below average, average and above average. Inspectors meet senior staff to gather further information and check factual details. Both quantitative and qualitative data are collected during the process of an inspection. At the end of the inspection period the Registered Inspector gives the headteacher and senior management team an oral report. A draft report is written and presented to the school governors and a final report is compiled within 25 working days. A summary of the final report is made available to all parents. 'Key Issues' are identified in the report, and the governors must prepare an Action Plan addressing these issues within 40 working days. They must report on progress to the parents at the next annual parent governor meeting. Schools judged as 'failing, or likely to fail to give their pupils an acceptable standard of education' are declared as 'requiring special measures' and the Action Plan is sent to the Secretary of State and Chief Inspector of Schools. LEAs are expected to work with such schools and are required to outline their plans to help them improve. Schools deemed to be failing receive a visit from HMI, and then further visits from OFSTED, to check whether they have improved sufficiently to be taken off the list. If not, the school will be closed and re-opened with a new name. Essentially it is deemed a new school and the measure is entitled 'Fresh Start'. The ultimate sanction is full closure, but this must be approved by the Secretary of State for Education. In October 1995, the first such school closure was Hackney Downs, a school in the London Borough of Hackney, in one of the most deprived areas of Europe.

Evaluation standards

If inspection is an example of external evaluation then it seems entirely appropriate to ask if the practice of inspection adopted by OFSTED actually conforms to the standards for evaluation. The most strongly articulated set of standards to provide guidance for effective evaluation are those produced by the Joint Committee on Standards for Educational Evaluation (1981, 1994) in the USA. Although inspection is not an evaluation strategy that features in educational evaluation in the USA, and the educational system in that country differs markedly from that found in England and Wales, the evaluation standards are sufficiently wide-ranging to encompass a variety of evaluation strategies. In essence, the evaluation standards endorsed by the Joint Committee (1994) focus on the overall quality of evaluations and are grouped into four primary criteria:

- Utility standards: an evaluation must be useful and serve the practical information needs of the intended users.
- Propriety standards: an evaluation should be conducted fairly and ethically, with due regard for the welfare of all those people involved including those who are likely to be affected by the results.
- Feasibility standards: an evaluation must be realistic, prudent, diplomatic and frugal.
- Accuracy standards: an evaluation should be carried out using valid and reliable methods of data collection.

The extent to which school inspections, as conducted by OFSTED, meet these criteria will be discussed in the remainder of this chapter. Where appropriate reference will be made to some of the key issues raised by educationalists and researchers during the early years of OFSTED. The fact that there is controversy surrounding this form of evaluation should come as no surprise to students of educational evaluation, for as McLaughlin notes, 'Evaluation embraces two separate dimensions. It is both a logic of enquiry and a part of a complex system of social and political relations' (quoted in Adelman, 1984: 5).

Utility standards

Practical evaluation studies are intended to serve the needs of policy-makers, planners and service providers. As Rossi and Freeman note, 'the worth of evaluations must be judged by their utility' (1993: 443). This means that evaluators need to address the information needs of the intended users of evaluation findings when engaged in designing and conducting evaluations. As the utility standard relating to 'evaluation impact' states: 'Evaluations should be planned, conducted and reported in ways that encourage follow-through by stakeholders so that the likelihood that the evaluation will be used is increased' (Joint Committee, 1994: 24). In order to maximize the chances of utilization, evaluators are urged to observe a number of utility standards, which cover, among other things, stakeholder identification, evaluator credibility, the scope and selection of information and report clarity and dissemination.

Stakeholder identification This involves identifying the primary groups either directly involved in, or likely to be affected by, an evaluation, in order to ensure that their needs are taken into account. In the case of schools inspection there is a wide array of stakeholders including senior school staff, teachers, governors, parents, pupils, the LEA and the government. Some consultation does take place with selected stakeholder groups. For example, inspectors undertake a survey of parents and hold a structured meeting with them prior to an inspection (OFSTED, 1996a). However, although some groups are consulted, they have no real influence over the nature or structure of an inspection.

While OFSTED inspectors are required to consult the school and the parents, there is no such requirement as far as LEAs are concerned. LEAs have extensive experience of local schools and provide some services such as psychological testing, statements of special educational need, advice and training for teachers and governors, and in some cases, advisers and local inspectors. They have a monitoring role over local schools and a duty to promote high standards. Thus LEAs have a detailed knowledge of their schools and so are capable of contributing contextual and historical information to the inspection process (DuQuesnay, 1995). The lack of involvement of LEAs in the consultation process has attracted some critical comment (Andersen, 1995).

Evaluator credibility According to this utility standard, evaluation findings are more likely to be accepted if they are seen as being produced by individual evaluators who are well informed, technically competent and trustworthy. Inspection, as a method of evaluation, needs to establish its credibility. The guidelines governing the activities of inspectors are of some help in this respect. The 1992 Education Act explicitly forbids inspectors from inspecting any school, teacher or governor with whom they have had connections in the past, thus effectively reducing the possibility of a conflict of interest jeopardizing the objectivity and integrity of the exercise (Harris, 1995). The inclusion of lay inspectors in inspection teams also enhances credibility by displaying openness to external review and guarding against accusations of a lack of impartiality in the inspection process (Perry, 1995).

Some of the early criticism levelled against OFSTED inspections has concerned the training and preparation of inspectors (O'Connor, 1995). It has been suggested that in some cases inspectors have been appointed with very little recent teaching experience. Furthermore, there are claims that mismatches have occurred between the expertise of individual inspectors and their inspection assignments, as for example, when inspectors with experience and knowledge in the secondary school sector are appointed to inspect primary schools. OFSTED inspectors receive one week's training and are then assessed through an attachment to a full school inspection. However, as Matthews (1995) and Donoughue (1996) claim, during this training would-be inspectors are trained to understand and apply the 'framework for inspection', not necessarily how to inspect. For example, Thomas (1996) notes that encounters and relationships with teachers during the course of an inspection are not focused upon in training, despite the fact that research suggests that this is a key factor in encouraging teachers to adopt new practices (Metcalf, 1994; Brimble-combe et al., 1996a; Russell, 1996).

In any type of evaluation the credibility issue is brought into sharp relief when there are a number of stakeholder groups with conflicting interests. In such a situation it is recommended that the evaluator adopts the role of 'expert witness' and 'provides the best possible knowledge on evaluation issues to the political process' (Rossi and Freeman, 1993: 419–20). Some critics of OFSTED have questioned the credibility of their findings and commented upon the similarities between OFSTED reports and official government policy (Montgomery, 1996). A case in point concerns the debate over the impact of class size on educational achievement. Empirical evidence from a methodologically rigorous long-term study in the USA demonstrates a strong correlation between small class size and high achievement, especially in reading and mathematics (Nye et al., 1993). This finding applied across all age groups but was particularly marked in relation to younger children, children from poor families and those for whom English was a second language. In contributing to the debate, OFSTED conceded that class size was an important factor at Key Stage 1 (i.e. pupils aged between 5 and 7 years) but challenged the findings of the USA study claiming that their own investigations revealed that other factors were of greater significance. Critics claim that OFSTED's findings lack credibility because they are not the product of a methodologically sound research design, such as a replication study, but are based on inspection data that were originally collected for a different purpose (Bassey, 1995; Brown, 1995). School effectiveness researchers have also criticized OFSTED for flawed methodology in some of their studies. For example, commenting on a study of reading in inner London primary schools, Mortimore and Goldstein claim that data are misused in order 'to press strongly held views about the teaching of reading' (1996: 29). Data collected as part of the inspection process are inadequate when it comes to measuring the relative effectiveness of reading schemes. A carefully controlled longitudinal study is what is called for.

Provision of information Utility standards require that the information collected should be selected so as to be 'responsive to the needs and interests' of the various stakeholders, and reports should provide essential information in a way that can be clearly understood. Without a doubt, a wide range of information is collected during the course of an inspection. The publication of the guidelines governing inspection and the wide dissemination of inspection reports mean that 'the secret garden of inspection has been thrown open to public view' (Matthews, 1995: 68).

The guidelines provided by OFSTED describe the criteria governing the collection of information. Despite some inconsistency in the use of the terms 'efficiency' and 'effectiveness' (Levacic and Glover, 1994) the framework for inspection is regarded by many as 'a suitable blueprint for evaluating schools' (Matthews, 1995). Indeed, there is evidence that headteachers find the written report and oral feedback useful for planning purposes (Maychell and Pathak, 1997). However, this is not to suggest that everything in the garden is rosy. For example, the provision of information in the form of crude raw data, as with the first publication of schools' performance league tables, caused widespread concern as no allowance was made for variations in the in-take characteristics of different school populations. Without some notion of 'value added' it is not possible to measure school effectiveness in any meaningful way. Furthermore, information obtained from classroom observations only provides a snapshot view. In commenting on inspection procedures Barber and Fuller note that, 'inspection teams are sometimes reaching conclusions on the basis of unrepresentative or cursory classroom visits' (OFSTED, 1995b: 23).

Not only should the information in reports be relevant to the needs of the intended users but also reports should be written using clear, jargon-free language. Although there is some evidence which suggests that parents find the reports fairly clear (Tabberer, 1995), a number of early OFSTED reports were criticized for their 'blandness, negative tone, unnecessary repetition and the use of language which was inappropriate for the audience' (OFSTED, 1995b: 25). This criticism resulted in the issuing of new advice on the style, format and composition of inspection reports. Despite this response independent research has revealed that not only are some reports still not easily understood by parents or governors (Ouston and Klenowski, 1996) but they read as though they are written to a formula (Wragg and Brighouse, 1996).

Propriety standards

The propriety standards drawn up by the Joint Committee (1994) endorse the view that evaluations should be conducted in a fair and ethical fashion, and that evaluators should have due regard for the dignity and welfare of all those people involved in the evaluation process. In referring to what is termed 'service orientation' the standards explicitly state that 'evaluations should be designed to assist organizations to address and effectively serve the needs of the full range of targeted participants' (1994: 81).

School inspections have a clear service orientation and mechanisms and procedures exist to identify areas for post-evaluation improvement within schools. For example, OFSTED reports contain 'key issues' and schools are required to address these in their 'action plans'. There is mounting evidence that this has had some impact on the way in which schools operate (Matthews, 1995). In monitoring a 10 per cent sample of action plans in the first year, OFSTED found that a large majority of the schools reviewed had made 'discernible progress' in addressing some of the key action points. However, it was also noted that, 'It was too early at the time of the survey to observe improvement in standards of achievement, but many schools were able to show that they had clear strategies for addressing this issue' (OFSTED, 1995b: 33).

Independent evaluations of the implementation of action plans have produced mixed findings. Wilcox and Gray (1996) found that 40 per cent of recommendations were either not implemented or only partially implemented nine months after the report. Recommendations directly related to teaching and learning were particularly slow to be implemented. Another survey of schools six months after inspection revealed that while most had begun to implement the majority of the key issues, only a quarter of the schools could be considered to have made substantial changes in this direction (Maychell and Pathak, 1997). The researchers reported that following inspection many headteachers in their sample felt that they had been left with insufficient advice on how to tackle the key issues for action identified by the inspection team.

As far as service orientation goes, inspection only has a limited contribution to make. Although inspection helps schools to identify weaknesses and shortcomings, it is not part of OFSTED's remit to give advice and guidance on strategies for post-inspection improvements. This lack of an advisory function is frequently commented upon. As Brooks and Hirsch assert, 'There seems little point in collecting ever more sophisticated information to identify ineffective schools, if schools are then given little or no assistance in finding out what they are doing wrong and working out how to change their approach' (1995: 46). This is a view expressed by a number of other commentators including Mortimore et al. (1988), Mortimore (1995) and Douse (1995). It has been suggested that teachers feel frustrated by the fact that inspection is not followed by advice and support (Earley et al., 1995; O'Connor, 1995). Feedback to teachers is crucial to improvement (OFSTED, 1995b) and Brimblecombe et al. (1996a) show that feedback affects intention to change, especially when it is constructive and prescriptive. In practice, many schools involve their LEA advisers in formulating action plans; however, advisers are somewhat disadvantaged by not having been involved in the original inspection (Bowring Carr, 1994).

Propriety standards require that evaluations are conducted with due respect for the human rights and general welfare of all the participants. OFSTED provides guidance for its inspectors on the proper conduct of inspections. Inspectors are required to respect the dignity and worth of teachers, and to treat them with courtesy and respect at all times (Bolton, 1995). There is evidence of schools reporting positive reactions to the experience of being inspected, with some headteachers and teachers commenting favourably on the manner in which the inspectors went about their task (Carpenter and Stoneham, 1995; Jeffrey and Wood, 1995; Tabberer, 1995). However, there are also reports of negative reactions from teaching staff who found inspectors to be impassive and unfriendly (Thomas, 1996).

There is a view that the inspection process itself is a cause of stress and anxiety for many teachers (Jeffrey and Wood, 1995; Passmore, 1997); women teachers and less senior staff appear to be disproportionately affected in this way (Brimblecombe et al., 1995). The process has been described as aggressive and destructive (Duffy, 1996). Reactions such as these are fairly commonplace in the world of practical evaluation. There are many features of the relationship between evaluators and stakeholders that provide a potential for conflict (Weiss, 1973a). As House notes, 'evaluators exercise special powers over people that can injure self-esteem, damage reputations and stunt careers' (1993: 164). Therefore, it is not surprising that teachers feel vulnerable and anxious when their competence as a teacher is assessed, especially as 'competence in teaching lies at the very heart of the professional self' (Gray and Wilcox, 1995: 135). Fitz-Gibbon describes the current system of inspection as demoralizing, insofar as it constitutes a form of 'Personnel Management by humiliation' producing 'ruined careers and devastated individuals' (1995a: 6). She advocates its replacement by a less expensive and more humane system for assessing individual teachers.

Feasibility standards

Feasibility standards ensure that evaluators pay due regard to practical, political and economic concerns when planning an evaluation. The data collection methods employed and the evaluation procedures followed should be practical and designed to keep disruption to a minimum. Inspection teams are allocated their own room or working area when visiting a school and inspectors do not enter the staffroom. Schools are notified of an inspection visit well in advance and thus have plenty of time in which to prepare the required documents. The general preparation and pre-inspection planning that takes place in a school can be seen as a form of self-evaluation that results in improvements occurring prior to inspection (OFSTED, 1995b; Wilcox and Gray, 1996; Maychell and Pathak, 1997). Earley et al. (1995) studied 170 schools and concluded that the majority were positive about the inspection process and felt that preparing for the actual inspection improved the quality of thought and planning that went into school management.

One of the feasibility standards refers to the need to establish the political viability of a planned evaluation. This involves anticipating the positions likely to be taken by the different stakeholder groups, in order to be able to gain their support at the outset and secure their continued co-operation. This was not the case with OFSTED inspections, which were introduced without wide consultation within the teaching profession. Consequently, the scheme met with considerable opposition from teachers. In many cases it was not that they did not see the value of what was being attempted, but that they were unhappy with the way the new scheme was being imposed upon them. Although the inspection framework has been improved and modified in response to some of the criticisms, it will take some time before the widespread hostility generated by its introduction is dissipated.

Accuracy standards

The methods used in any evaluation exercise should be both appropriate and reliable. Many of the accuracy standards for programme evaluation listed by the Joint Committee (1994) have a resonance as far as inspection is concerned. A key issue here concerns the validity and reliability of the information obtained during the inspection process. This requires giving careful consideration to what can actually be gleaned from quantitative measures and qualitative observations. For example, pupil progress is not something that is easily measured during the course of an inspection (Mortimore and Goldstein, 1996). Much of what is judged by inspectors to be evidence of learning is, in fact, observation of the conditions for learning. It is not pupil progress that is being measured but the process of learning that is being observed. Furthermore, as Fitz-Gibbon notes, 'The link between process and outcome is tenuous indeed in a complex system like education and many ways of teaching may produce good outcomes' (1995b: 99).

In some ways inspection is a form of non-participant observation. Given the emphasis placed upon qualitative observational data in the inspection process, particularly in relation to classroom observations, it is perhaps somewhat surprising to find that the issue of the reactive effects of the observer's presence is largely overlooked in OFSTED publications. The presence of an OFSTED inspector in the classroom can affect the behaviour of both pupils and teachers (Brimblecombe et al., 1995, 1996a, 1996b).

As noted previously, inspection is a 'time-constrained' form of evaluation, which has implications as far as accuracy standards are concerned. Time to weigh the evidence, interpret contradictory trends and determine where the evidence is sufficiently corroborative is short (Wilcox and Gray, 1994). Nixon and Ruddock (1993) described the ways in which intuition interacts with connoisseurship, experience and observation to form professional judgement: like good qualitative research practice it requires reflection and the following up of clues. It should go hand in hand with systematic investigation, thus providing a form of triangulation on the data. However, given the tight time schedules and criteria-focused model adopted by OFSTED there is little opportunity for working in this way. This is unfortunate as critical, reflective work, rather more intellectual than managerial, has much to contribute to the general debate on quality in education. Nixon and Ruddock (1993) suggest that it is precisely this element which gives local inspections their diagnostic edge, and defines their functions in terms of school improvement as well as public accountability. The sort of reflective analysis required in research, with researchers revisiting their data, is just not available to OFSTED inspectors working to a five-day time scale.

Summary

Much of what passes for evaluation in public sector organizations is a managerial version of performance assessment, in which the concept of accountability figures largely. This is nowhere more evident than in the field of education. Evaluation and accountability have been key themes in the development of educational policies in the UK in recent years, as witnessed by the level of debate surrounding educational standards in schools and the performance of teachers. In this chapter we have briefly described four broad approaches to measuring school effectiveness: research studies, performance monitoring and assessment, self-evaluation and inspection. Given the changes introduced to the school inspection system by the setting up of OFSTED, we have concentrated on inspection as a method of external evaluation. Drawing on the relevant research literature we have discussed the extent to which inspection meets the four basic criteria of utility, propriety, feasibility and accuracy, which in themselves may be seen to provide a set of general standards by which educational evaluations can be judged.

7   Evaluation Utilization

In the preceding chapters we have concentrated on defining the nature and scope of evaluation research and identifying some of the practical difficulties, technical concerns and theoretical issues encountered when undertaking this type of research, particularly in the fields of criminal justice, health care and education. We have noted how there is considerable debate between evaluators on such topics as the definition of evaluation, the adoption of experimental and non-experimental research designs, and the application of quantitative and qualitative research methods. However, there is a general consensus that one of the major defining characteristics of evaluation research is that it is intended to be useful. Evaluation theorists may offer different definitions of evaluation, but 'Nearly all the literature on evaluation speaks of it as an attempt to serve a decision maker' (Cronbach, 1982: 5). As a form of applied research, the primary purpose of an evaluation is to assess the impact of a social programme, with a view to providing information to help those people responsible for making decisions about the future of the programme. As Rossi and Freeman proclaim, 'In the end, the worth of evaluations must be judged by their utility' (1993: 443). The issue of the utility of inspection as a form of evaluation was discussed in the previous chapter with specific reference to education. Here we focus on the more general question of the utilization of evaluation research findings.

The utilization problem has been the subject of much comment (Leviton and Hughes, 1981; Bedell et al., 1985; Greene, 1988; Weiss, 1988a; 1988b; Patton, 1988c; Alkin, 1990). At the heart of the utilization issue is the fact that, 'Evaluation is a political act in a context where power, ideology, and interests are paramount and influence decisions more than evaluative feedback' (Shadish et al., 1991: 448). The recognition that political factors have an important influence on the utilization of evaluation findings is a principal feature of Patton's utilization-focused approach. For Patton, politics is a feature of all stages of the evaluation process, from the original conceptualization of the evaluation questions through to the issue of the implementation of the findings. The political dimension of the evaluation enterprise cannot be ignored. As Patton asserts, 'To be innocent of the political nature of evaluation is to become a pawn in someone else's game, wittingly or unwittingly – or perhaps more commonly, to miss the game all together' (1986: 291). His brand of utilization-focused evaluation places utility at a premium. The whole process becomes interactive, as evaluators are encouraged to work closely with stakeholders. Patton, on his own admission, is not prescribing a formal model for conducting evaluations, but is recommending a particular approach to evaluation that recommends collaboration between researchers and the sponsors or users of research. It is a recommendation that many would-be evaluators would do well to follow.

In a general sense, focusing on utility gives rise to three main questions. In what ways are evaluation findings useful? What are the major factors affecting utilization? What can be done to increase the influence of evaluation findings?

Use of evaluation findings

In the early years of evaluation research there was a general assumption that policy makers and programme managers would be grateful recipients of information provided by evaluators and would readily base their decisions on the findings of evaluation studies. According to this view, successful programmes would continue to be supported and programmes that were found to be ineffective, or had unintended negative effects, would be identified and either modified or discontinued. In reality, this did not prove to be the case. Indeed, it is highly unlikely to find decisions about the future of programmes taken purely on the basis of the results of a single evaluation study. However, this does not necessarily mean that evaluations do not have an influence.

Carol Weiss (1988a), one of the foremost writers on the impact of research findings on policy, describes four ways in which evaluation information is used in the decision-making process. First, the information provided by evaluators can serve as a warning that something is going wrong. For example, if early research findings suggest that some groups are not receiving the designated services, or intermediate outcome measures are not being achieved, then corrective action can be taken before the situation worsens. Second, evaluation findings can provide guidance for improving a programme. In cases where there are a number of different ways of delivering a service or treatment, a comparative analysis may help to identify which approach works the best. A third contribution evaluation can make is by way of offering a new way of looking at a familiar problem; Weiss refers to this as 'reconceptualization'. Finally, evaluation can be used to mobilize support for a project or programme.

In addressing the utilization issue, Rossi and Freeman (1993) endorse the conventional distinction between three broad types of utilization: direct or instrumental, conceptual and persuasive. Direct or instrumental utilization can be said to take place when evaluation findings are used by programme planners or managers to make observable changes in the way a programme operates. Although, as stated above, programmes are rarely discontinued on the basis of evaluation findings alone, evaluations can have an impact on budgets or lead to changes and adjustments to the internal structure of a programme (Shadish et al., 1991). Instrumental changes can be partial, such as when a programme management team decides only to act on selected recommendations, or incremental, as is the case when small adjustments are introduced over a period of time (Smith, 1988). Conceptual utilization, or reconceptualization to use Weiss' terminology, occurs when an evaluation affects how people think about a programme. It is not just the findings of an evaluation that can have a conceptual impact, but the very fact that an evaluation is being conducted can cause those involved in a programme to reflect on why tasks and activities are organized in a particular way. Finally, persuasive utilization refers to the use of evaluative information to support or challenge a particular stance taken towards a programme.

It is possible that different stakeholder groups will hold different views about the ways in which a piece of evaluative research may be used. According to Weiss, the concept of 'research utilization' is in need of clarification. The social science literature contains many 'diverse images of the processes and purposes of utilization' (Weiss, 1986: 31). Weiss identifies seven perspectives on research utilization. Although she is referring to social science research in general, the different models she identifies clearly have relevance in the context of evaluation research. The seven different meanings of research utilization are described as follows:

- The knowledge-driven model: This model derives from the physical sciences where basic research provides the foundation for applied research which eventually leads to practical action.
- The problem-solving model: According to this model empirical research findings provide the kind of information decision-makers need. Where research is commissioned to address a specific problem its findings can have a direct impact. Published research findings from studies in similar areas may also be used to inform debates and guide future action.
- The interactive model: The underlying assumption is that it is not only social researchers who provide knowledge for decision-makers. Social scientists engage in an interactive search for knowledge along with politicians, administrators, clients, practitioners, journalists, pressure group activists and the like.
- The political model: In some circumstances the political beliefs and ideological positions adopted by decision-makers may make them unreceptive to certain research findings. Thus, research becomes 'ammunition for the side that finds its conclusions congenial and supportive' (Weiss, 1986: 36).

- The tactical model: This model of the use of research has nothing to do with the content or findings of a study, but refers to how the fact that research is being undertaken can be used by decision-makers to deflect criticism or delay the taking of action.
- The enlightenment model: For Weiss, this represents the mechanism by which social science research findings are most likely to find their way into policy-making circles. 'The imagery is that of social science generalizations and orientations percolating through informed publics and coming to shape the way in which people think about social issues' (1986: 38). Therefore, it is not individual studies that are seen as exerting a direct influence, but more a case of the concepts and theories generated within social science in general that inform decision-makers.
- The intellectual enterprise model: In this interpretation of the use of research, social science is viewed as one element in the intellectual enterprise of a society. Both researchers and policy-makers influence, and are themselves influenced by, trends in popular thinking.

Weiss admits that it is not possible to single out any one of these perspectives as offering a full explanation of research utilization; each makes a partial contribution to our understanding of the use that can be made of social science research.

The uses of evaluative research can be viewed from the perspectives identified by Weiss. For example, evaluation can serve a problem-solving function. Programme managers may commission an evaluation because they lack the necessary information to decide between alternative courses of action. In such cases, the evaluator is engaged as a technical expert capable of providing decision-makers with knowledge and information to enable them to solve problems and make informed choices. This is a somewhat simplistic view of the role of evaluation, which effectively ignores the existence of the social and political realities in which programmes operate. There is an assumption that decision-makers are clear about the objectives of their policy or programme, that these objectives are shared by all the relevant stakeholder groups and that those people responsible for commissioning the evaluation have a good idea as to what new knowledge is required. Evaluations are more likely to have a direct impact on programme decisions in local, small-scale studies where there is a close, collaborative relationship between the evaluator and the programme managers.

The interactive model is also applicable in the context of evaluative research. Programme sponsors, administrators and practitioners do not rely solely on the results of evaluation studies when making decisions, but they draw their information from a myriad of sources. Evaluators can and do have an influence, but those responsible for taking decisions also draw on information they receive through reading the professional journals, talking to colleagues, exchanging experiences with their counterparts working on similar projects and listening to their own clients or service users.

It is almost a truism to state that evaluation is a highly political process. Stakeholder groups may seek to use evaluation findings in order to strengthen their arguments or justify their actions. Alternatively, they may disregard or discredit any evaluation evidence that challenges their established position. Consequently, evaluation results may be totally ignored or decision-makers may be selective when it comes to acting upon their recommendations of evaluators. As Weiss herself notes,

> Findings tend to be listened to when they confirm what decision makers already believe or disclose what they are pre-disposed to accept . . . It is rarely the case that decision makers act upon findings that disconfirm their existing beliefs or which suggest a radical and political or ideologically unpalatable change in direction. (1975: 19)

The political model of research utilization recognizes the fact that not only are there conflicts of interests and values between different groups in any evaluation setting, but that also some groups will have the power to influence the evaluation process. Where large organizations are concerned, evaluative research can have a symbolic function, as opposed to an instrumental function. As Eaton explains, evaluation research can be considered to serve a symbolic function when there is a 'ritualistic avowal of the value of research by staff members in organizational committees and in policy statements' (1969: 506) a situation that can quickly change once research findings question existing practices, challenge organizational policies and threaten the position of powerful interest groups (1969: 506). In a different context, Owen (1993) refers to the 'symbolic use' of evaluation research, as is the case when an evaluation is commissioned by an individual or organization for reasons other than the improvement of a programme or service. This fits the tactical model of research utilization, in which the commissioners have no real interest in the substantive findings, but have ulterior motives for instigating an evaluation. For example, they may use research as a delaying tactic to 'buy themselves time' before they have to make a decision, or an individual may commission a study in order to create a favourable impression among senior colleagues.

Rossi and Freeman describe evaluation as a 'real-world activity' (1993: 403). What is of primary importance is the extent to which evaluation findings lead to changes in programmes and policies that ultimately improve the human condition. Instrumental utilization is clearly a key objective. Indeed, programme evaluation can be described as the social 'engineering model in full flower' (Bulmer, 1982: 159). However, as Weiss (1978) noticed early on, the social engineering approach to research utilization has its limitations. She maintains that 'enlightenment' is a more accurate description of the impact research has on policy decision-making. Decisions, particularly in the case of public social policy, require a wide scope of information that cannot be supplied by a single evaluation study (Weiss, 1988a). Whatever the context, evaluation can serve an enlightenment function. In the case of a process evaluation, enlightenment might occur as a result of the evaluator explaining how a programme actually works and describing the mechanisms by which desired outcomes are achieved. Impact evaluations can also be enlightening by illustrating whether or not a programme works. However, given the incremental, pluralistic, political and interactive nature of the policy-making process it would be unrealistic to expect a single evaluation study to bring about a major change in policy. Rather, results from a number of studies conducted over a period of time have a gradual cumulative effect as they find their way into the various policy debates. In general, for Owen (1993) it is through the process of enlightenment that evaluations first begin to display a use value.

Having outlined the different ways in which evaluation research can be utilized we now turn to a consideration of the major factors that are likely to affect utilization.

Factors affecting utilization

Many evaluation theorists have commented on the major factors that limit the use of evaluation results (Weiss, 1972; Leviton and Hughes, 1981; Caulley, 1993). Following a review of the research literature on evaluation utilization, Alkin (1985) identified 50 factors related to utilization, which he grouped into four main categories. These are based on the characteristics of the evaluator, the involvement of potential users in the evaluation process, the circumstances in which the evaluation is conducted and the characteristics of the evaluation itself.

How an evaluator approaches an evaluation can affect utilization. For example, not all evaluators share the same level of commitment when it comes to trying to ensure that direct or instrumental use is made of evaluation findings. Looking at how evaluators view the purposes and functions of evaluation, Shadish and Epstein (1987) distinguish between 'academic evaluators' and 'service evaluators'. Academically-oriented evaluators place considerable emphasis upon evaluation as a research-based activity. Consequently, they stress the importance of maintaining the scientific integrity of evaluation research designs, ensuring that methodological procedures are adhered to and making a contribution to social science theory. In contrast, service-oriented evaluators are described as being more concerned with serving the needs of the stakeholders and to this end they are more likely to get involved in the decision-making process at the programme level. In their survey of evaluation researchers, Shadish and Epstein found that those researchers who saw themselves first and foremost as professional evaluators, in general, tended towards a service-oriented model and displayed a strong interest in conducting formative evaluations. Those researchers who described themselves primarily by reference to their particular academic discipline were found to be the ones who had a preference for undertaking summative evaluations.

Clearly, whether the evaluator adopts an academic-research perspective or a service perspective will have implications for utilization for a number of reasons. First, as Weiss notes, an 'academic orientation sometimes leads evaluators to stop short of drawing conclusions when they report their results' (1972: 111). They see their task as providing knowledge by collecting and analysing data in accordance with established procedures in the social sciences. While they report the findings, they do not see it as part of their brief to make recommendations for action.

Second, the extent to which evaluators encourage the potential users of evaluation to take part in the evaluation process can affect utilization. An evaluation that does not ask the 'right' questions will not produce the information that users require in order to help them improve their programmes. As Patton argues, in his stakeholder-oriented approach to evaluation, the problem of utilization is one of 'getting the right information to the right people' (1986: 299). Utilization-focused evaluation aims at bridging the gap between knowledge and action. This entails the evaluator developing a good rapport with the stakeholders and taking the necessary steps to actively involve them in the evaluation. If the evaluation is focused on the problems and concerns of the stakeholders then there is a greater likelihood that its findings will be acted upon. Patton describes this collaborative decision-making process, involving both information users and evaluators, as an 'active-reactive-adaptive' process. As he asserts, 'effective evaluators trying to enhance utilization decide how to act with regard to goals by reacting and adapting to particular situations and specific stakeholders' (1986: 309). It is the interaction between the evaluator and the potential users throughout all stages of the evaluation process that allows a rapport to develop and thus ensures that the findings of the evaluation are likely to be used (Owen, 1993).

It is not only evaluator characteristics that influence utilization; consideration also needs to be given to the characteristics of the potential users of evaluation results. For evaluation to have an impact, decision-makers must be receptive to evaluation findings and believe that evaluation can make a difference. In organizations where there is already an established culture of monitoring and evaluation, research findings are more likely to feed into the decision-making process. As Shadish et al. (1991) note in discussing the use component of evaluation theory, programme staff can provide an obstacle to utilization when their patterns of working are determined not in the interests of efficacy, but out of force of habit or for reasons of convenience. However, it should not be assumed that where an evaluative culture exists, research findings are always readily accepted. As described above, when discussing the political and tactical models of research utilization, findings may be overlooked or discounted when they challenge or threaten dominant values and vested interests.

The discussion of user characteristics can be broadened to take into account what Alkin (1985) describes as the wider contextual characteristics associated with evaluation utilization. By and large, these refer to features of the organizational setting in which evaluation is conducted. Weiss (1972) argues that organizations may fail to modify their practices in the light of evaluation findings for reasons of feasibility, acceptability and ideology. Managers may feel that it is not feasible to implement all or some of the recommended changes contained in an evaluation report. They may feel that introducing too many changes too quickly might undermine the stability of the organization. Organizations are concerned with ensuring their long-term survival as well as achieving short-term goals. Evaluation findings are only likely to be used if they are acceptable to programme managers. For example, if programme managers believe that proposed changes would be either unpopular with sponsors or alter the nature of the relationship between programme practitioners and clients, they stand little chance of being implemented. Organizations can also be resistant to change on account of their ideological commitments. Indeed, negative findings may be ignored and a grossly ineffective programme may be condoned if it conforms to the prevailing value system (Weiss, 1973b).

There are a number of factors relating to the evaluation itself that have an influence on utilization. First, there is the issue of timeliness. If evaluation information is to be of any use to decision-makers then it needs to be made available to them at the appropriate time, that is well before they have to make a decision. Evidence suggests that lack of timeliness is one of the main reasons why evaluation findings are not used (Davis and Salasin, 1975). There are various reasons why information might not be available on time. Programme managers may delay commissioning an evaluation, thus giving the evaluator insufficient time in which to complete the exercise. Practical difficulties may be encountered in the course of conducting an evaluation, with the result that the final report is delayed. Unforeseen circumstances may force programme managers to make radical changes to a programme before the evaluation is completed.

A second aspect of an evaluation that is likely to influence utilization concerns the perceived quality of the findings. Once decision-makers are convinced of the relevance of a particular study, Weiss and Bucuvalas (1980a, 1980b) suggest that they apply a truth test and a utility test in order to gauge the potential usefulness of the results. The truth test deals with the issue of the trustworthiness of the findings and consists of two components: research quality and conformity to user expectations. In the case of the former, stakeholders are keen to establish whether or not an evaluation is methodologically sound. For if action is to be taken on the basis of evaluation findings, then 'it is valuable to have research evidence of sufficient merit to withstand methodological criticism and convince others of one's case' (Weiss and Bucuvalas, 1980a: 253). As regards conformity to user expectations, potential users consider the extent to which evaluation findings are compatible with their own experience, knowledge and values.

The utility test is also composed of two interdependent components. These are referred to as action orientation and challenge to the status quo. As regards the former, potential users of evaluation findings look to see if the research provides 'explicit guidance and clear direction for feasible reform' (1980a: 256). Obviously the chances of utilization are enhanced if the evaluation provides clear recommendations for practical action. The extent to which evaluation challenges established practices and procedures constitutes the second type of utility question posed by potential users. The relationship between the two types of utility is described as follows: 'Action Orientation is more important for usefulness when a study does not challenge existing practice, and a challenging study is more likely to be taken into account when it is not action-oriented' (1980a: 256).

A third feature of an evaluation that is likely to have implications for utilization concerns the communication of evaluation findings. There can be no doubt that, 'Dissemination is a definite responsibility of evaluation researchers' (Rossi and Freeman, 1993: 452). Evaluation stands little chance of making a difference if decision-makers do not read final evaluation reports. Poorly structured or badly written reports are unlikely to impress.

From this brief description of the various factors affecting utilization it is possible to begin to identify some of the steps evaluators need to take in order to maximize the chances of their findings being used. In the next section we look at some guidelines for good practice, with special reference to report writing and the dissemination of findings.

How to maximize utilization

There is a great deal of sound advice available for the evaluator who is about to embark on a programme evaluation. Alkin suggests some general guidelines for evaluation that include the following: identify the key decision-makers; make sure the evaluation addresses the questions stakeholders raise; limit the study to variables over which the decision-makers have some control; communicate results early and ensure reports are short, concise and clear (1990: 227). The guidelines have implications as far as utilization is concerned.

Drawing on Solomon and Shortell (1981), Rossi and Freeman (1993: 449) list five rules evaluators should follow in order to maximize utility. First, *evaluators must understand how decision-makers operate*. Information should be presented in a form and manner most appropriate for the target audience. For example, key decision-makers are unlikely to have time to wade through lengthy, detailed technical evaluation reports; an executive summary is often more effective. Second, *evaluation results must be timely and available when needed*. In order to produce information for decision-making purposes the evaluator may be called upon to make data available before the final analysis has been completed. While methodological purists might view this as a serious breach of scientific protocol, the more pragmatically inclined would probably maintain that some information is better than no information at all. With formative evaluation research designs and action research projects anyway, there is usually a gradual accumulation of information. As Garaway (1995) observes, there needs to be 'a tolerance for imperfection'. A third rule states that *evaluations must respect stakeholders' programme commitments*. One way of increasing utilization is by encouraging the major stakeholder groups to participate in the evaluation process from an early stage. This will ensure that the evaluation is sensitive to the different views and interests of the various stakeholder groups. Fourth, *utilization and dissemination plans should be part of the evaluation design*. To increase the likelihood of evaluation findings being used, evaluators are advised to discuss with potential users how results can be interpreted and how they, as decision-makers, can best convey these findings to other interested parties. Finally, *evaluations should include an assessment of utilization*. It is recommended that, at the outset, evaluators and potential users should decide on what basis they intend judging the usefulness of the evaluation.

Clearly, good dissemination of evaluation findings is the key to increasing the chances of utilization. The final report is not the only means of conveying information to stakeholders. For example, on completion of a summative study, evaluators may choose to give an oral presentation of their findings in addition to producing a full report. In formative evaluations, where there is regular contact between evaluators and programme staff, feedback may often take place through informal conversations. Evaluators may also provide management committees with more formal briefings at their regular meetings. Whether conducting a summative or formative study, there is a case for providing stakeholders with some information during the process of an evaluation so as to prepare them for what the final report might contain and thus spare them any unpleasant surprises (Barkdoll, 1992; Robinson, 1996).

The final report constitutes the end product of an evaluation and it is important that it is clearly presented and well written. The form of the report may be prescribed by the commissioners of the evaluation or left to the evaluator to determine. Although there is no set structure for

TABLE 7.1 *Structure of a typical evaluation report*

Title page:
- title of the programme, its location and duration
- name of the organization commissioning the study
- name(s) of the evaluator(s)
- date of submission of the report

Contents page:
- a list of main sections and sub-headings
- an index of all graphs, figures and tables

Executive summary:
- a brief overview of the main findings and recommendations
- reference to those features of the research design or methodology that have implications when it comes to interpreting the findings

Introduction:
- terms of reference

About the programme:
- description of the origin of the programme, its main elements and intended objectives
- explanation of the rationale behind the programme
- outline of the circumstances in which the programme operates

About the evaluation:
- the nature, scope and type of evaluation undertaken
- statement of the main evaluation questions addressed
- reference to other evaluations of similar programmes

Methodology:
- discussion of choice of research design
- description of type of outcome measures used, nature of data collection instruments employed and reference to issues of reliability and validity
- outline of data collection schedule
- methods used to analyse the data

Findings:
- results
- discussion of findings
- recommendations for action

Appendices:
- examples of research instruments used (questionnaires, rating scales etc.)
- graphs, figures and tables not included in the main body of the report
- technical information relating to research design or data analysis issues
- references

evaluation reports, general advice concerning layout, contents and presentation is generally available (Morris and Fitz-Gibbon, 1978; Connor, 1993). Table 7.1 presents a typical structure for a final evaluation report.

If an evaluation is to make a difference then it is essential that the information provided by the evaluator be easily understood. An evaluation report differs markedly in style from a paper an evaluator might submit to an academic journal. For example, when writing for sponsors and stakeholders, technical terms should be kept to a minimum and

TABLE 7.2 *Assessing the quality of evaluation reports*

Meeting needs:	Does the evaluation adequately address the information needs of the commissioning body and fit the terms of reference?
Relevant scope:	Is the rationale of the programme and its set of outputs, results and outcomes/impacts examined fully, including both intended and unexpected policy interactions and consequences?
Defensible design:	Is the evaluation design appropriate and adequate to ensure that the full set of findings, along with methodological limitations is made accessible for answering the main evaluation questions?
Reliable data:	To what extent are the primary and secondary data collected/selected appropriate and comprehensive, offering an adequate degree of validity and reliability for the intended use?
Sound analysis:	Is quantitative and qualitative information appropriately and systematically analysed according to professional standards so that evaluation questions are answered in a valid way?
Credible findings:	Do findings follow logically from, and are they justified by, the data analysis and interpretations based on carefully described assumptions and rationale?
Impartial conclusions:	Are recommendations fair, unbiased by personnel or stakeholders' views, and sufficiently detailed to be operationally applicable?
Clear report:	Does the report clearly describe the programme being evaluated, including its context and purpose, together with the procedures and findings of the evaluation, so that information provided can easily be understood?

Source: Monnier (1997)

where necessary a glossary of terms provided. It is also a good idea to include an executive summary in a final report as it is highly likely that many politicians, decision-makers and programme staff will not read the whole report.

The evaluator seeking to establish what Alkin et al. (1979: 254) call an 'information dialogue' may decide to produce separate reports, or summaries, in different styles and formats, for different target audiences and stakeholder groups. Thus, it is possible to distinguish between 'primary dissemination' and 'secondary dissemination' (Rossi and Freeman, 1993). The former applies in the case of the production and publication of full, technically detailed reports, whereas the latter refers to the communication of evaluation findings in ways that are tailored to the needs of specific stakeholders. Secondary dissemination does not only involve specially written reports, but takes many different forms including 'memos, oral reports complete with slides, and sometimes even movies and videotapes' (Rossi and Freeman, 1993: 452). To reach a wider audience through the mass media, the main findings of an evaluation may be issued in the form of a press release.

Whatever methods of dissemination are chosen, there will always be some form of formal, written report produced at the end of an evaluation. This report will be subjected to close scrutiny by the various stakeholder groups looking for information to further their own interests. 'An evaluation report ordinarily is not regarded as a neutral document' (Berk and Rossi, 1990: 14). Users of evaluation, as well as evaluation researchers, are concerned with assessing the quality of evaluation reports. In Table 7.2, Monnier (1997) describes eight criteria to be taken into account when evaluating evaluations. Clearly, if evaluators want to maximize the impact of their evaluations then they need to identify the salient evaluation questions, adopt rigorous and systematic methodological procedures, and be aware of the need to present information in a way that can be easily understood by different stakeholder groups.

Summary

Evaluations can and do make a difference. However, to be effective, evaluators not only need to have the necessary technical skills and a deep understanding of the application of different research methods and methodologies, but they also need to be able to communicate their findings in ways which sponsors and stakeholders find accessible.

References

Adelman, C. (ed.) (1984) *The Politics and Ethics of Evaluation*, London: Croom Helm.

Albrecht, G.L. (1994) 'Subjective health assessment', in C. Jenkinson (ed.) *Measuring Health and Medical Outcomes*, London: UCL Press. pp. 7–26.

Alkin, M. (1985) *A Guide for Evaluation Decision Makers*, Beverly Hills, CA: Sage.

Alkin, M. (1990) *Debates on Evaluation*, Newbury Park, CA: Sage.

Alkin, M., Daillak, R. and White, P. (1979) *Using Evaluations: Does Evaluation Make a Difference?*, Beverly Hills, CA: Sage.

Andersen, K. (1995) 'Refuting the blistering attack', *Times Educational Supplement*, 13 October.

Anderton, K.J. (1985) *The Effectiveness of Home Watch Schemes in Cheshire*, Cheshire: Cheshire Constabulary.

Andrews, D.A., Zinger, I., Hoge, R.D., Bonta, J., Gendreau, P., Cullen, F.T. (1990) 'Does correctional treatment work? A clinically relevant and psychologically informed meta-analysis', *Criminology*, 28 (3): 369–429.

Audit Commission (1989) *The Probation Service: Promoting Value for Money*, London: HMSO.

Babbie, E. (1995) *The Practice of Social Research*, 7th edn, Belmont, USA: Wadsworth Publishing Company. (1st edn, 1973.)

Baker, R. (1991) 'Audit and standards in general practice', *British Medical Journal*, 303: 32–4.

Baldwin, S., Godfrey, C. and Propper, C. (eds) (1994) *Quality of Life: Perspectives and Policies*, London: Routledge.

Barclay, G.C. (ed.) (1991) *A Digest of Information on the Criminal Justice System*, London: Home Office Research and Statistics Department.

Barkdoll, G.L. (1992) 'Strong medicine and unintended consequences', *Evaluation Practice*, 13 (1): 53–5.

Barone, T.E. (1992) 'On the demise of subjectivity in education inquiry', *Curriculum Inquiry*, 22: 25–38.

Bassey, M. (1995) 'Inspectors ask the wrong question', *Times Educational Supplement*, 17 November.

Becker, M., Diamond, M.D. and Sainfort, F. (1993) 'A new client centred index for measuring quality of life in persons with severe and persistent mental illness', unpublished paper, Wisconsin, quoted in Albrecht (1994) op. cit. p. 18.

Bedell, J.R., Ward, Jr, J.C., Archer, R.P. and Stokes, M.K. (1985) 'An empirical evaluation of a model of knowledge utilization', *Evaluation Review*, 9 (2): 109–26.

Bennett, T. (1988) 'An assessment of the design, implementation and effectiveness of neighbourhood watch in London', *Howard Journal of Criminal Justice*, 27 (4): 241–55.

Bennett, T. (1990) *Evaluating Neighbourhood Watch*, Aldershot: Gower.

Bennett, T. (1991) 'The effectiveness of a police-initiated fear-reducing strategy', *British Journal of Criminology*, 31 (1): 1–14.

Bennett, T. (1992) 'A national survey of the organization and use of community constables', *British Journal of Criminology*, 32 (2): 167–82.

Berk, R.A. (1995) 'Publishing evaluation research', *Contemporary Sociology: A Journal of Reviews*, 24 (1): 9–12.

Berk, R.A. and Rossi, P.H. (1990) *Thinking About Program Evaluation*, Newbury Park, CA: Sage.

Berk, R.A. and Sherman, L.W. (1988) 'Police responses to family violence incidents: an analysis of an experimental design with incomplete randomization', *Journal of the American Statistical Association*, 83: 70–6.

Berk, R.A., Boruch, R.F., Chambers, D.L., Rossi, P.H. and Witte, A.D. (1985) 'Social policy experimentation: a position paper', *Evaluation Review*, 9 (4): 387–429.

Bickman, L. (1987), 'The functions of program theory', in L. Bickman (ed.), *Using Program Theory in Evaluation*, San Francisco: Jossey-Bass.

Biklen, S.K. and Bogdan, R. (1986) 'On your own with naturalistic evaluation', in D.D. Williams (ed.), *Naturalistic Evaluation, New Directions in Program Evaluation*, Vol. 30, San Francisco: Jossey-Bass.

Blagg, H. and Smith, D. (1989) *Crime, Penal Policy and Social Work*, London: Longman.

Blagg, H., Pearson, G., Sampson, A., Smith, D. and Stubbs, P. (1988) 'Inter-agency co-operation: rhetoric and reality', in T. Hope and M. Shaw (eds), *Communities and Crime Reduction*, London: HMSO.

Blaxter, M. (1990) *Health and Lifestyles*, London: Tavistock/Routledge.

Bolton, E. (1995) 'HMI 1976–92', in T. Brighouse and B. Moon (eds), *School Inspection*, London: Pitman. pp. 15–34.

Bond, S. and Thomas, L. (1992) 'Measuring patients' satisfaction with nursing care', *Journal of Advanced Nursing*, 17: 52–63.

Booth, T. (1985) *Home Truths: Old People's Homes and the Outcome of Care*, Aldershot: Gower.

Boruch, R.F. (1987) 'Conducting social experiments', in D.S. Cordray, H.S. Bloom and R.J. Light (eds), *Evaluation Practice in Review*, New Directions for Program Evaluation, No. 34, San Francisco: Jossey-Bass.

Bottomley, A.K. and Pease, K. (1986) *Crime and Punishment: Interpreting the Data*, Milton Keynes: Open University Press.

Bottoms, A.E. (1981) 'The suspended sentence in England 1967–1978', *British Journal of Criminology*, 21 (1): 1–26.

Bowling, A. (1991) *Measuring Health: A Review of Quality of Life Measurement Scales*, Milton Keynes: Open University Press.

Bowring Carr, C. (1994) 'Detached and distrusted', *Times Educational Supplement*, 7 June.

Box, S. (1981) *Deviance, Reality and Society*, 2nd edn, London: Holt, Rinehart and Winston. (1st edn, 1971.)

Bracken, M.B. (1987) 'Clinical trials and the acceptance of uncertainty', *British Medical Journal*, 294: 1111–12.

Bradshaw, S. (1987) 'Phaneuf's nursing audit', in A. Pearson (ed.), *Nursing Quality Measurement*, Chichester: HM&M/John Wiley. pp. 42–52.

Brannen, J. (ed.) (1995) *Mixing Methods: Qualitative and Quantitative Research*, Aldershot: Avebury.

Brantingham, P.J. and Faust, F.L. (1976) 'A conceptual model of crime prevention', *Crime and Delinquency*, 22: 130–46.

Brimblecombe, N., Ormstone, M. and Shaw, M. (1995) 'Teachers' perceptions of school inspections: a stressful experience', *Cambridge Journal of Education*, 25 (1): 53–6.

Brimblecombe, N., Ormstone, M. and Shaw, M. (1996a) 'Teachers' intention to change as a result of OFSTED school inspections', *Educational Management and Administration*, 24 (4): 339–54.

Brimblecombe, N., Ormstone, M. and Shaw, M. (1996b) 'Teachers' perceptions of inspection', in J. Ouston, P. Earley and B. Fidler (eds), *Ofsted Inspections: The Early Experience*, London: David Fulton. pp. 126–35.

British Medical Association (1989) *An Evaluation of the Six Experimental Sites by the Central Consultants and Specialists Committee of the British Medical Association*, Resource Management Initiative, London: BMA.

Brody, S.R. (1976) *The Effectiveness of Sentencing – A Review of the Literature*, Home Office Research Study No. 35, London: HMSO.

Brooks, St J. and Hirsch, D. (eds) (1995) *Schools Under Scrutiny*, Centre for Educational Research, Paris: OECD.

Brown, B. (1995) 'No way to judge the effect of class sizes', *Times Educational Supplement*, 24 November.

Brown, S. (1994) 'School effectiveness research and the evaluation of schools', *Evaluation and Research in Education*, 8: 1/2, 55–68.

Brownlee, I.D. (1991) *Leeds Young Adult Offenders Project: A Second Evaluation Report, 1990–91*, Leeds: NCH and West Yorkshire Probation Service.

Brownlee, I.D. and Joanes, D. (1993) 'Intensive probation for young adult offenders: evaluating the impact of a non-custodial sentence', *British Journal of Criminology*, 33 (2): 216–30.

Bryman, A. (1988) *Quantity and Quality in Social Research*, London: Unwin Hyman.

Bulmer, M. (1982) *The Uses of Social Research: Social Investigation in Public Policy-Making*, London: George Allen and Unwin.

Bulmer, M. (1986) 'The value of qualitative methods', in M. Bulmer et al. (eds), *Social Science and Social Policy*, London: Allen and Unwin. pp. 180–203.

Burgess, R.G. (1982) 'Some role problems in field research', in R.G. Burgess (ed.), *Field Research: A Sourcebook and Field Manual*, London: George Allen and Unwin. pp. 45–9.

Burgess, R.G. (1984) *In the Field: An Introduction to Field Research*, London: George Allen and Unwin.

Calnan, M. (1987) *Health and Illness*, London: Tavistock.

Calnan, M. (1988) 'Towards a conceptual framework of lay evaluation of health care', *Social Science and Medicine*, 27 (9): 927–33.

Campbell, D.T. (1969) 'Reforms as experiments', *American Psychologist*, 14: 404–29.

Campbell, D.T. (1979) 'Assessing the impact of planned social change', *Evaluation and Program Planning*, 2: 67–90.

Campbell, D.T. (1988) *Methodology and Epistemology for Social Science: Selected Papers*, Chicago: Chicago University Press.

Campbell, D.T. and Boruch, R.F. (1975) 'Making the case for randomized assignments to treatment by considering the alternatives: six ways in which quasi-experimental evaluations in compensatory education tend to under-estimate effects', in A. Lumsdaine and C.A. Bennett (eds), *Evaluation of Experience: Some Critical Issues in Assessing Social Programs*, New York: Academic Press.

Campbell, D.T. and Stanley, J.C. (1963) *Experimental and Quasi-Experimental Designs for Research*, Chicago: Rand McNally and Company.

Carnie, J. (1990) *Sentencers' Perceptions of Community Service by Offenders*, Edinburgh: Scottish Office Central Research Unit.

Carpenter, B. and Stoneham, C. (1995) 'Inspection effectiveness', *British Journal of Special Education*, 21 (2): 70–2.

Carr, W. and Kemmis, S. (1986) *Becoming Critical: Education, Knowledge and Action Research*, London: Falmer Press.

Carr-Hill, R. (1992) 'The measurement of patient satisfaction', *Journal of Public Health Medicine*, 14: 236–49.

Cartwright, A. (1964) *Human Relations and Hospital Care*, London: Routledge and Kegan Paul.

Cartwright, A. (1967) *Patients and their Doctors*, London: Routledge and Kegan Paul.

Cartwright, A. and Anderson, R. (1981) *General Practice Revisited: A Second Study of Patients and Their Doctors*, London: Tavistock.

Cartwright, A. and Windsor, J. (1992) *Outpatients and their Doctors*, London: HMSO.

Caulley, D. (1993) 'Evaluation: does it make a difference?', *Evaluation Journal of Australasia*, 5 (2): 3–15.

Chambers, D.E., Wedel, K.R. and Rodwell, M.K. (1992) *Evaluating Social Programs*, Boston: Allyn and Bacon.

Cheetham, J., Fuller, R., McIvor, G. and Petch, A. (1992) *Evaluating Social Work Effectiveness*, Buckingham: Open University Press.

Chelimsky, E. (1985) 'Comparing and contrasting auditing and evaluation: some notes on their relationship', *Evaluation Review*, 9 (4): 483–503.

Chen, H.T. (1990) *Theory-Driven Evaluations*, Newbury Park, CA: Sage.

Chen, H.T. (1996) 'A comprehensive typology for program evaluation', *Evaluation Practice*, 17 (2): 121–30.

Chen, H.T. and Rossi, P.H. (1981) 'The multi-goal, theory-driven approach to evaluation: a model linking basic and applied social science', in H.E. Freeman and M.A. Solomon (eds), *Evaluation Studies Review Annual*, Vol. 6, Newbury Park, CA: Sage.

Chen, H.T. and Rossi, P.H. (1983) 'Evaluating with sense: the theory-driven approach', *Evaluation Review*, 7: 283–302.

CIPFA (Chartered Institute of Public Finance and Accountancy) (1988) *Performance Indicators in Schools: A Contribution to the Debate*, London: CIPFA.

Clarke, M.J. and Stewart, L.A. (1994), 'Obtaining data from randomised controlled trials: how much do we need for reliable and informative meta-analyses?', *British Medical Journal*, 309: 1007–10.

Clarke, R.V.G. (1983) 'Situational crime prevention: its theoretical basis and practical scope', in M. Tonry and N. Morris (eds), *Crime and Justice: An Annual Review of Research*, Vol. 4, Chicago: Chicago University Press.

Clarke, R.V.G. and Cornish, D.B. (1972) *The Controlled Trial in Institutional Research: Paradigm or Pitfall?*, Home Office Research Study No. 15, London: HMSO.

Clarke, R.V.G. and Sinclair, I. (1974) 'Towards more effective treatment evaluation', in Council of Europe, *Collected Studies in Criminological Research*, Vol. XII. pp. 55–82.

Cochrane, A.L. (1972) *Effectiveness and Efficiency: Random Reflections on Health Services*, London: Nuffield Provincial Hospitals Trust.

Cohen, S. (1979) 'The punitive city: notes on the dispersal of social control', *Contemporary Crisis*, 3: 339–69.

Cohen, S. (1985) *Visions of Social Control: Crime, Punishment and Classification*, Cambridge: Polity Press.

Connell, J.P. and Kubisch, A.C. (1997) 'Applying a theory of change approach to the evaluation of community initiative: progress, prospects and problems', unpublished paper.

Connor, A. (1993) *Monitoring and Evaluation Made Easy: A Handbook for Voluntary Organisations*, Edinburgh: HMSO.

Cook, T.D. (1983) 'Quasi-experimentation: its ontology, epistemology and methodology', in G. Morgan (ed.), *Beyond Method: Strategies for Social Research*, Beverly Hills, CA: Sage.

Cook, T.D. and Campbell, D.T. (1976) 'The design and conduct of quasi-experiments and true experiments in field settings', in M.D. Dunnette (ed.), *Handbook of Industrial and Organizational Psychology*, 2nd edn, Chicago: Rand McNally.

Cook, T.D. and Campbell, D.T. (1979) *Quasi-Experimentation: Design and Analysis Issues for Field Settings*, Chicago: Rand McNally.

Cook, T.D. and Reichardt, C.S. (1979) *Qualitative and Quantitative Methods in Evaluation Research*, Beverly Hills, CA: Sage.

Copas, J.B. (1994) 'On using crime statistics for prediction', in M. Walker (ed.), *Statistics of Crime*, Oxford: Oxford University Press.

Cordray, D.S. and Lipsey, M.W. (1986) 'Program evaluation and program research', in *Evaluation Studies: A Review Annual*, Beverly Hills, CA: Sage. pp. 17–31.

Corimer, W.H. and Corimer, L.S. (1979) *Interviewing Strategies for Helpers*, Monterey, CA: Brooks/Cole.

Cornish, D.B. and Clarke, R.V.G. (1975) *Residential Treatment and its Effects on Delinquency*, Home Office Research Study No. 32, London: HMSO.

Coulter, A. (1991) 'Evaluating the outcomes of health care', in J. Gabe, M. Calnan and M. Bury (eds), *The Sociology of the Health Service*, London: Routledge. pp. 115–39.

Cousins, J.B. and Earl, L.M. (1995) *Participatory Evaluation in Education: Studies in Evaluation Use and Organizational Learning*, London: Falmer Press.

Cracknell, B. (1996) 'Evaluating development aid', *Evaluation*, 2 (1): 23–34.

Cranberg, L. (1979) 'Do retrospective controls make clinical trials "inherently" fallacious?', *British Medical Journal*, 2: 1265–6.

Crawford, A. and Jones, M. (1995) 'Inter-agency co-operation and community-based crime prevention', *British Journal of Criminology*, 35 (1): 17–33.

Crawford, A. and Jones, M. (1996) 'Kirkholt revisited: some reflections on the transferability of crime prevention initiatives', *Howard Journal of Criminal Justice*, 35 (1): 21–39.

Creswell, J.W. (1994) *Research Design: Qualitative and Quantitative Approaches*, Thousand Oaks, CA: Sage.

Cronbach, L.J. (1982) *Designing Evaluations of Educational and Social Programs*, San Francisco: Jossey-Bass.

Cronbach, L.J., Ambron, S.R., Dornbusch, S.M., Hess, R.D., Hornik, R.C., Phillips, D.C., Walker, D.F. and Weiner, S.S. (1980) *Toward Reform of Program Evaluation*, San Francisco: Jossey-Bass.

Dalley, G. and Carr-Hill, R. (1991) *Pathways to Quality, a Study of Quality Management Initiatives in the NHS*, York: Centre for Health Economics, University of York.

Daly, J. and McDonald, I. (1992) 'Introduction: the problem as we saw it', in J. Daly, I. McDonald and E. Willis (eds), *Researching Health Care: Designs, Dilemmas, Disciplines*, London: Tavistock/Routledge. pp. 1–11.

Davis, H.R. and Salasin, S.E. (1975) 'The utilization of evaluation', in E.L. Struening and M. Guttentag (eds), *Handbook of Evaluation Research*, Vol. I, Beverly Hills, CA: Sage. pp. 621–66.

Day, P. (1993) 'Accountability', in N. Thomas, N. Deakin and J. Doling (eds), *Learning From Innovation: Housing and Social Care in the 1990s*, Birmingham: Birmingham Academic Press. pp. 86–104.

Dennis, M.L. (1990) 'Assessing the validity of randomized field experiments', *Evaluation Review*, 14: 347–73.

Dennis, M.L. and Boruch, R.F. (1989) 'Randomized experiments for planning and testing projects in developing countries: threshold conditions', *Evaluation Review*, 13: 292–309.

Denzin, N.K. (1970) *The Research Act in Sociology*, London: Butterworths.

Denzin, N.K. (1978) *Sociological Methods: A Sourcebook*, 2nd edn, New York: McGraw-Hill.

Denzin, N.K. (1989) *Interpretive Interactionism*, Newbury Park, CA: Sage.

Department of Health (1989) *Working For Patients*, Cmnd 555, London: HMSO.

Department of Health (1991) *The Patient's Charter*, London: HMSO.

DES (1988) *Education Reform Act: Local Management of Schools*, Circular 7/88, London: DES.

Deutscher, I. (1977) 'Towards avoiding the goal trap in evaluation research', in F.G. Caro (ed.), *Readings in Evaluation Research*, New York: Russell Sage. pp. 221–38.

de Vaus, D.A. (1996) *Surveys in Social Research*, 4th edn, London: UCL Press.

Dexter, L.A. (1970) *Elite and Specialized Interviewing*, Evanston, IL: Northwestern University.

DHHS (US Department of Health and Human Services), Office of Disease Prevention and Promotion (1992) *A Framework for Cost-Utility Analysis of Government Health Care Programs*, Washington, DC: Government Printing Office.

DHSS (Department of Health and Social Security) (1983) *National Health Service Management Inquiry* (Griffiths Report), London: HMSO.

DHSS (1985) *Performance Indicators for the National Health Service: Guidance for Users*, London: DHSS.

d'Houtard, A. and Field, M.G. (1984) 'The image of health: variations in perception by social class in a French population', *Sociology of Health and Illness*, 6: 30–60.

Diehl, L. and Perry, D.J. (1986) 'A comparison of randomized concurrent control groups with matched historical controls: are historical controls valid?', *Journal of Clinical Oncology*, 4: 114–20.

Dingwall, R. (1992) 'Don't mind him – he's from Barcelona: qualitative methods in health studies', in J. Daly, I. McDonald and E. Willis (eds), *Researching Health Care: Designs, Dilemmas, Disciplines*, London: Tavistock/Routledge. pp. 161–75.

Doig, B. and Littlewood, J. (eds) (1992) *Policy Evaluation: The Role of Social Research*, London: HMSO.

Doll, R. (1973) 'Monitoring the National Health Service', *Proceedings of the Royal Society of Medicine*, 66: 729–40.

Donabedian, A. (1980) *Explorations in Quality Assessment and Monitoring, Volume 1: The Definition of Quality and Approaches to its Assessment*, Ann Arbor: Health Administration Press.

Donabedian, A. (1988) 'Quality assessment and assurance: unity of purpose, diversity of means', *Inquiry*, 25: 173–92.

Donoughue, C. (1996) '"A fit and proper person" – the training of inspectors', in J. Ouston, P. Earley and B. Fidler (eds), *Ofsted Inspections: The Early Experience*, London: David Fulton. pp. 33–42.

Douse, M. (1995) *Ofsted & Onward*, Reading: CBfT.

Dowds, L. and Mayhew, P. (1994) *Participation in neighbourhood watch: Findings from the 1992 British Crime Survey*, Research Findings No. 11, Home Office Research and Statistics Department, London: Home Office.

Drummond, M.F. (1989) 'Output measurement for resource allocation decisions in health care', *Oxford Review of Economic Policy*, 5: 1.

Drummond, M.F., Stoddart, G.L. and Torrance, G.W. (1987) *Methods for the Economic Evaluation of Health Care Programmes*, Oxford: Oxford University Press.

Duffy, M. (1996) 'Someone's watching', *Times Educational Supplement*, 8 March.

Dunford, J.E. (1998) *Her Majesty's Inspectorate of Schools of Schools Since 1944*, London: Woburn Press.

DuQuesnay, H. (1995) 'The LEA of the future: school accountability, inspection and support', in T. Brighouse and B. Moon (eds), *School Inspection*, London: Pitman. pp. 105–119.

Earley, P., Fidler, B. and Ouston, J. (1995) 'Secondary heads fear planning blight', *Times Educational Supplement*, 10 January.

Eaton, J.W. (1969) 'Symbolic and substantive evaluative research', in H.C. Schulberg, A. Sheldon and F. Baker (eds), *Program Evaluation in the Health Fields*, New York: Behavioral Publications, Inc. pp. 506–24.

Ebrahim, S. (1990) 'Measurement of impairment, disability and handicap', in A. Hopkins and D. Costain (eds), *Measuring the Outcomes of Medical Care*, London: Royal College of Physicians. pp. 27–41.

Egger, M. and Davey-Smith, G. (1995) 'Misleading meta-analysis: lessons from "an effective, safe, simple" intervention that wasn't', *British Medical Journal*, 310: 752–4.

Eglin, P.A. (1987) 'The meaning and use of official statistics in the explanation of deviance', in R.J. Anderson, J.A. Hughes and W.W. Sharrock (eds), *Classic Disputes in Sociology*, London: Allen and Unwin.

Ekblom, P. (1989) 'Evaluating crime prevention: the management of uncertainty', in C. Kemp (ed.), *Current Issues in Criminological Research*, British Criminological Conference Proceedings, Vol. 2, Bristol: Bristol and Bath Centre for Criminal Justice.

Ekblom, P. (1992) 'The safer cities programme impact evaluation: problems and progress', *Studies on Crime and Crime Prevention*, 1: 35–51.

Ekblom, P. and Pease, K. (1995) 'Evaluating crime prevention', in M. Tonry and D.P. Farrington (eds), *Building a Safer Society: Strategic Approaches to Crime Prevention*, Crime and Justice: A Review of Research, Vol. 19, Chicago: University of Chicago Press. pp. 585–662.

Elden, M. and Chisholm, R.F. (1993) 'Emerging varieties of action research: introduction to the special issue', *Human Relations*, 46 (2): 121–41.

Elden, M. and Levin, M. (1991) 'Cogenerative learning: bringing participation into action research', in W.F. Whyte (ed.), *Participatory Action Research*, Newbury Park, CA: Sage.

Ellis, R. and Whittington, D. (1993) *Quality Assurance in Health Care: A Handbook*, London: Edward Arnold.

Epstein, A.M., Hall, J.A., Son, L.H. and Conant, L. (1989) 'Using proxies to evaluate quality of life: can they provide information about patients' health status and satisfaction with medical care?', *Medical Care*, 27: 91–8.

Evason, E. and Whittington, D. (1991) 'Patient satisfaction studies: problems and implications explored in a pilot study in Northern Ireland', *Health Education Journal*, 50 (2): 73–97.

Farmer, A. (1993) 'Preventive care: cardiovascular disease', in M. Lawrence and T. Schofield (eds), *Medical Audit in Primary Health Care*, Oxford: Oxford University Press. pp. 110–21.

Farrington, D.P. and Tarling, R. (eds) (1985) *Prediction in Criminology*, Albany, New York: SUNY Press.

Feek, W. (1988) *Evaluation*, London: Bedford Square Press and National Council for Voluntary Organisations.

Fein, E., Staff, I.L. and Kobylenski, S. (1993) 'The evaluator as power merchant', *Evaluation Practice*, 14 (1): 9–13.

Fetterman, D.M. (ed.) (1988) *Qualitative Approaches to Evaluation in Education: The Silent Scientific Revolution*, New York: Praeger.

Fetterman, D.M. (1994a) 'Empowerment evaluation', *Evaluation Practice*, 15 (1): 1–15.

Fetterman, D.M. (1994b) 'Steps of empowerment evaluation', *Evaluation and Program Planning*, 17 (3): 305–13.

Fielding, N.G. and Fielding, J.L. (1986) *Linking Data*, Qualitative Research Methods Series, Vol. 4, Beverly Hills, CA: Sage.

Fink, A. (1993) *Evaluation Fundamentals: Guiding Health Programs, Research and Policy*, Newbury Park, CA: Sage.

Firestone, W.A. (1990) 'Accommodation: toward a paradigm-praxis dialectic', in E.G. Guba (ed.), *The Paradigm Dialog*, Newbury Park, CA: Sage. pp. 105–24.

Fitz-Gibbon, C.T. (ed.) (1990) *Performance Indicators*, BERA Dialogues 2, Clevedon: Multilingual Matters.

Fitz-Gibbon, C.T. (1995a) 'Mental cruelty and inadequate methodology?', *Education Today and Tomorrow*, 47 (2): 6–7.

Fitz-Gibbon, C.T. (1995b) 'Ofsted scmofsted', in T. Brighouse and B. Moon (eds), *School Inspection*, London: Pitman.

Fitz-Gibbon, C.T. (1996) *Monitoring Education: Indicators, Quality and Effectiveness*, London: Cassell.

Fitz-Gibbon, C.T. and Morris, L.L. (1987) *How to Design a Program Evaluation*, Newbury Park, CA: Sage.

Fitz-Gibbon, C.T. and Morris, L.L. (1996) 'Theory-based evaluation', *Evaluation Practice*, 17 (2): 177–84.

Fitzpatrick, R. (1990) 'Measurement of patient satisfaction', in A. Hopkins and D. Costain (eds), *Measuring the Outcomes of Medical Care*, London: Royal College of Physicians. pp. 19–26.

Fitzpatrick, R. (1994) 'Applications of health status measures', in C. Jenkins (ed.), *Measuring Health and Medical Outcomes*, London: UCL Press. pp. 27–41.

Fitzpatrick, R. (1997) 'The assessment of patient satisfaction', in C. Jenkinson (ed.), *Assessment and Evaluation of Health and Medical Care: A Methods Text*, Buckingham: Open University Press. pp. 85–101.

Fitzpatrick, R. and Hopkins, A. (1983) 'Problems in the conceptual framework of patient satisfaction research: an empirical exploration', *Sociology of Health and Illness*, 5 (3): 297–311.

Fitzpatrick, R., Ziebland, S., Jenkinson, C., Mowat, A. and Mowat, A. (1992) 'The importance of sensitivity to change as a criterion for selection of health status measures', *Quality in Health Care*, 1: 89–93.

Folkard, M.S., Fowles, A.J., McWilliams, B.C., McWilliams, W., Smith, D.D., Smith, D.E. and Walmsley, G.R. (1974) *IMPACT. Volume I*, Home Office Research Study No. 24, London: HMSO.

Folkard, M.S., Smith, D.E. and Smith, D.D. (1976) *IMPACT. Volume II*, Home Office Research Study No. 36, London: HMSO.

Forrester, D., Chatterton, M. and Pease, K. (1988) *The Kirkholt Burglary Prevention Project*, Rochdale, Crime Prevention Unit Paper No. 13, London: Home Office.

Foster, J. and Hope, T. (1993) *Housing, Community and Crime: The Impact of the Priority Estates Project*, Home Office Research Study No. 131, London: HMSO.

Fowkes, F.G.R. (1982), 'Medical audit cycle', *Medical Education*, 16: 228–38.

Fowler, F.J. (1988) *Survey Research Methods*, London: Sage.

Frost, H., Klaber Moffett, J.A., Moser, J.S. and Fairbank, J.C.T. (1995) 'Randomised controlled trial for evaluation of fitness programme for patients with chronic low back pain', *British Medical Journal*, 310: 151–4.

Fullan, M. and Hargreaves, A. (1992) *What's Worth Fighting For in Your School? Working Together for Improvement*, Buckingham: Open University Press.

Fuller, R. and Petch, A. (1995) *Practitioner Research: The Reflexive Social Worker*, Buckingham: Open University Press.

Gage, N. (1989) 'The paradigm wars and their aftermath', *Educational Researcher*, 18: 4–10.

Garaway, G.B. (1995) 'Participatory evaluation', *Studies in Educational Evaluation*, 21: 85–102.

Giddens, A. (1976) *New Rules of Sociological Method*, New York: Basic Books.

Gilbert, J.P., Light, R.J. and Mosteller, F. (1975) 'Assessing social innovations: an experimental base for policy', in C. Bennett and A.A. Lumsdaine (eds), *Evaluation and Experiment: Some Critical Issues in Assessing Social Programs*, New York: Academic Press.

Gilling, D. (1993) 'Crime prevention discourse and the multi-agency approach', *International Journal of the Sociology of Law*, 21: 145–57.

Glaser, B. and Strauss, A. (1967) *The Discovery of Grounded Theory*, Chicago: Aldine.

Goddard, A. and Powell, J. (1994) 'Using naturalistic and economic evaluation to assist service planning: a case study in the United Kingdom', *Evaluation Review*, 18 (4): 472–92.

Gold, R.L. (1969) 'Roles in sociological field observations', in G.J. McCall and J.L. Simmons (eds), *Issues in Participant Observation: A Text and Reader*, London: Addison-Wesley. pp. 30–8.

Goldman, A.E. and McDonald, S.S. (1988) *The Group-Depth Interview: Principles and Practice*, Englewood Cliffs, NJ: Prentice-Hall.

Goodinson, S. and Singleton, J. (1989) 'Quality of life: a critical review of current concepts, measures and their clinical implications', *International Journal of Nursing Studies*, 26 (4): 327–41.

Gorden, R.L. (1980) *Interviewing: Strategy, Techniques and Tactics*, 3rd edn, New York: Dorsey Press.

Gray, J. and Jesson, D. (1990) 'The negotiation and construction of performance indicators: some principles, proposals and problems', *Evaluation and Research in Education*, 4 (2): 93–108.

Gray, J. and Wilcox, B. (1995) 'The methodologies of school inspection: issues and dilemmas', in T. Brighouse and B. Moon (eds), *School Inspection*, London: Pitman. pp. 127–42.

Greene, J.G. (1988) 'Stakeholder participation and utilization in program evaluation', *Evaluation Review*, 12 (2): 91–116.

Greene, J.G. (1994) 'Qualitative program evaluation: practice and promise', in N.K. Denzin and Y.S. Lincoln (eds), *Handbook of Qualitative Research*, Thousand Oaks, CA: Sage. pp. 530–54.

Greene, J.G. and McClintock, C. (1985) 'Triangulation in evaluation: design and analysis issues', *Evaluation Review*, 9 (5): 523–47.

Greenwood, D.J., Whyte, W.F. and Harkavy, I. (1993) 'Participatory action research as a process and as a goal', *Human Relations*, 46 (2): 175–91.

Grimley Evans, J. (1992) 'Quality of life assessments and elderly people', in A. Hopkins (ed.), *Measures of the Quality of Life*, London: Royal College of Physicians. pp. 107–20.

Gruel, L. (1975) 'The human side of evaluating human service programs: problems and prospects', in M. Guttentag and E.L. Struening (eds), *Handbook of Evaluation Research*, Beverly Hills, CA: Sage. pp. 11–28.

Guba, E.G. (1972) 'The failure of educational evaluation', in C.H. Weiss (ed.), *Evaluating Action Programs*, Boston: Allyn and Bacon. pp. 250–66.

Guba, E.G. (1978) *Toward a Methodology of Naturalistic Inquiry in Educational Evaluation*, Monograph Series 8, Los Angeles: UCLA, Center for the Study of Evaluation.

Guba, E.G. (1985) 'The context of emergent paradigm research', in Y.S. Lincoln (ed.), *Organizational Theory and Inquiry: The Paradigm Revolution*, Beverly Hills, CA: Sage.

Guba, E.G. (1986) 'What have we learned about naturalistic evaluation?', *Evaluation Practice*, 8 (1): 22–43.

Guba, E.G. (ed.) (1990) *The Paradigm Dialog*, Newbury Park, CA: Sage.

Guba, E.G. and Lincoln, Y.S. (1981) *Effective Evaluation: Improving the Usefulness of*

Evaluation Results Through Responsive and Naturalistic Approaches, San Francisco: Jossey-Bass.

Guba, E.G. and Lincoln, Y.S. (1988) 'Do inquiry paradigms imply inquiry methodologies?', in D.M. Fetterman (ed.), *Qualitative Approaches to Evaluation in Education: The Silent Scientific Revolution*, New York: Praeger. pp. 89–115.

Guba, E.G. and Lincoln, Y.S. (1989) *Fourth Generation Evaluation*, Newbury Park, CA: Sage.

Guyatt, G., Kirschner, B. and Jaeschke, R. (1992) 'Measuring health status: what are the necessary measurement properties?', *Journal of Clinical Epidemiology*, 45: 1341–5.

Halpern, S. (1985) 'What the public thinks of the NHS', *Health and Social Services Journal*, 95: 702–4.

Hammersley, M. and Atkinson, P. (1983) *Ethnography: Principles in Practice*, London: Tavistock.

Harré, R. (1972) *The Philosophies of Science*, Oxford: Oxford University Press.

Harris, N.S. (1995) 'Quality control and accountability to the consumer: an evaluation of the Education (Schools) Act 1992', in T. Brighouse and B. Moon (eds), *School Inspection*, London: Pitman. pp. 46–66.

Haynes, R.B. (1988) 'Selected principles of the measurement and setting of priorities of death, disability and suffering in clinical trials', *American Journal of Medical Sciences*, 296: 364–9.

Henderson-Stewart, D. (1990) 'Performance measurement and review in local government', in M. Cave, M. Kogan and R. Smith (eds), *Output and Performance Measurement in Government: The State of the Art*, London: Jessica Kingsley.

Henerson, M.E., Morris, L.L. and Fitz-Gibbon, C.T. (1987) *How to Measure Attitudes*, Newbury Park, CA: Sage.

Herman, J.L., Morris, L.L. and Fitz-Gibbon, C.T. (1987) *Evaluator's Handbook*, Newbury Park, CA: Sage.

Hickson, D.J. (1987) 'Decision making at the top of organizations', *Annual Review of Sociology*, 13.

Higginson, I. and McCarthy, M. (1989) 'Evaluation of palliative care: steps to quality assurance?', *Palliative Medicine*, 3: 267–74.

Hine, J. (1997) 'Trying to unravel the Gordian Knot: an evaluation of community service orders', in G. Mair (ed.), *Evaluating the Effectiveness of Community Penalties*, Aldershot: Avebury. pp. 96–119.

HMSO (1956) *Committee of Enquiry into the Cost of the National Health Service: the Guillebaud Report*, Cmnd 663, London: HMSO.

HMSO (1979) *Report of the Royal Commission on the National Health Service*, Cmnd 7615, London: HMSO.

HMSO (1982) *Efficiency and Effectiveness in the Civil Service: The Financial Management Initiative*, London: HMSO.

HMSO (1984) *Better Schools*, Cmnd 9469, London: HMSO.

HM Treasury (1989) *The Government's Expenditure Plans*, Department of Health, London: HMSO.

Hoinville, G. and Jowell, R. in association with Airey, C., Brook, L., Courtney, C. et al. (1987) *Survey Research Practice*, London: Heinemann.

Home Office (1977) *Review of Criminal Justice Policy 1976*, London: HMSO.

Home Office (1978) *The Sentence of the Court: A Handbook for the Courts on the Treatment of Offenders*, 3rd edn, London: HMSO.

Home Office (1983) 'Reconvictions of those given Community Service Orders', *Home Office Statistical Bulletin*, London: HMSO.

Home Office (1988) *Tackling Offending: An Action Plan*, London: Home Office.

Home Office (1990a) *Crime, Justice and Protecting the Public*, Cmnd 965, London: HMSO.

Home Office (1990b) *Partnership in Crime Prevention*, London: HMSO.

Hope, T. (1988) 'Support for neighbourhood watch: a British Crime Survey analysis', in T. Hope and M. Shaw (eds), *Communities and Crime Reduction*, London: HMSO. pp. 146–61.

Hopkins, A. (1991) 'Approaches to medical audit', *Journal of Epidemiology and Community Health*, 45: 1–3.

House, E.R. (1993) *Professional Evaluation: Social Impact and Political Consequences*, Newbury Park, CA: Sage.

Hudson, J. (1977) 'Problems of measurement in criminal justice', in L. Rutman (ed.), *Evaluation Research Methods: A Basic Guide*, Beverly Hills, CA: Sage. pp. 73–100.

Hughes, J.A. (1976) *Sociological Analysis: Methods of Discovery*, London: Nelson.

Hughes, J. and Humphrey, C. (1990) *Medical Audit in General Practice: A Practical Guide to the Literature*, London: King Edward's Hospital Fund for London.

Hulme, G. (1989) 'Performance evaluation and performance indicators for schools', in R. Levacic (ed.), *Financial Management in Education*, Milton Keynes: Open University Press. pp. 189–98.

Humphrey, C., Carter, P. and Pease, K. (1992) 'A reconviction predictor for probationers', *British Journal of Social Work*, 22: 33–46.

Hunt, S., McEwen, J. and McKenna, S. (1986) *Measuring Health Status*, London: Croom Helm.

Hyman, H.H., Cobb, W.J., Feldman, J.J., Hart, C.W. Stember, C.H. (1954) *Interviewing in Social Research*, Chicago: University of Chicago Press.

Illsey, R. (1980) *Professional or Public Health?*, London: Nuffield Provincial Hospitals Trust.

Jeffrey, B. and Wood, S.P. (1995) 'Panic on parade', *Times Educational Supplement*, Update, 8 September.

Jenkinson, C. and McGee, H. (1997) 'Patient assessed outcomes: measuring health status and quality of life', in C. Jenkinson (ed.), *Assessment and Evaluation of Health and Medical Care: A Methods Text*, Buckingham: Open University Press. pp. 64–84.

Jick, T.D. (1983) 'Mixing qualitative and quantitative methods: triangulation in action', in J. Van Maanen (ed.), *Qualitative Methodology*, Beverly Hills, CA: Sage. pp. 135–47.

Joint Committee on Standards for Educational Evaluation (1981) *Standards for Evaluations of Educational Programs, Projects and Material*, New York: McGraw-Hill.

Joint Committee on Standards for Educational Evaluation (1994) *Program Evaluation Standards*, 2nd edn, Thousand Oaks, CA: Sage.

Jones, L., Leneman, L. and Maclean, U. (1987) *Consumer Feedback for the NHS: A Literature Review*, London: King's Fund.

Judd, C.M. and Kenny, D.A. (1981) *Estimating the Effects of Social Interventions*, Cambridge: Cambridge University Press.

Jupp, V. (1989) *Methods of Criminological Research*, London: Unwin Hyman.

Kaplan, R.M. (1995) 'Utility assessment for estimating quality-adjusted life years', in F.A. Sloan (ed.), *Valuing Health Care: Costs, Benefits and Effectiveness of Pharmaceuticals and other Medical Technologies*, Cambridge: Cambridge University Press. pp. 31–60.

Kaplan, R.M. and Anderson, J.P. (1988) 'The quality of well-being scale: rationale for a single quality of life index', in S.R. Walker and R.M. Rosser (eds), *Quality of Life: Assessment and Application*, Lancaster: MTP Press. pp. 51–77.

Kaplan, R.M. and Bush, J.W. (1982) 'Health-related quality of life measurement for evaluation research and policy analysis', *Health Psychology*, 1 (1): 61–80.

Karabinas, A., Monaghan, B. and Sheptycki, J.W.E. (1996) 'An evaluation of Craigmillar Youth Challenge', *Howard Journal of Criminal Justice*, 35 (2): 113–29.

Keat, R. and Urry, J. (1975) *Social Theory as Science*, London: Routledge.

Kelman, H.R. (1976) 'Evaluation of health care quality by consumers', *International Journal of Health Services*, 6: 431.

Kincey, J., Bradshaw, P. and Ley, P. (1975) 'Patients' satisfaction and reported acceptance of advice in general practice', *Journal of the Royal College of General Practitioners*, 25: 558.

Kind, P., Rosser, R. and Williams, A. (1982) 'Valuation of quality of life: some psychometric evidence', in M. W. Jones-Lee (ed.), *The Value of Life and Safety*, Leiden: North Holland.

Knivett, T., Cripps, L., Merrington, S. and Hawley, A. (1989) *The Cambridgeshire 4B Offender Unit: A Report on the First Two Years*, Cambridge: Cambridgeshire Probation Service.

Kober, A. (1995) 'The nature of clinical audit and progress made', in M. Kogan and S. Redfern et al. (eds), *Making Use of Clinical Audit: A Guide to Practice in the Health Professions*, Buckingham: Open University Press.

Kogan, M., Redfern, S. and Kober, A. (1995) 'Making audit a workable system', in M. Kogan and S. Redfern et al. (eds), *Making Use of Clinical Audit: A Guide to Practice in the Health Professions*, Buckingham: Open University Press. pp. 128–45.

Krueger, R.A. (1994) *Focus Groups: A Practical Guide for Applied Research*, 2nd edn, Thousand Oaks: Sage.

Kuhn, T. (1970) *The Structure of Scientific Revolutions*, Chicago: University of Chicago Press.

Larsen, D. and Rootman, I. (1976) 'Physician role performance and patient satisfaction', *Social Science and Medicine*, 16: 29–32.

Lawrence, M. (1993) 'What is medical audit', in M. Lawrence and T. Schofield (eds), *Medical Audit in Primary Health Care*, Oxford: Oxford University Press. pp. 1–13.

Lawton, D. and Gordon, P. (1987) *HMI*, London: Routledge & Kegan Paul.

Laycock, G.K. (1984) *Reducing Burglary: A Study of Chemists' Shops*, Crime Prevention Unit Paper No. 1, London: Home Office.

Laycock, G. and Heal, K. (1989) 'Crime prevention: the British experience', in D. Evans (ed.), *The Geography of Crime*, London: Routledge.

Levacic, R. and Glover, D. (1994) *Ofsted Assessment of School's Efficiency*, Open University: Buckingham.

Levine, A. and Levine, M. (1977) 'The social context of evaluative research: a case study', *Evaluation Quarterly*, 1 (4): 515–42.

Leviton, L.C. and Hughes, E.F.X. (1981) 'Research on the utilization of evaluations: a review and synthesis', *Evaluation Review*, 5 (4): 525–48.

Lewis, C. (1992) 'Crime statistics: their use and misuse', in *Social Trends 22*, London: HMSO. pp. 13–23.

Ley, P. (1982) 'Satisfaction, compliance and communication', *British Journal of Clinical Psychology*, 21: 241–54.

Lincoln, Y.S. (1991) 'The arts and sciences of program evaluation', *Evaluation Practice*, 12 (1): 1–8.

Lincoln, Y.S. (1992) 'Sympathetic connections between qualitative methods and health research', *Qualitative Health Research*, 2 (4): 375–91.

Lincoln, Y.S. and Guba, E.G. (1985) *Naturalistic Inquiry*, Newbury Park, CA: Sage.

Lincoln, Y.S. and Guba, E.G. (1986) 'Research, evaluation and policy analysis: heuristics for disciplined inquiry', *Policy Studies Review*, 5: 546–65.

Linder-Pelz, S. (1982) 'Social psychological determinants of patient satisfaction: a test of five hypotheses', *Social Science and Medicine*, 16: 583–9.

Lipsey, M.W. (1992) 'Juvenile delinquency treatment: a meta-analytic inquiry into the variability of effects', in T.D. Cook, H. Cooper, D.S. Cordray, H.

Hartmann, L.V. Hedges, R.J. Light, T.A. Louis and F. Mosteller (eds), *Meta-Analysis for Explanation*, New York: Russell Sage Foundation. pp. 83–127.

Lipton, D., Martinson, R. and Wilks, J. (1975) *Effectiveness of Correctional Treatment: A Survey of Treatment Evaluation Studies*, Springfield: Praeger.

Lloyd, C., Mair, G. and Hough, M. (1994) *Explaining Reconviction Rates: A Critical Analysis*, Home Office Research Study No. 136, London: HMSO.

Locker, D. and Dunt, D. (1978) 'Theoretical and methodological issues in sociological studies of consumer satisfaction with medical care', *Social Science and Medicine*, 12: 283–92.

Lofland, J. and Lofland, L.H. (1984) *Analyzing Social Settings*, 2nd edn, Belmont, CA: Wadsworth. (1st edn, 1971.)

Love, A. (1991) *Internal Evaluation*, London: Sage.

Lurigio, A. and Rosenbaum, D.P. (1986) 'Evaluation research in community crime prevention: a critical look at the field', in D.P. Rosenbaum (ed.), *Community Crime Prevention: Does it Work?*, London: Sage. pp. 19–44.

Mair, G. (1988) *Probation Day Centres*, Home Office Research Study No. 100, London: HMSO.

Mair, G. (1991) 'What works – nothing or everything? Measuring the effectiveness of sentences', *Home Office Research Bulletin*, No. 30, London: Home Office. pp. 3–8.

Mair, G. (ed.) (1997) *Evaluating the Effectiveness of Community Penalties*, Aldershot: Avebury.

Mair, G. and Nee, C. (1992) 'Day centre reconviction rates', *British Journal of Criminology*, 32 (3): 329–39.

Mair, G., Lloyd, C., Nee, C. and Sibbitt, R. (1994) *Intensive Probation in England and Wales: An Evaluation*, Home Office Research Study No. 133, London: HMSO.

Maitland, P. and Keegan, A. (1988) *The Sherborne House Day Centre: A Non-Custodial Programme for High Tariff Young Offenders*, London: Inner London Probation Service.

Mark, M.M. and Cook, T.D. (1984) 'Design of randomized experiments and quasi-experiments', in L. Rutman (ed.), *Evaluation Research Methods: A Basic Guide*, 2nd edn, Beverly Hills, CA: Sage.

Mark, M.M. and Shotland, R.L. (1985) 'Stakeholder-based evaluation and value judgements', *Evaluation Review*, 9 (5): 605–26.

Marsland, D. (1993) 'Technical progress and ideological conflict in evaluation research', paper presented at the British Sociological Association Annual Conference, 1993.

Martindale, D. (1974) *Sociological Theory and the Problem of Values*, Columbus: Charles E. Merrill.

Martinson, R. (1974) 'What works? Questions and answers about prison reform', *Public Interest*, 35: 22–54.

Martinson, R. (1979) 'New findings, new views: a note of caution regarding sentencing reform', *Hofstra Law Review*, 7: 243–58.

Mathison, S. (1994) 'Rethinking the evaluator role: partnerships between organizations and evaluators', *Evaluation and Program Planning*, 17 (3): 299–304.

Matthews, P. (1995) 'Aspects of inspection, improvement and OFSTED', in T. Brighouse and B. Moon (eds), *School Inspection*, London: Pitman. pp. 66–79.

Matza, D. (1969) *Becoming Deviant*, New York: Wiley.

May, T. (1993) *Social Research: Issues, Methods and Process*, Buckingham: Open University Press.

Maychell, K. and Pathak, S. (1997) *Planning for Action*, Slough: NFER.

Maxwell, R.J. (1992) 'Dimensions of quality revisited: from thought to action', *Quality in Health Care*, 1: 171–7.

McCall, G.J. and Simmons, J.L. (1969) *Issues in Participant Observation: A Text and Reader*, London: Addison-Wesley.

McDowell, I. and Newell, C. (1987) *Measuring Health: A Guide to Rating Scales and Questionnaires*, Oxford: Oxford University Press.

McGhee, A. (1961) *The Patient's Attitude to Nursing Care*, E. and S. Livingstone: Edinburgh.

McIver, S. and Carr-Hill, R. (1989) *The NHS and its Customers*, York: Centre for Health Economics.

McIvor, G. (1990) 'Community service and custody in Scotland', *Howard Journal of Criminal Justice*, 29 (2): 101–13.

McIvor, G. (1992) *Sentenced to Serve: The Operation and Impact of Community Service by Offenders*, Aldershot: Avebury.

McIvor, G. (1995) 'Practitioner evaluation in probation', in J. McGuire (ed.), *What Works: Reducing Reoffending: Guidelines from Research and Practice*, Chichester: John Wiley and Sons.

McKillip, J. (1987) *Need Analysis: Tools for the Human Services and Education*, Newbury Park, CA: Sage.

Meenan, R.F., Gertman, P.M. and Mason, J.H. (1980) 'Measuring health status in arthritis: the Arthritis Impact Measurement Scales', *Arthritis and Rheumatism*, 23: 146–52.

Merton, R.K. and Kendall, P.L. (1946) 'The focus interview', *American Journal of Sociology*, 51 (6): 541–57.

Metcalf, C. (1994) 'Inspection and quality: the contribution of research', paper presented at the British Educational Research Association Conference, September 1994.

Miles, M.B. and Huberman, A.M. (1984) *Qualitative Data Analysis*, London: Sage.

Miles, M.B. and Huberman, A.M. (1988) 'Drawing valid meaning from qualitative data: toward a shared craft', in D.M. Fetterman (ed.), *Qualitative Approaches to Evaluation in Education: The Silent Scientific Revolution*, New York: Praeger.

Miller, D.C. (1991) *Handbook of Research Design and Social Measurement*, 5th edn, Newbury Park, CA: Sage.

Mirrlees-Black, C., Mayhew, P. and Percy, A. (1996) *The 1996 British Crime Survey*, Home Office Statistical Bulletin, London: HMSO.

Monnier, E. (1997) 'Vertical partnerships: the opportunities and constraints which they pose for high quality evaluations', *Evaluation*, 3 (1): 110–17.

Montgomery, J. (1996) 'Appraisal study warns against pay link', *Times Educational Supplement*, 10 May.

Moores, B. and Thompson, A. (1986) 'What 1357 hospital inpatients think about aspects of their stay in British acute hospitals', *Journal of Advanced Nursing*, 11: 87–102.

Morgan, D.L. (ed.) (1993) *Successful Focus Groups: Advancing the State of the Art*, Newbury Park, CA: Sage.

Morgan, D.L. (1997) *Focus Groups as Qualitative Research*, 2nd edn, London: Sage. (1st edn, 1988.)

Morrell, D.C. (1970) 'Methods of assessing quality of medical care', in J. Collins (ed.), *Resources in Medicine*, London: Kings Fund.

Morris, L.L. and Fitz-Gibbon, C.T. (1978) *How to Present an Evaluation Report*, Beverly Hills, CA: Sage.

Mortimore, P. (1991) 'The nature and findings of research on school effectiveness in the primary sector', in S. Riddell and S. Brown (eds), *School Effectiveness Research: Its Messages for School Improvement*, Edinburgh: HMSO.

Mortimore, P. (1995) 'Your local critical friend', *Education*, 7 July.

Mortimore, P. (1997) 'Neither whingers nor pessimists', *Times Educational Supplement*, 31 October.

Mortimore, P. and Goldstein, H. (1996) *'The teaching of reading in 45 inner London primary schools: a critical examination of OFSTED research'*, London: Institute of Education, University of London.

Mortimore, P., Sammons, P., Stoll, L. Lewis, D. and Ecob, R. (1988) *School Matters*, Wells, Somerset: Open Books.

Moser, C. and Kalton, G. (1983) *Survey Methods in Social Investigation*, London: Heinemann.

Mulkay, M., Ashmore, M. and Pinch, T. (1987) 'Measuring the quality of life: a sociological invention concerning the application of economics to health care', *Sociology*, 21 (4): 541–64.

Mynors-Wallis, L.M., Gath, D.H., Lloyd-Thomas, A.R. and Tomlinson, D. (1995) 'Randomised controlled trial comparing problem solving treatment with amitriptyline and placebo for major depression in primary care', *British Medical Journal*, 310: 441–45.

Nachmias, D. (1979) *Public Policy Evaluation: Approaches and Methods*, New York: St. Martin's Press.

National Audit Office (1989) *Review of the Crown Prosecution Service*, London: HMSO.

Neave, G. (1988) 'On the cultivation of quality, efficiency and enterprise: an overview of recent trends in higher education in Western Europe, 1986–1988', *European Journal of Education*, 23, 1/2.

Newell, D.J. (1992) 'Randomised controlled trials in health care research', in J. Daly, I. McDonald and E. Willis (eds), *Researching Health Care: Designs, Dilemmas, Disciplines*, London: Routledge.

Nichols, P. (1991) *Social Survey Methods*, Oxford: Oxfam.

Nixon, J. and Ruddock, J. (1993) 'The role of professional judgement in the local inspection of schools', *Research Papers in Education*, 8 (1): 136–48.

Norman, I. (1995) 'Making a start on clinical audit: cycles and spirals', in M. Kogan and S. Redfern et al. (eds), *Making Use of Clinical Audit: A Guide to Practice in the Health Professions*, Buckingham: Open University Press. pp. 41–54.

Norman, I. and Redfern, S. (1995) 'What is audit?', in M. Kogan and S. Redfern et al. (eds), *Audit: A Guide to Practice in the Health Professions*, Buckingham: Open University Press. pp. 1–20.

Nuttall, D., Goldstein, H., Prosser, R. and Rasbash, J. (1989) 'Differential school effectiveness', *International Journal of Educational Research*, 13: 7, 769–76.

Nye, B.A., Achilles, C.M., Zacharias, J.B. and Fulton, B.D. (1993) 'Class size research: from experiment to field study to policy application', paper presented to American Evaluation Research Association, 1993 (STAR study).

Oakes, J. (1989) 'School context and organization', in R.J. Shavelson et al. (eds), *Indicators for Monitoring Mathematics and Science Education*, Santa Monica: Rand Co. pp. 25–39.

Oakley, A. (1992) *Social Support in Motherhood: The Natural History of a Research Project*, Oxford: Blackwell.

O'Boyle, C.A., McGee, H., Hickey, A., O'Malley, K. and Joyce, C.R.B. (1992) 'Individual quality of life in patients undergoing hip replacement', *Lancet*, 339: 1088–91.

O'Connor, M. (1995) 'Revelations after the storm', *Times Educational Supplement*, 20 January.

OFSTED (1992; 1994; 1995a) *Framework for the Inspection of Schools*, London: HMSO.

OFSTED (1995b) *Inspection Quality 1994/5*, Keele and Touche Ross, OFSTED: London.

OFSTED (1996a) *Consultation on Arrangements for the Inspection of Maintained Schools from September 1997*, London: OFSTED.

Oldfield, M. (1996) *The Kent Reconviction Study*, Maidstone: Kent Probation Service, Research and Information Department.

O'Neill, I.T. (1995) 'Implementation frailties of Guba and Lincoln's fourth generation evaluation theory', *Studies in Educational Evaluation*, 21: 5–21.

OPCS (1978) *Royal Commission on the National Health Service: Patients' Attitudes to the Hospital Service*, London: HMSO.

Oppenheim, A.N. (1992) *Questionnaire Design and Attitude Measurement*, London: Pinter.

Ouston, J. and Klenowski, V. (1996) 'Parents' responses to school inspectors' in J. Ouston, P. Earley and B. Fidler (eds), *Ofsted Inspections: The Early Experience*, London: David Fulton. pp. 135–48.

Owen, J.M. (1993) *Program Evaluation: Forms and Approaches*, St Leonards, NSW: Allen and Unwin.

Packwood, T. and Kober, A. (1995) 'Clinical audit and managing health systems', in M. Kogan and S. Redfern et al. (eds), *Making Use of Clinical Audit: A Guide to Practice in the Health Professions*, Buckingham: Open University Press. pp. 106–27.

Palfrey, C., Phillips, C., Thomas, P. and Edwards, D. (1992) *Policy Evaluation in the Public Sector: Approaches and Methods*, Aldershot: Avebury.

Palmer, T.B. (1975) 'Martinson revisited', *Journal of Research on Crime and Delinquency*, 12: 133–52.

Parkes, C. (1985) 'Terminal care: home, hospital or hospice?', *Lancet*, 1: 155–7.

Parlett, M. and Hamilton, D. (1976) 'Evaluation as illumination: a new approach to the study of innovative programs' in G.V. Glass (ed.), *Evaluation Studies Review Annual*, Vol. 1, Beverly Hills, CA: Sage. pp. 140–57.

Passmore, B. (1997) 'Stressed out heads reach for Prozac', *Times Educational Supplement*, 7 November.

Patrick, D.L. and Deyo, R.A. (1989) 'Generic and disease-specific measures in assessing health status and quality of life', *Medical Care*, 27: 217–32.

Patrick, D.L. and Erikson, P. (1993) *Health Status and Health Policy: Quality of Life in Health Care Evaluation and Resource Allocation*, Oxford: Oxford University Press.

Patton, MQ. (1975) *Alternative Evaluation Research Paradigm*, Grand Fork: University of North Dakota.

Patton, M.Q. (1980) *Qualitative Evaluation Methods*, Beverly Hills, CA: Sage.

Patton, M.Q. (1981) *Creative Evaluation*, Beverly Hills, CA: Sage.

Patton, M.Q. (1982) *Practical Evaluation*, Beverly Hills, CA: Sage.

Patton, M.Q. (1986) *Utilization-Focused Evaluation*, 2nd edn, Newbury Park, CA: Sage.

Patton, M.Q. (1987) *How to use Qualitative Methods in Evaluation*, Newbury Park, CA: Sage.

Patton, M.Q. (1988a) 'Paradigms and pragmatism', in D.M. Fetterman (ed.), *Qualitative Approaches to Evaluation in Education: The Silent Scientific Revolution*, New York: Praeger.

Patton, M.Q. (1988b) 'How primary is your identity as an evaluator?', *Evaluation Practice*, 9 (2): 87–92.

Patton, M.Q. (1988c) 'The evaluator's responsibility for utilization', *Evaluation Practice*, 9 (2): 5–24.

Patton, M.Q. (1989) 'A context and boundaries for a theory-driven approach to validity', *Evaluation and Program Planning*, 12: 375–77.

Patton, M.Q. (1990) *Qualitative Evaluation and Research Methods*, 2nd edn, Newbury Park, CA: Sage.

Patton, M.Q. (1996) 'A world larger than formative and summative', *Evaluation Practice*, 17 (2): 131–44.

Patton, M.Q. (1997) *Utilization-Focused Evaluation*, 3rd edn, Newbury Park, CA: Sage.

Pawson, R. (1989) *A Measure for Measures: A Manifesto for an Empirical Sociology*, London: Routledge.

Pawson, R. (1997) 'Evaluation methodology: back to basics', in G. Mair (ed.), *Evaluating the Effectiveness of Community Penalties*, Aldershot: Avebury. pp. 151–73.

Pawson, R. and Tilley, N. (1992) 'Re-evaluation: rethinking research on corrections and crime', *Yearbook of Correctional Education 1992*, Vancouver: Simon Fraser University. pp. 19–49.

Pawson, R. and Tilley, N. (1993) 'OXO, Tide, brand X and new improved evaluation', paper presented at the British Sociological Association Annual Conference, University of Essex.

Pawson, R. and Tilley, N. (1994) 'What works in evaluation research?', *British Journal of Criminology*, 34 (3): 291–306.

Pawson, R. and Tilley, N. (1997) *Realistic Evaluation*, London: Sage.

Pearson, G., Blagg, H., Smith, D., Sampson, A. and Stubbs, P. (1992) 'Crime, community and conflict: the multi-agency approach', in D. Downes (ed.), *Unravelling Criminal Justice*, London: Macmillan.

Pease, K. (1985) 'Community service orders', in M. Tonry and N. Morris (eds), *Crime and Justice: An Annual Review of Research*, Vol. 6, Chicago: University of Chicago Press.

Pease, K. (1994) 'Crime prevention', in M. Maguire, R. Morgan and R. Reiner (eds), *The Oxford Book of Criminology*, Oxford: Clarendon Press. pp. 659–703.

Pease, K., Billingham, S. and Earnshaw, I. (1977) *Community Service Assessed in 1976*, Home Office Research Study No. 39, London: HMSO.

Pease, K., Durkin, P., Earnshaw, I., Payne, D. and Thorpe, J. (1975) *Community Service Orders*, Home Office Research Studies, No. 29, London: HMSO.

Péladeau, N. and Mercier, C. (1993) 'Approches qualitative et quantitative en evaluation de programmes', *Sociologie et Sociétés*, 25 (2): 111–24.

Perry, P. (1995) 'The formation of OFSTED', in T. Brighouse and B. Moon (eds), *School Inspection*, London: Pitman. pp. 35–46.

Phillips, C., Palfrey, C. and Thomas, P. (1994) *Evaluating Health and Social Care*, London: Macmillan.

Phillpotts, G.J.O. and Lancucki, L.B. (1979) *Previous Convictions, Sentence and Reconviction: A Statistical Study of a Sample of 5,000 Offenders convicted in January 1971*, Home Office Research Study No. 53, London: HMSO.

Powell, R.A. and Single, H.M. (1996) 'Focus groups', *International Journal of Quality in Health Care*, 8 (5): 499–504.

Poyner, B. (1991) 'Situational crime prevention in two parking facilities', in R.V.G. Clarke (ed.), *Situational Crime Prevention: Successful Case Studies*, New York: Harrow and Heston.

Preston, R. (1980) 'Social theology and penal theory and practice: the collapse of the rehabilitative ideal and the search for an alternative', in A.E. Bottoms and R.H. Preston (eds), *The Coming Penal Crisis*, Edinburgh: Scottish Academic Press.

Prior, L. (1985) 'The social production of mortality statistics', *Sociology of Health and Illness*, 7: 220–35.

Quantz, R.A. (1992) 'On critical ethnography', in M.D. LeCompte, W.L. Millray and J. Preissle (eds), *The Handbook of Qualitative Research in Education*, New York: Academic Press. pp. 447–505.

Race, K.E., Hotch, D.F. and Parker, T. (1994) 'Rehabilitation program evaluation: use of focus groups to empower clients', *Evaluation Review*, 18 (6): 730–40.

Raynor, P. (1988) *Probation as an Alternative to Custody*, Aldershot: Avebury.

Raynor, P. and Vanstone, M. (1994) *Straight Thinking on Probation: Third Interim Report*, Bridgend: Mid Glamorgan Probation Service.

Raynor, P., Smith, D. and Vanstone, M. (1994) *Effective Probation Practice*, London: Macmillan.

Reichardt, C.S. and Gollob, H.F. (1989) 'Ruling out threats to validity', *Evaluation Review*, 13: 3–17.

Reicken, H.W. and Boruch, R.F. (eds) (1974) *Social Experimentation: A Method for Planning and Evaluating Social Intervention*, New York: Academic Press.

Reiss, A.J. (1971) 'Systematic observation and natural social phenomena', in H.L. Costner (ed.), *Sociological Methodology*, San Francisco: Jossey-Bass.

Reynolds, D. (1995) 'The effective school: an inaugural lecture', *Evaluation and Research in Education*, 9: 2, 57–73.

Rhodes, T., Holland, J. and Hartnoll, R. (1991) *Hard to Reach or Out of Reach: An Evaluation of an Innovative Model of HIV Outreach Health Education*, London: Tufnell Press.

Rice, S.A. (1929) 'Contagious bias in the interview', *American Journal of Sociology*, 35 (3): 420–3.

Roberts, C.H. (1989) *Young Offender Project: First Evaluation Report*, Worcester: Hereford and Worcester Probation Service.

Roberts, H. (1990) 'Performance and outcome measures in the health service', in M. Cave, M. Kogan and R. Smith (eds), *Output and Performance Measurement in Government: The State of the Art*, London: Jessica Kingsley.

Robinson, S. (1996) 'Evaluating the progress of clinical audit', *Evaluation*, 2 (4): 373–92.

Robson, C. (1993) *Real World Research*, Oxford: Blackwell.

Rosenbaum, D.P. (ed.) (1986) *Community Crime Prevention: Does it Work?*, London: Sage.

Rosenbaum, D.P. (1987) 'The theory and research behind neighbourhood watch', *Crime and Delinquency*, 33 (1): 103–34.

Rosser, R., Cottee, M., Rabin, R. and Selai, C. (1992) 'Index of health-related quality of life', in A. Hopkins (ed.), *Measures of the Quality of Life*, London: Royal College of Physicians. pp. 81–90.

Rossi, P.H. and Freeman, H.E. (1993) *Evaluation: A Systematic Approach*, 5th edn, Newbury Park, CA: Sage. (1st edn, 1979.)

Rossi, P. and Wright, S. (1979) *Evaluation: A Systematic Approach*, Beverly Hills, CA: Sage.

Rossman, G.B. and Wilson, B.L. (1985) 'Numbers and words: combining quantitative and qualitative methods in a single large-scale evaluation study', *Evaluation Review*, 9 (5): 627–43.

Royal College of General Practitioners (1985) *Assessing Quality of Care in General Practice*, London: Royal College of General Practitioners.

Royal Commission on the National Health Service (1979) (The Merrison Report), Cmnd 7615, London: HMSO.

Russell, I.T., Fell, M., Devlin, H.B., Glass, N.J. and Newell, D.J. (1977) 'Day-case surgery for hernias and haemorrhoids – a clinical, social and economic evaluation', *Lancet*, 1, 844–7.

Russell, S. (1996) 'Schools experience of inspection', in J. Ouston, P. Earley and B. Fidler (eds), *Ofsted Inspections: The Early Experience*, London: David Fulton. pp. 97–110.

Sackett, D.L. and Torrance, G.W. (1978) 'The utility of different health states', *Journal of Chronic Diseases*, 31: 697–704.

Sainsbury, E. (1985) 'Measures of effectiveness in probation practice', in E. Sainsbury (ed.), *Research and Information in the Probation Service*, Sheffield: University of Sheffield.

Sammons, P., Hill, J. and Mortimore, P. (1995) *Key Characteristics of Effective Schools*, London: OFSTED and the Institute of Education: London.

Sampson, A., Stubbs, P., Smith, D., Pearson, G. and Blagg, H. (1988) 'Crime, localities and the multi-agency approach', *British Journal of Criminology*, 28 (4): 473–93.

Schwandt, T. (1994) 'Constructivist, interpretivist approaches to human inquiry', in N.K. Denzin and Y.S. Lincoln (eds), *Handbook of Qualitative Research*, Thousand Oaks, CA: Sage. pp. 118–37.

Schwarz, D., Flamant, R. and Lellouch, J. (1980) *Clinical Trials*, London: Academic Press.

Schlesselman, J.J. (1982), *Case-Control Studies: Design, Conduct, Analysis*, Oxford: Oxford University Press.

Scott, J. (1990) *A Matter of Record: Documentary Sources in Social Research*, Cambridge: Polity Press.

Scriven, M. (1967) 'The methodology of evaluation', in R.W. Tyler, R.M. Gagne and M. Scriven (eds), *Perspectives of Curriculum Evaluation*, Chicago: Rand McNally. pp. 39–83.

Scriven, M. (1980) *The Logic of Evaluation*, Inverness, CA: Edgepress.

Scriven, M. (1991a) *Evaluation Thesaurus*, 4th edn, Newbury Park, CA: Sage.

Scriven, M. (1991b) 'Beyond formative and summative evaluation', in G.W. McLaughin and D.C. Phillips (eds), *Evaluation and Education: At Quarter Century*, Chicago, IL: University of Chicago Press. pp. 19–64.

Scriven, M. (1993) *Hard Won Lessons in Program Evaluation*, New Directions for Program Evaluation, No. 58, San Francisco: Jossey-Bass.

Scriven, M. (1996) 'Types of evaluation and types of evaluator', *Evaluation Practice*, 17 (2): 151–61.

Sechrest, L. (1992) 'Roots: back to our first generations', *Evaluation Practice*, 13 (1): 1–8.

Shadish, W.R. and Epstein, R. (1987) 'Practice of program evaluation practice among members of the Evaluation Research Society and Evaluation Network', *Evaluation Review*, 11: 555–90.

Shadish, W.R., Cook, T.D. and Leviton, L.C. (1991) *Foundations of Program Evaluation: Theories of Practice*, Newbury Park, CA: Sage.

Shaw, C.D. (1990) *Medical Audit: A Hospital Handbook*, London: King's Fund Centre.

Singer, L.R. (1991) 'A non-punitive paradigm of probation practice: some sobering thoughts', *British Journal of Social Work*, 21: 611–26.

Skogan, W.G. and Maxfield, M.G. (1981) *Coping with Crime: Individual and Neighbourhood Reactions*, Beverly Hills, CA: Sage.

Slevin, M., Plant, H., Lynch, D., Drinkwater, J. and Gregory, W.M. (1988) 'Who should measure quality of life, the doctor or the patient', *British Journal of Cancer*, 57: 109–12.

Sloan, F.A. (1995) 'Introduction', in F.A. Sloan (ed.), *Valuing Health Care: Costs, Benefits and Effectiveness of Pharmaceuticals and other Medical Technologies*, Cambridge: Cambridge University Press. pp. 1–14.

Smith, A., Preston, D., Buchanan, D. and Jordan, S. (1997) 'When two worlds collide', *Evaluation*, 3 (1): 49–68.

Smith, G. and Cantley, C. (1985a) 'Policy evaluation: the use of varied data in a study of a psychogeriatric service', in R. Walker (ed.), *Applied Qualitative Research*, Aldershot: Gower. pp. 156–74.

Smith, G. and Cantley, C. (1985b) *Assessing Health Care: A Study in Organisational Evaluation*, Milton Keynes: Open University Press.

Smith, J.K. (1983) 'Quantitative versus qualitative research: an attempt to clarify the issue', *Educational Researcher*, 12 (3): 6–13.

Smith, J.K. (1989) *The Nature of Social and Educational Inquiry: Empiricism versus Interpretation*, Norwood, NJ: Ablex.

Smith, L.J.F. (1982) 'Day training centres', *Home Office Research and Planning Unit Bulletin*, No. 14, London: HMSO. pp. 34–7.

Smith, M.F. (1988) 'Evaluation utilization revisited', in J. McLaughlin, L. Weber, R. Covert and R. Ingle (eds), *Evaluation Utilization*, San Francisco: Jossey-Bass.

Smith, M.L. (1986) 'The whole is greater: combining qualitative and quantitative approaches in evaluation studies', in D.D. Williams (ed.), *Naturalistic Evaluation, New Directions in Program Evaluation*, Vol. 30, San Francisco: Jossey-Bass. pp. 37–54.

Smith, P. (1995) 'Outcome-related performance indicators and organizational control in the public sector', in J. Holloway, J. Lewis and G. Mallory (eds), *Performance Measurement and Evaluation*, London: Sage.

Solomon, M.A. and Shortell, S.M. (1981) 'Designing health policy research for utilization', *Health Policy Quarterly*, 1: 261–73.

Spencer, D. (1996) 'Independent Heads give the nod to value added tests', *Times Educational Supplement*, 11 September.

Spitzer, W.O., Dobson, A.J., Hall, J. et al. (1981) 'Measuring the quality of life of cancer patients: a concise QL index for use by physicians', *Journal of Chronic Disease*, 34: 585–99.

Stake, R.E. (ed.) (1975) *Evaluating the Arts in Education: A Responsive Approach*, Columbus, OH: Merrill.

Stake, R.E. (1980) 'Program evaluation, particularly responsive evaluation', in W.B. Dockrell and D. Hamilton (eds), *Rethinking Educational Research*, London: Hodder and Stoughton. pp. 72–87.

Stake, R.E. (1981) 'Case study methodology: an epistemological advocacy', in W. Welch (ed.), *Case Study Methodology in Educational Evaluation*, Minnesota Research and Evaluation Center: Minneapolis.

Stake, R.E. and Trumbull, D.J. (1982) 'Naturalistic generalizations', *Review Journal of Philosophy and Social Science*, 7: 1–12.

Stewart, A.L. and Ware, J.E. (1992) *Measuring Functioning and Well-being: The Medical Outcomes Approach*, London: Duke University Press.

Stewart, D. and Shamdasani, P. (1990) *Focus Groups: Theory and Practice*, London: Sage.

Stimson, G. and Webb, B. (1975) *Going to See the Doctor*, London: Routledge and Kegan Paul.

St Leger, A.S., Schnieden, H. and Walsworth-Bell (1992) *Evaluating Health Services' Effectiveness*, Milton Keynes: Open University Press.

Stockdale, J.E. and Gresham, P.J. (1995) *Combating Burglary: An Evaluation of Three Strategies*, Crime Detection and Prevention Series, Paper No. 59, Police Research Group, Home Office, London: HMSO.

Strauss, A. and Corbin, J. (1990) *Basics of Qualitative Research: Grounded Theory Procedures and Techniques*, Newbury Park, CA: Sage.

Streiner, D.L. and Norman, G.R. (1995) *Health Measurement Scales: A Practical Guide to Their Development and Use*, 2nd edn, Oxford: Oxford University Press.

Stufflebeam, D.L. and Shinkfield, A.J. (1985) *Systematic Evaluation: A Self-Instructional Guide to Theory and Practice*, Dordrecht: Kluwer Nijhoff.

Suchman, E.A. (1967) *Evaluative Research*, New York: Russell Sage.

Sudman, S. and Bradburn, N.M. (1974) *Response Effects in Surveys*, Chicago: Aldine.

Tabberer, R. (1995) *Parents' Perceptions of OFSTED's Work*, London: NFER.

Taylor, R.B. (1994) *Research Methods in Criminal Justice*, New York: McGraw-Hill.

Thomas, G. (1996) 'The new schools' inspection system: some problems and possible solutions', *Educational Management and Administration*, 24 (4): 355–69.

Tilley, N. (1993) 'Crime prevention and the safer cities story', *Howard Journal of Criminal Justice*, 32 (1): 40–57.

Trochim, W.M.K. (1984) *Research Design for Program Evaluation: The Regression-Discontinuity Approach*, Beverly Hills, CA: Sage.

Van Maanen, J. (1983) 'The fact of fiction in organizational ethnography', in J. Van Maanen (ed.), *Qualitative Methodology*, Beverly Hills, CA: Sage, pp. 37–55.

Van Straelen, F.W.M. (1978) 'Prevention and technology', in J. Brown (ed.), *Cranfield Papers*, London: Peel Press.

Varah, M. (1987) 'Probation and community service', in J. Harding (ed.), *Probation and the Community: A Practice and Policy Reader*, London: Tavistock.

Vass, A.A. (1981) 'Community service for juveniles? A critical comment', *Probation Journal*, 28: 44–9.

Vass, A.A. (1984) *Sentenced to Labour: Close Encounters with a Prison Substitute*, St Ives: Venus Academic.

Vass, A.A. (1990) *Alternatives to Prison: Punishment, Custody and the Community*, London: Sage.

Vass, A.A. and Weston, A. (1990) 'Probation day centres as an alternative to custody: a "Trojan horse" examined', *British Journal of Criminology*, 30: 189–206.

Walker, N. (1968) *Crime and Punishment in Britain: The Penal System in Theory, Law and Practice*, 2nd edn, Edinburgh: Edinburgh University Press. (1st edn, 1965.)

Warner, K. and Luce, B. (1982) *Cost-Benefit and Cost-Effectiveness Analysis in Health Care*, Ann Arbor, MI: Health Administration Press.

Washnis, G.J. (1976) *Citizen Involvement in Crime Prevention*, London: Lexington Books.

Weiss, C.H. (1970) 'The politicization of evaluation research', *Journal of Social Issues*, 26: 57–68.

Weiss, C.H. (1972) *Evaluation Research*, Englewood Cliffs, NJ: Prentice Hall.

Weiss, C.H. (1973a) 'Evaluation in the political context', paper presented at the annual meeting of the American Psychological Association in Montreal.

Weiss, C.H. (1973b) 'Where politics and evaluation research meet', *Evaluation*, 1: 37–45.

Weiss, C.H. (1975) 'Interviewing in evaluation research', in E.L. Struening and M. Guttentag (eds), *Handbook of Evaluation Research: Volume I*. pp. 355–95.

Weiss, C.H. (1978) 'Improving the linkage between social research and public policy, in L.E. Lynn (ed.), *Knowledge and Policy: The Uncertain Connection*, Washington, DC: National Academy of Sciences. pp. 23–81.

Weiss, C.H. (1983a) 'The stakeholder approach to evaluation: origins and promise', in A. Bryk (ed.), *Stakeholder-Based Evaluation*, San Francisco: Jossey-Bass. pp. 3–14.

Weiss, C.H. (1983b) 'Toward the future of stakeholder approaches in evaluation', in A. Bryk (ed.), *Stakeholder-Based Evaluation*, San Francisco: Jossey-Bass. pp. 83–96.

Weiss, C.H. (1986) 'The many meanings of research utilization', in M. Bulmer et al. (eds), *Social Science and Social Policy*, London: Allen and Unwin. pp. 31–40.

Weiss, C.H. (1988a) 'Evaluation for decisions: Is anybody there? Does anybody care?', *Evaluation Practice*, 9 (1): 5–19.

Weiss, C.H. (1988b) 'If program decisions hinged only on information: a response to Patton', *Evaluation Practice*, 9 (2): 87–92.

Weiss, C.H. (1995) 'Nothing as practical as good theory: exploring theory-based evaluation for comprehensive community initiatives for children and families', in J.P. Connell, A.C. Kubisch, L.B. Schorr and C.H. Weiss (eds), *New Approaches to Evaluating Community Initiatives: Concepts, Methods and Contexts*, Washington, DC: Aspen Institute. pp. 65–92.

Weiss, C.H. (1997) 'How can theory-based evaluation make greater headway?', *Evaluation Review*, 21 (4): 501–24.

Weiss, C.H. and Bucuvalas, M.J. (1980a) *Social Science Research and Decision-Making*, New York: Columbia University Press.

Weiss, C.H. and Bucuvalas, M.J. (1980b) 'Truth tests and utility tests: decision-makers frames of reference for social science research', *American Sociological Review*, 45: 302–13.

West, J.S.M. (1976) 'Community service orders', in J.F.S. King and W. Young (eds), *Control Without Custody*, Cambridge: Cambridge Institute of Criminology.

Whitehead, J.T. and Lab, S.P. (1989) 'A meta-analysis of juvenile correctional treatment', *Journal of Research in Crime and Delinquency*, 26 (3): 276–95.

Whitehead, M. and Baker, R. (1992) 'Measuring patient satisfaction for audit in general practice', *Quality Health Care*, 3, 151.

Whitehead, P. (1990) *Community Supervision for Offenders: A New Model of Probation*, Aldershot: Avebury.

Wholey, J.S. (1987) 'Evaluability assessment: developing program theory', in L. Bickman (ed.), *Using Program Theory in Evaluation: New Directions for Program Evaluation*, No. 33, San Francisco: Jossey-Bass.

Wholey, J.S. (1996) 'Formative and summative evaluation: related issues in performance measurement', *Evaluation Practice*, 17 (2): 145–9.

Whyte, W.F. (ed.) (1991) *Participatory Action Research*, Newbury Park, CA: Sage.

Wiklund, I., Gorkin, L., Pawitan, Y., Schron, E., Schoenberger, J., Jared, L. L. and Shumaker, S. (1992) 'Methods for assessing quality of life in the cardiac arrhythmia suppression trial (CAST)', *Quality of Life Research*, 1 (3): 187–201.

Wilcox, B. (1992) *Time-Constrained Evaluation*, London: Routledge.

Wilcox, B. (1993) 'Inspection, time-constrained evaluation and the production of credible knowledge', in R.G. Burgess (ed.), *Educational Research and Evaluation for Policy and Practice?*, London: Falmer Press. pp. 81–101.

Wilcox, B. and Gray, J. (1994) 'Reactions to inspections: a study of three variants', *Cambridge Journal of Education*, 24 (2): 245–59.

Wilcox, B. and Gray, J. (1995) 'The methodologies of school inspection: issues and dilemmas', in T. Brighouse and B. Moon (eds), *School Inspection*, London: Pitman. pp. 127–43.

Wilcox, B. and Gray, J. (1996) *Inspecting Schools: Holding Schools to Account and Helping Schools to Improve*, Buckingham: Cassell.

Wilcox, B., Gray, J. and Tranmer, M. (1993) 'LEA frameworks for the assessment of schools: an interrupted picture', *Educational Research*, 35 (3): 211–21.

Wilkin, D.L., Hallam, L. and Doggett, M. (1993) *Measures of Need and Outcome for Primary Health Care*, Oxford: Oxford University Press.

Wilkins, L.T. (1969) *Evaluation of Penal Measures*, New York: Random House.

Williams, A. (1985) 'Economics of coronary by-pass grafting', *British Medical Journal*, 291: 326–9.

Williams, A. (1987) 'Measuring quality of life', in G. Teeling Smith (ed.), *Health Economics: Prospects for the Future*, Beckenham: Croom Helm.

Williams, A. and Kind, P. (1992) 'The present state of play about QALYs', in A. Hopkins (ed.), *Measures of the Quality of Life*, London: Royal College of Physicians. pp. 21–34.

Williams, B. (1994) 'Patient satisfaction: a valid concept?', *Social Science and Medicine*, 38 (4): 509–16.

Williams, R.G.A. (1983) 'Concepts of health: an analysis of lay logic', *Sociology*, 17: 185–204.

Williams, S.J. and Calnan, M. (1991) 'Convergence and divergence: assessing criteria of consumer satisfaction across general practice, dental and hospital care settings', *Social Science and Medicine*, 33 (6): 707–16.

Willis, A. (1977) 'Community service as an alternative to imprisonment: a cautionary view', *Probation Journal*, 24, 120–6.

Woodward, C.A. (1992) 'Broadening the scope of evaluation: why and how', in J. Daly, I. McDonald and E. Willis (eds), *Researching Health Care: Designs, Dilemmas, Disciplines*, London: Tavistock/Routledge. pp. 93–113.

Wragg, E. and Brighouse, T. (1996) *A New Model of School Inspection*, Exeter: Exeter University.

Yin, R.K. (1977) *Evaluating Citizen Crime Prevention Programs*, Santa Monica: Sage.

Young, W. (1979) *Community Service Orders: The Development and Use of a New Penal Measure*, London: Heinemann.

Zelditch, Jr, M. (1962) 'Some methodological problems of field studies', *American Journal of Sociology*, 67 (5): 566–76.

Ziebland, S. (1994) 'Measuring changes in health status', in C. Jenkinson (ed.), *Measuring Health and Medical Outcomes*, London: UCL Press. pp. 42–53.

Ziebland, S., Fitzpatrick, R. and Jenkinson, C. (1992) 'Assessing short term outcome', *Quality in Health Care*, 1: 141–2.

Zimmerman, D.H. and Wieder, D.L. (1977) 'The diary: diary–interview method', *Urban Life*, 5 (4): 479–98.

Index